MacArthur Strikes Back

General Douglas MacArthur, Allied Commander in Chief, Southwest Pacific Theater.

MacArthur Strikes Back

Decision at Buna, New Guinea 1942–1943

Harry A. Gailey

PRESIDIO

Published by Presidio Press, Inc.
505 B San Marin Drive, Suite 160
Novato, CA 94945-1340

Library of Congress Cataloging-in-Publication Data

Gailey, Harry A.
    MacArthur Strikes Back : Decision at Buna, New Guinea
    1942–1943 / Harry A. Gailey.
            p.   cm.
    Includes bibliographical references and index.
    ISBN 0-89141-702-8
    1. World War, 1939–1945—Campaigns—New Guinea. 2. United
    States—Armed Forces—History—World War, 1939–1945. 3. Aus-
    tralia—Armed Forces—History—World War, 1939–1945. I. Title.

D767.95 .G35 2000
940.54'26—dc21
                                                    00-038521

Maps by Donald DeWald
All photos courtesy National Archives unless otherwise noted.

Printed in the United States of America

To the Australian and American citizen soldiers who, in the deadly Papuan campaign, reversed the tide of Japanese aggression during the Pacific war

Contents

I. The Japanese Tide 1
II. MacArthur Arrives 17
III. Return to Ioribaiwa 35
IV. Milne Bay 59
V. Changing Commands 73
VI. On to Kododa 87
VII. Enter the 32d Division 101
VIII. Sanananda-Gona Operation 117
IX. Buna Operations: First Phase 135
X. Eichelberger Arrives, Harding Departs 155
XI. Sanananda Stalemate 171
XII. Clearing the Buna Approaches 189
XIII. Final Offensives 213
Epilogue 233
Notes 237
Bibliography 251
Index 257

MAPS

Papuan Campaign 38
Japanese Offensive at Milne Bay 64
Oivi-Gorari 31 October–8 November 118
Approach to the Beachhead 128
Sanananda Front December 1942 184
Warren Front 17–28 December 200
Urbana Front 204
Sanananda Operations Final Phase 227

Chapter I
The Japanese Tide

The successful surprise attack on Pearl Harbor assured the Japanese of virtual naval supremacy in the vast Pacific area. That disaster was compounded by the loss on 10 December 1941 of the *Prince of Wales* and *Renown* by enemy air attacks. Without these capital ships, and threatened by a large Japanese force including carriers, the Royal Navy retreated to the Indian Ocean and ultimately to eastern Africa. United States naval presence in the crucial areas astride the Japanese advance was represented by the weak Asiatic Fleet, whose most powerful ship was the heavy cruiser *Houston*. Combined with air superiority, this command of the sea allowed the Japanese to move with impunity against selected island targets.

The unpreparedness of the Allies was obvious from the beginning of the various operations. As early as 1911, U.S. military planners had decided that the Philippines could not be held if the Japanese mounted a full-scale attack. Consequently, little had been done to build up Philippine defenses before Gen. Douglas MacArthur arrived in 1935 to command the Philippine forces. By the onset of the European war, he had convinced the military planners in Washington that with reinforcements of men, planes, and materiel, he could blunt any Japanese attack and defend Luzon until help arrived. Unfortunately, the buildup of forces proceeded slowly, and the U.S. and Philippine army strength was far below what was necessary when the Japanese struck. MacArthur's air units were destroyed in the first few days. With total control of the air and with naval superiority, the Japanese expected an easy victory. Much to their surprise, MacArthur's forces retreated to the Bataan Peninsula and held off the much superior Japanese army until 9 April 1942. The neighboring island fortress of Corregidor was overrun on 6 May.

This temporary local setback did little to derail the Japanese offensives. Guam was occupied by their South Seas Detachment on 8 December 1941 and Wake Island, after a spirited defense, on the twenty-third of the same month. On the mainland, Hong Kong fell on the day after Pearl Harbor. To protect the Dutch East Indies and Malaya, the Allies hastily put together the ABDA defense coalition, comprising Australian, British, Dutch, and American naval, air, and ground forces under the command of one of Britain's most distinguished soldiers, Gen. Sir Archibald Wavell. His was a more hopeless task than the one he had faced earlier in North Africa. With few trained troops and with outclassed and outnumbered aircraft, he was supposed to defend all of Southeast Asia, to include the East Indies, and blunt any advance toward Australia. The key to Wavell's plan to halt the Japanese was Singapore, referred to by overly optimistic observers as the Gibraltar of the Orient. However, the Commonwealth forces were unable to contain the Japanese advance overland down the Malay Peninsula, resulting in the surrender of the Singapore garrison of 64,000 men on 15 February 1942.[1]

Even before the collapse of Malaya, Japanese units had begun a step-by-step conquest of the East Indies. Although the Dutch had more than 100,000 men available, they were scattered throughout the major islands. The air force available to Allied commanders was quickly neutralized. The ABDA navy—small in size, with its largest ship the U.S. heavy cruiser *Houston*—was greatly handicapped by its command structure. Japanese amphibious forces landed on Tarakan Island on 10 January, then continued to Borneo and Sumatra. Resistance on Java ended on 8 March 1942. By mid-March the most important islands in the East Indies were under Japanese control.

The hopelessly outclassed ABDA fleet was mauled in a number of engagements, the last being the disastrous Java Sea battle of 27 January. The so-called Bismarcks Barrier was broken and the remnants of the ABDA command were scattered. Many of the British retired to Ceylon, and the American and Australian units that could escape found their way to Australia. General George Brett, who had been Wavell's chief deputy in the ABDA command structure, became the commander of all U.S. forces in Australia (USAFIA). At this juncture, most of these were members of air units that had escaped from the East Indies.[2]

At the request of Australian prime minister John Curtin, the area around Darwin, in northern Australia, was incorporated into the ABDA command zone on 24 January. Five days later another organization designed to provide naval protection of areas east of Australia was created. This was the ANZAC area, and within it a composite Australian-American naval force was to operate in conjunction with the U.S. fleet based at Pearl Harbor. Although the structure of the new command was designed to carry out necessary specific missions, the means to do so were not available. Vice Admiral Herbert Leary, U.S. Navy, the commander, had available only the Australian cruisers *Canberra, Hobart,* and *Australia* and the U.S. cruiser *Chicago,* as well as four destroyers and a few corvettes. In addition, he had a squadron of B-17s, which arrived at Townsville on 17 February. These were the newest, most reliable bombers available to the Allied forces.[3]

The collapse of Allied resistance in all areas presented the Japanese High Command with a unique opportunity to cut the long supply lines to Australia and New Zealand without minimizing its naval threat to Hawaii. The southern Solomon Islands were undefended, and farther eastward, New Caledonia, Fiji, and Samoa at this early stage could have been seized as easily as the central Pacific conquests. The Free French administration on New Caledonia was extremely apprehensive. It expected the Japanese at any moment. There was only a token French and Australian force there, numbering fewer than 2,000 men. It was not until 17 March that the U.S. 132d and 182d Infantry Regiments landed at Noumea on that same island.

As late as July, Gen. George Kenney, on his way to Australia to take command of the U.S. Air Corps units there, reported on the sad defense of the vital air links at Canton Island and Fiji. Both were "practically defenseless against any organized attacks." He believed that if either of these links were taken out, the air route would be gone and the ship distance to Australia would increase by at least another thousand miles to stay out of the range of Japanese bombers.[4]

Had the Japanese acted earlier, their submarines and aircraft would thus have been in position to wreak havoc on any supply or troop convoy bound for Australia. The Japanese, however successful in most other regions and fully confident of future victories, chose to divide their naval forces, sending Admiral Nagumo's carriers into the Indian Ocean, thus postponing any serious assault on the U.S. bases at Midway and Hawaii. At the same time, they made the decision to move southward from the East Indies, first to New Britain and from there to occupy key positions in Papua New Guinea. The next step was to seize the major Solomon Islands in a leisurely fashion.

It is doubtful whether the Japanese planners ever seriously considered invading the arid north of Australia. To do so would commit them to a major continental war, and with the bulk of their forces committed to China and Manchuria, the inadequate forces available would have become bogged down in the vastness of the Australian continent. The Japanese wanted to isolate Australia, but it was not until later that they realized that by committing so much to the New Britain and New Guinea campaigns, they left the South Pacific supply routes open. Not until the summer of 1942 did they realize their mistake and sought in part to remedy the situation by constructing an airfield on Guadalcanal. By then the United States, realizing the extreme vulnerability of its supply routes, had moved troops to Fiji and New Caledonia and decided to check any further eastward Japanese movement by seizing Guadalcanal.

Once the Japanese High Command decided upon a strategy to isolate Australia, they moved rapidly to seize the small town of Rabaul, in eastern New Britain. Rabaul had been the capital of the Australian territories of Papua and New Britain until an earthquake in June 1941 caused the government to be moved to Lae, in New Guinea. In March 1941, the tiny garrison was augmented by an Australian Imperial Force (AIF) battalion. Two 6-inch coastal defense guns were emplaced as well as an antiaircraft battery. Two small airfields were also constructed, and eventually four Lockheed Hudson bombers (American A-29s) and ten Wirraway (Australian-built North American AT-6s) training planes were stationed there.

The worsening diplomatic situation in the Pacific caused the Australian government in November 1941 to order all women and children evacuated. The first Japanese air attack against Rabaul came on 4 January 1942; this was followed in the next two weeks by three more raids concentrated on the airfields and military installations. The most devastating attack was mounted on the twentieth and another on the twenty-second, by planes from the aircraft carriers *Kaga* and *Akagi*, in preparation for the landing of Japanese infantry the following day. The superior Japanese Zero fighters had little trouble destroying the puny Australian air units at Rabaul.[5]

The Japanese South Seas Detachment of more than 5,000 men had been designated to capture Rabaul. It departed Guam on 16 January escorted by units of the Japanese Fourth Fleet, which included the two carriers *Kaga* and *Akagi*. At Truk the task force was joined by another alternate force, which was to land at Kavieng, on New Ireland.

That naval landing force met little opposition from the small Australian garrison at Kavieng, whose members later attempted an escape by boat but were soon captured. The South Seas Detachment began landing at Simpson Harbor and Karavia, on New Britain, after midnight on 23 January. Soon, further landings were made at Ruluana Point and at Vulcan Island.

The Australian defenders, who had only rifles and machine guns, fought bravely, but by midmorning their situation was hopeless and they began a fighting withdrawal. The 1,400-man garrison exacted a terrible toll from the Japanese, who suffered more than 3,000 casualties on the beaches before the Australians began their retreat.

After giving up the settled areas of Rabaul, bands of Australians moved into the hills, followed by the Japanese. Many were caught and massacred. Eventually, four hundred of the defenders reached the south coast after a torturous journey through nearly impassable jungle and swamps. Daring souls in schooners and small boats ran the gauntlet of Japanese naval and air patrols to effect their rescue.[6]

With the loss of Rabaul, the paper-thin defense of the northern area had received a near mortal blow. All that was left were the few troops in the Bulolo Valley and the garrison at Port Moresby, in New Guinea. Almost immediately the Japanese began construction on the airfields and improvement of harbor facilities at Rabaul. Ultimately they would have five airfields, and the harbor would be able to hold and service a large portion of the Japanese fleet. Rabaul would also become headquarters for the Eighteenth Area Army. Thus it became the key Japanese base in the southern Pacific and the prime target for later Allied air and naval attacks.

Across the Arafura Sea from Papua lay the arid Northern Territories of the vast Australian continent. The population there, estimated at only 7,000 people in 1940, was scattered, maintaining the large cattle ranches that provided the major source of income for the area. The small city of Darwin was the seat of administration; it was also the port of entry for European airlines and the major seaport in the north. An oil tank farm was located there.

The defenses of the city were minimal. There was a fort with 6-inch guns, a naval dock, and a small air force station. It was the key to any defense of the Northern Territories, and at the beginning of the war it came under the ABDA command of General Wavell. By then most of the women and children had been evacuated.

Despite the importance of Darwin, the Australian government, with most if its army in the Middle East, could afford only minimal reinforcements for the city. By February 1942, Darwin had a garrison of 14,000 men, and two Royal Australian Air Force (RAAF) squadrons were located there. It soon became a base for Allied naval vessels, and a trickle of U.S. forces began to arrive even before the first Japanese air attacks.[7] By then the harbor was congested, largely because of difficulties with the powerful Australian labor unions over unloading the ships on an emergency basis.

The Japanese High Command had brought together the greatest naval concentration since Pearl Harbor to support the occupation of the island of Timor, just north of Australia. The task force was built around four aircraft carriers. The planes from these brought the war for the first time directly to Australia. The first air raid struck Darwin without warning in midmorning on 19 February, when eighty-one bombers accompanied by eighteen Zero fighters bombed and strafed the harbor. The U.S. destroyer *Peary* was sunk and the transport *Neptunia,* loaded with explosives, blew up. A second raid followed shortly, with fifty-four bombers attacking the air stations as well as ships in the harbor.

The raids created a panic among the population. Many townspeople fled south, and even military personnel at the RAAF stations joined them. Six ships were sunk, three were beached, and two were damaged. Two U.S. ships were also sunk in adjacent waters. The RAAF, after having nineteen planes destroyed, would not be a factor for weeks. The military and civilian casualties were high; the official account was 193 killed and 443 wounded.[8] Included among the wounded was President Roosevelt's personal envoy, ex–Secretary of War Brig. Gen. Patrick Hurley.

Hoping to bolster public opinion, the official report minimized the damage. Many observers of the raid and later commentators placed the casualties at a much higher number. From the government's position at the time, it was believed necessary to keep the announced figures as low as possible, because the attack and fears of invasion had caused panic throughout the Northern Territories. In retrospect, these fears were groundless. The air strikes were probably meant to negate any offensive preparations for an Allied attack on the Japanese then landing on Timor.

Nevertheless, by 23 February, administration of the northern portion of the Northern Territories was placed under military control. The Japanese would return in eleven further raids in the following days. None of these was as large or did the damage that the first had done. However, a number of people were killed and wounded, and the oil tanks and airfield were damaged. By then the worst of the panic was over, and many of those who had fled into the interior returned to the city.

Soon after the first air raids on Darwin, the Japanese struck at the small town of Broome, near Roebuck Bay, on the northwest coast, where there were only two hundred houses with a normal population of four hundred people. There was a small RAAF fueling facility there, and it was a base for Qantas Airways. A few U.S. Air Corps personnel began arriving to man the few planes stationed at Broome in February, but these were but a small part of the influx during that month. Thousands of evacuees from Malaya, Singapore, and the East Indies passed through the port. Many of those from the East Indies were brought by Dutch flying boats. Because there was not enough housing for the refugees in town, many of them stayed on the aircraft anchored in the bay until transportation into the interior could be arranged.

On 3 March, a flight of nine Zero fighters systematically strafed the port and the airfield. Sixteen Dornier flying boats were destroyed and eight planes, including four U.S. heavy bombers, were lost. The exact number of casualties was never established. The official release indicated seventy killed and a large unspecified number wounded. Other sources placed the number killed at more than two hundred, including many women and children.[9] The panic that had gripped Darwin earlier was repeated at Broome. Fear of further attacks and a Japanese landing caused many people, including servicemen, to attempt to escape into the interior.

Japanese submarines were active off the east coast of Australia, and in the early months of the war they sank a number of Allied merchant ships. The Japanese Naval High Command, however, never utilized its submarines armed with the devastating long lance torpedoes in the same manner as the Germans and the United States to interdict merchant shipping. Actions by the submarines, however, added to the general tension and fears of the Australian civilian population.

The most jarring of submarine attacks occurred on 31 May, when five Japanese monster attack submarines moved into position eight miles east of Sydney and launched four midget submarines. Two of these evaded the antitorpedo boom net protecting the harbor. Another became tangled in the boom, and its commander exploded his submarine, thus alerting the defenses. Only one submarine was able to do any damage. It fired a torpedo at the U.S. cruiser *Chicago,* which evaded it. The torpedo went under a Dutch submarine and struck the seawall. Its detonation sank the *Kuttabul,* a ferryboat, and killed twenty-one sailors. The *Chicago* fired a number of rounds at what was believed to be a submarine, without effect, and one of its 5-inch shells ricocheted into a Sydney residential area. Only one of the midget submarines survived the attack. The material damage of the battle of Sydney was slight, but the action showed a jittery Australia how vulnerable even its largest city was to enemy attack.[10]

Despite the losses of Singapore and the Dutch East Indies, whose possession had figured largely in the planning for the defense of Australia, there was a positive factor in planning that defense; it was known to high-level military planners but not many civilians. This was the island of New Guinea, the second largest island in the world, located immediately north of the Australian continent. Fifteen hundred miles long, it was a shield against any easy invasion of the Northern Territories. The southeastern part, Papua, occupying one-third of the total area, was administered by Australia. The interior was inhospitable, dominated by the high mountains of the Owen Stanley Range as well as jungle and swamps. Although an estimated 100,000 people representing numerous Melanesian tribes inhabited Papua, there were only a few thousand whites; they had settled there to exploit the mineral resources and manage the various plantations along the northern coastal plain. The main town was Port Moresby, on the south coast, which before the war had a population of fewer than 3,000 people, most of whom were natives. There were only a few villages, including Buna, Gona, Lae, and Salamaua, along the north coast. Away from Port Moresby, only native trails connected the north and south coasts. The obstacles to any army effectively operating in Papua were immense. If the Japanese abandoned any idea of invading Australia directly and instead hoped to isolate the north by occupying New Guinea, they would find the island itself a formidable enemy, unless they could take Port Moresby by an amphibious operation. This was a situation well appreciated by Australia's military planners.

Although later developments showed that there was no immediate cause for the panic that had gripped civilians and some of the military, the situation in the early months of the war nevertheless was grim. The situation was largely the fault of Australian patriotism and loyalty to Great Britain, which had allowed the majority of its regular army, the Australian Imperial Force, to be hastily sent to the Middle East in the early stages of the European war. There, the Australian divisions had an enviable record as part of the Western Desert Force and later the Eighth Army in North Africa. At the time of the attack on Pearl Harbor, 121,000 men of the AIF were serving overseas, leaving only 37,000 to defend Australia.[11] To be sure there was the home defense organization, the Australian Military Force (AMF) and the Volunteer Defense Corps (VDC). The former was made up primarily of a citizens' militia force, poorly equipped and numbering only 132,000 men at the start of the Pacific conflict.[12] The VDC comprised generally overage citizens, many of whom were veterans of World War I. The Australian government had immediately developed plans for the expansion of both defense forces, but adequate training would take time, and in early 1942 there appeared to many to be little time left.

The condition of the Royal Australian Air Force was even worse than that of the ground forces. The number of planes and crews available in early 1942 had been reduced drastically by the decision to provide the British in Malaya with air support. In all, 165 planes were lost in the futile defense of Malaya and Singapore. There were only 175 first-line aircraft available after those debacles, backed by a reserve force of 198 planes. Aside from the Catalina patrol bombers and fifty-three Hudson light bombers of the first line, the majority of planes of the small air force were Wirraways, advanced trainers that were hardly a match for Japanese Zero fighters. Compounding the problem was the severe shortage of trained aircrews—not enough at first to man even the few planes available.[13] There was a rush to obtain more aircraft from the United States and Britain, but those promised would not arrive until later, and many of them would prove to be of questionable value. Production of the Wirraways was increased, with a target number of five hundred per month, and delivery of more Hudson light bombers from the United States began in January.

The most obvious solution to the dilemma facing Prime Minister John Curtin and his military staff was to secure the recall of those Australian divisions serving elsewhere. Australia had borne an inordinate share of the ABDA defense. The government, agreeing with the wishes of General Wavell and believing that the Japanese could be checked, had dispatched two brigades of the 8th Division to Malaya. The 15,000-man contingent, after considerable fighting toward the end of the campaign, was forced to surrender when Singapore was lost. Further, in compliance with requests from Wavell, two of the remaining three battalions of the 8th Division had been sent to reinforce the Dutch garrisons at Amboina and Timor, and the third was sent to Rabaul. After heroic but ultimately futile actions, these units were overrun by superior Japanese forces.

Prior to the Japanese attack, Australians had been confident in the might of the British Empire: The British would protect them from any serious threat. They had already witnessed and participated in the inability of Commonwealth forces to halt the Japanese. They would soon discover how difficult it would be to regain control of the Australian divisions sent to the European theater. The major problem facing the Curtin government very early, therefore, was to convince Prime Minister Winston Churchill to release the Australian units then in the Middle East. This was agreed to only reluctantly, because it meant a considerable reduction of the available Commonwealth forces defending Egypt and the Suez Canal.[14]

An agreement had been reached on 8 December that the 6th and 7th Divisions would be shifted to Malaya, to arrive there by March 1942. With the loss of Malaya, these units then became available to the high command for the defense of Australia. Prime Minister Curtin had to resist pressure from Wavell, Churchill, and even President Roosevelt to prevent one of these Australian divisions from being diverted to aid in the defense of Burma. Curtin not only refused this proposal, he demanded that the 9th Division should also be sent home. To agree to this, Churchill responded, would weaken the already precarious British position in North Africa.

A compromise was eventually secured. Two brigades of the 6th Division would temporarily be posted to Ceylon, which, it was feared, would soon be targeted for invasion. The 7th Division and one brigade of the 6th would be returned to Australia. The 9th would stay in the Middle East; its place in Australia's defense would be taken by a U.S. division.[15]

To provide such assistance, the U.S. 32d and 41st Divisions were hastily prepared for embarkation. The 41st arrived in Australia in April and the 32d the following month. The leading elements of the

Australian divisions had already landed in mid-March.[16] Thus by the end of April, the military situation, although still serious, had improved dramatically from the dark days of February.

Although the Australian chiefs of staff were relatively well informed as to the possible choices the Japanese had for further action against Australia, if they were successful in the East Indies and Burma, they were less sure of what military responses could be made to counter them. An "Appreciation" by the chiefs of staff on 17 February reflected their dilemma. Recognizing that they had available less than half the troops necessary to defend Australia, they planned to concentrate on the vital area between Brisbane and Melbourne, the industrial heartland of the continent. They expected the Japanese to attempt to occupy Port Moresby sometime in March, followed by an invasion aimed at Darwin the following month. The main defense proposed would be along the so-called Brisbane Line, which stretched from Brisbane in the east to Adelaide to the southwest, following roughly the course of the Darling River. The Australian War Cabinet, however, on 5 March decided that despite the concentration of the bulk of the army elsewhere, Darwin and Port Moresby should be defended to "the fullest extent possible."[17] At that juncture there were only 35,800 troops in the Northern Territories. To defend Port Moresby, there was the 30th Infantry Brigade, a field artillery regiment, and coastal and antiaircraft units, a total of only 6,500 men.[18]

Prime Minister Curtin had recognized early in the conflict that the major effort in the Pacific war would be borne by the United States. His correspondence with Prime Minister Churchill over the use of Australian troops only convinced him further that Australia's defense ultimately would depend on assistance not from Britain but from the United States. With the collapse of the ABDA command, it was imperative that there be a complete reorganization of the ANZAC command structure. Thus on 26 February, the Combined Australian and New Zealand Chiefs of Staff, in a long memorandum, concluded that a new supreme commander, "preferably a United States officer," of the ANZAC area should be appointed immediately.[19] Even before this, Curtin had communicated to President Roosevelt his wish that Gen. Douglas MacArthur be assigned as commander of Allied forces in the Southwest Pacific. This request only reinforced the decision already made to order MacArthur from the Philippines. The capture of the most distinguished American soldier by the Japanese would be a grave loss and a psychological victory for the enemy.

Roosevelt responded to Curtin's request by sending a personal message to MacArthur on Corregidor on 21 February, ordering him as soon as practicable to leave for Mindanao to inspect the defenses there, then proceed to Australia. At first reluctant to obey, MacArthur eventually agreed, although he postponed his departure for three weeks. Finally on 11 March, MacArthur, accompanied by his family and seventeen senior staff officers, left Corregidor in four battered PT (patrol-torpedo) boats. These officers would form the nucleus of what would later be called the "Bataan Gang," MacArthur's closest advisers in the Southwest Pacific Command.

After running the Japanese blockade, the party landed at Cagayan, on Mindanao. Of the first four B-17s sent to meet MacArthur's party, one had crashed, two never reached Cagayan, and the one that finally landed was in such bad condition that it was not usable. Finally two more B-17s arrived, held together, as the general recalled, "with chewing gum and bailing wire."[20] These were the rickety planes that transported MacArthur and his party on the long flight to Batchelor Field, south of Darwin. There MacArthur met reporters on 17 March and made a simple factual statement concluding with a phrase concerning his future plans for the Philippines: "I shall return."[21]

From Darwin, the general and his family proceeded to Alice Springs by rail. Most of his staff was flown to Melbourne, the site of Australian army, navy, and air force headquarters, as well as those of American general George Brett.

As soon as Brett learned that MacArthur was safely in Australia, he telephoned Prime Minister Curtin to inform him that, in accordance with President Roosevelt's instructions, he had assumed command of all U.S. forces in Australia. Further, he passed on Roosevelt's suggestion that MacArthur be nominated as supreme commander of all forces in the Southwest Pacific.[22] This was a foregone conclusion because of Curtin's earlier request. The Australian

War Cabinet agreed to the proposal, and Curtin informed London and Washington.

MacArthur left Alice Springs almost immediately by train for Melbourne. Arriving at the Spencer Street railway station, he was greeted by the service leaders, a guard of honor, and thousands of cheering spectators who saw in him, the most distinguished American general, the promise that the United States would not abandon Australia. In a short speech, he promised to do his best and, if given the resources, gain victory over Australia's enemies.

His first message to the Australian people was on 26 March at the federal parliamentary dinner at Canberra, where the American ambassador in a brilliant ceremony had earlier presented him with the Medal of Honor, to add to his already immense collection of decorations. MacArthur underscored the promise of America when he said: "My presence here is tangible evidence of our unity. I have come as a soldier in a great crusade of personal liberty as opposed to perpetual slavery. My faith in ultimate victory is invincible, and I bring to you the unbreakable spirit of the free man's code in support of our just cause."[23]

Earlier he had met with Prime Minister Curtin. From the first, Curtin's support for MacArthur's appointment was justified by their personal liking for each other. At the conclusion of their meeting, MacArthur put his arm on Curtin's shoulder and said: "We two, you and I, will see this thing through together. We can do it and we will do it. You take care of the rear and I will handle the front."[24] The support from the Australian prime minister never wavered during the dark days of the war.

Although MacArthur had established his headquarters in the AMP building, a nine-story insurance building in Melbourne where he and his staff had begun work almost immediately, the reality was that he commanded nothing. He had received no directive from Washington, and his relationship with the Australian military was still unclear. As the days went by without clarification of his status, he became more and more frustrated. He had believed that he had been ordered from the Philippines to assume overall command of the war against Japan. As the days passed, he came to believe that there was a conspiracy against him. He believed he had been tricked into leaving the Philippines and that there was a plot engineered by the navy to keep him from command.[25]

In this belief he was partially correct. The delay in announcing his actual command status was because there was no agreement in Washington on who should command the Allied war effort in the Pacific. On 24 March, the Combined Chiefs recognized the Pacific as an area of U.S. responsibility.[26] The formidable Adm. Ernest King, chief of naval operations, wanted Adm. Chester Nimitz to be appointed to control the Pacific war. His argument was that the war would be primarily naval in nature and therefore the navy should be in charge. However, Nimitz was junior to MacArthur and still unproven in his new command in Hawaii.

After many delays, it was finally decided on 30 March to divide the command responsibilities into two parts. Nimitz would control the Pacific Ocean Areas (POA) and MacArthur, from his headquarters in Australia, would command the offensives to recapture the islands north of Australia, the Dutch East Indies, and ultimately the Philippines. This Southwest Pacific theater and Nimitz's zone of operations, abutting each other as they were, would need—and it was hoped would get—maximum cooperation from the two commands. MacArthur was notified of his appointment as commander in chief of the Southwest Pacific theater on 31 March. However, this was preliminary, and it was not until details of command relations were further clarified that the Australian government agreed on 14 April. Four days later, MacArthur formally assumed command.[27]

Chapter II
MacArthur Arrives

The brave front that MacArthur showed in public masked serious doubts he had, particularly during the early weeks of his command. Then, too, he brought with him certain deficiencies, although he would not admit them. For all of the important commands he had held previously, none had equaled the difficult position he had just assumed. He had never commanded such a large body of multinational troops. His only active tactical command had been as a young brigadier general in World War I. In the losing battle for the Philippines, he had provided strategic rather than tactical insights; the actual tactical maneuvers he left to his subordinates. He had remained on Corregidor, never visiting Bataan, which earned him the unjust title of "Dugout Doug."

MacArthur also did not at this time understand or fully appreciate airpower. His dilatory attitude on 8 December had been largely responsible for the destruction of his considerable bomber force in the Philippines. Now in Australia, he found it difficult to work with his chief air officer, Lt. Gen. George Brett. Further, he had a longstanding personal antipathy with many in Washington, particularly Chief of Staff George C. Marshall. Finally, he was an American chauvinist, who preferred to command American troops. But the situation in early 1942 presented him with mainly Australian units. To his credit he would overcome these deficiencies, but it would take time for him to learn the intricacies of warfare in the arena in which he would operate over the next two years.

At the start of his new command, MacArthur had three pressing problems. The first of these was the organization of an adequate headquarters staff for the Southwest Pacific Command, located at first in Melbourne and later in Brisbane. General Marshall had recommended that all Allied governments be represented on his staff. In this he was reflecting President Roosevelt's desire that Dutch and particularly Australian officers be selected. MacArthur did not heed this advice; rather he appointed only U.S. officers, and he reserved the most important positions for the "Bataan Gang." He continued Maj. Gen. Richard Sutherland as his chief of staff, with Brig. Gen. Richard Marshall as the deputy. As his G-2, he kept his Philippine adviser, Col. Charles Willoughby.

Later in June, MacArthur explained to Marshall the reasons for excluding foreign officers from his headquarters staff. He stated that he could find no qualified Dutch officer in Australia and that the Australians, faced with an ever expanding army, were hard pressed to find suitable officers for their own staffs.[1] These reasons were only partly true. There were Australians available, many with more combat experience than those chosen by MacArthur. Undoubtedly, MacArthur wanted to be surrounded by men he knew and trusted. He probably also realized that the bulk of the war in the Pacific, after the early defensive phase had passed, would be the responsibility of the United States, and he did not want to prejudice future operations by having Australians functioning in senior staff positions in an organizational system with which they were not familiar.

At this juncture, MacArthur had to be content with subordinate field commanders not of his choosing. He divided the command of U.S. Army units into two sections. To command those already in Australia, he designated Maj. Gen. Julian Barnes. Showing how out of touch he was with the reality of the situation in the Philippines, he planned to exercise command there through Maj. Gen. Jonathan Wainwright. He was obsessed with the idea of an early return to the Philippines.

MacArthur had not informed Washington that he still intended to direct operations in the Philippines. Washington, therefore, assumed that Wainwright retained overall command in the Philippines and treated him as such. Marshall, in late March, vetoed MacArthur's desire to conduct Philippine affairs from a distance.

He informed MacArthur that his command responsibilities did not include the Philippines and should concentrate exclusively on the problem of defending Australia.[2]

In the command restructuring, Vice Adm. Herbert Leary was continued as the commander of the miniscule Allied fleet, and General Brett retained command of the Allied air forces. MacArthur was uncomfortable with Leary and did not understand fully the Naval High Command's viewpoint, which was dictated largely by the need to defend Hawaii. To his general negative attitude toward airpower he added a personal dislike of his air commander, and he minimized the extreme problems faced by both Australian and U.S. air units. Not until Brett was replaced in July by Maj. Gen. George Kenney would MacArthur find an air corps commander in whom he could place explicit trust.

It would have been unreasonable for MacArthur to insist upon having U.S. commanders for the Allied ground forces, because the bulk of the troops available were Australian, even after the arrival of the two U.S. National Guard divisions. On 23 March, Gen. Sir Thomas Blamey arrived in Australia from the Middle East, where he had served with distinction as the commander of the AIF during the desert war. Three days later he was appointed commander in chief of the Australian army, and in MacArthur's reorganization he soon became commander of Allied land forces.

The structure of the Australian army was not greatly altered by the Allied reorganization except that there was a more rational division of command responsibilities. The available land force was divided into two armies, one corps, a Northern Territories Force, and a New Guinea Force.[3] General Sir Vernon Sturdee remained chief of the General Staff, and Maj. Gen. Sir Edmund Herring continued as commander of the Northern Territories Force; Maj. Gen. Basil Morris was commanding officer of the New Guinea Force. Not until August would Morris be replaced by Maj. Gen. Sir Sydney Rowell, and Brig. Cyril Clowes would be appointed to command the army units designated to defend Milne Bay.

This duality of command, although it would later prove cumbersome, served the immediate purpose of a primarily defensive posture forced upon the Allies in early 1942. In the ensuing months,

MacArthur would make changes in the command structure of the U.S. forces, gaining men whom he trusted, particularly in his air arm. However important the organization of his headquarters was, and the correlated need for good relations with his Australian subordinates, his main concern during this early period was obtaining men and materiel first for defense and later for a hoped-for offensive that would end the immediate threat to Australia. In this he directly confronted the decisions by higher command in Washington and London, which had assigned priorities to the various theaters; the needs of Australia as seen by MacArthur could not be met.

Before Pearl Harbor, President Roosevelt and his advisers had envisioned the probability of war not with Japan but with the European Axis powers. The Lend-Lease program and decisions to provide protection to British North Atlantic convoys showed clearly that the United States was on a collision course with the Axis. The "Victory Program," designed by then Col. Albert Wedemeyer of the General Staff in mid-1941, was based upon the need to conduct a war in Europe; therefore, the European area was given first priority. The spread of the conflict to Asia and the Pacific did not alter these decisions, particularly with the hopes envisioned for an early second front to aid the Soviet Union in its desperate defense against the German army. On 18 March, Marshall informed MacArthur of the fixed limits on U.S. troop commitments to his theater. Two U.S. infantry divisions had already been allotted to Australia, and the air corps units would be brought up to strength.

This information was not well received by MacArthur, who believed that the United States, which had a total of thirty-three divisions by 1941 and a large air force, could send more reinforcements to Australia.[4] In this he minimized the losses suffered by the navy at Pearl Harbor, the length of the supply route, and the crucial need to secure the land bases to protect that route. In a meeting with Curtin, on 20 March, MacArthur pressed the prime minister to ask Winston Churchill for an aircraft carrier and the assignment of two British divisions to Australia.

Churchill was surprised that MacArthur would seek to circumvent the chain of command to appeal directly for aid, and he indicated his displeasure to President Roosevelt, who in turn conveyed the prime minister's feelings to Marshall. The chief of staff then reprimanded MacArthur for cutting through the accepted norm of diplomacy. In part to mollify MacArthur, he stated that he understood MacArthur's delicate position as commander in chief and also as an adviser to the government, which had made no secret of its displeasure at the inadequacy of the forces being provided for Australian defense.[5]

Marshall's March communication did not silence MacArthur and his demand for more troops and equipment. However, his chance of changing the policy and receiving more support immediately had been dealt a severe blow when the British government on 14 April accepted the U.S.-sponsored Bolero plan, which called for the buildup of U.S. forces in Britain as soon as possible. President Roosevelt agreed that Bolero would take precedence over other theaters' requests, and explained this to MacArthur in a personal letter.

MacArthur believed that his superiors in Washington did not appreciate the gravity of his situation. His concern no doubt was reinforced by the Japanese occupation of Lae and Salamaua, in northwest Papua, on 8 March. Then on 8 May he repeated his need for more support. He wanted a minimum of three first-line divisions, two British aircraft carriers, and at least five hundred more planes. Four days later he communicated his fears and needs to Curtin in a succinct appraisal of the situation: He had a vast continent to defend with poor communication infrastructures. Adding to the difficulties was the fact that the majority of its defenders were poorly trained. He compared this to the Japanese potential, which allowed them, if they wished, to move large numbers of troops to any part of New Guinea or northern Australia.

The prime minister passed on these requests to the Australian foreign minister Herbert Evatt, who relayed them to the joint staff mission in Washington. Churchill had earlier pointed out that Britain did not have available the two aircraft carriers and noted that his primary concern was with India. However, he promised to direct two divisions to Australia if the continent was invaded. General Marshall repeated his earlier contention that MacArthur had enough force to defend Australia. He stated that MacArthur had a total of 400,000 men and, with the arrival of the 32d and 41st Divisions, had more than 100,000 U.S. troops; in addition, he would soon be receiving 535 aircraft. Marshall did not address the quality of these forces; nor did the president, who followed up Marshall's reply with a direct communication supporting Marshall's position. These replies to MacArthur's requests closed this phase of his demands. It was now obvious that he would have to make do with what was then available.[6]

The inadequacy of MacArthur's defense forces applied with even more gravity to his air units. During the early phase of air action in the north and at Port Moresby, it was the responsibility of the Royal Australian Air Force, whose resources were pitifully small. The main airfield at Port Moresby had not been finished until February. At first just a few Hudson medium bombers and Catalina patrol planes operated from there, making token raids on the main Japanese base at Rabaul. On 19 March, RAAF Fighter Squadron 75, flying Curtis P-40 Kittyhawks, arrived and was greeted by antiaircraft fire from the nervous army gunners. The RAAF pilots soon made their presence felt defending the airfield. For the next forty-four days, the patched-up planes of Squadron 75 engaged the superior Japanese Zero fighters and bombers, which made almost daily raids on Port Moresby. The daily average of serviceable planes was only five. In addition, they attacked targets of opportunity at Lae and Salamaua and escorted U.S. bombers on their attacks on Japanese positions. In doing so, Squadron 75 lost thirty aircraft and twelve pilots. In turn, they destroyed thirty-five enemy planes.[7]

American planes were sent north generally to the area around Townsville, where Australian and U.S. engineers were hurriedly constructing new airfields. The U.S. units in late May were turned over to the operational control of the commanding general of the Northern Territories; later, when units were assigned to Port Moresby, they were placed under the commanding general of New Guinea Force. By the end of June, there were 20,000 U.S. Air Corps personnel in the north, but there would not be a separate U.S. Air Corps until September, and even then it would depend upon Australian communications and headquarters personnel. At this time the paper strength of the U.S. Air Corps was two heavy-, two medium-, and one light-bombardment group. One of the heavy-bombardment groups, the 43d, was not ready for an equal share of bombing missions until September, and the 38th Bomber Group received its B-25 medium bombers that same month. Many of the bomber squadrons operated with a melange of planes—mostly medium bombers such as the Douglas A-20s, Martin B-26s, and North American B-25s—putting an added burden on the supply and repair system, which was at best primitive. Of the three U.S. fighter squadrons, two were equipped with Bell P-39s and P-400s, the other with P-40s.[8]

Even more than with the ground forces, the air services had to be content with either inferior aircraft or planes that in the main were not wanted in other theaters. The Lockheed Hudson bomber, although it would do yeoman service in Europe as an antisubmarine patrol craft, was slow and had a limited bomb capacity and low operating ceiling. There were only a few A-20s available, and these were good basically for only low-level attack and were like most of the bombers—relatively easy prey for the dominant Japanese Zeros flying out of Rabaul. The B-26 was called by many the "Widow Maker" because of the difficulty that pilots had controlling it. Nevertheless, as the members of the 22d Bombardment Group showed, in the hands of trained pilots it was the best bomber available, at least until the arrival of a significant number of B-25s later in the year.

All Allied fighter aircraft were inferior to their Japanese counterparts, the Zero and the Oscar. The P-39 and its export version, the P-400, were severely handicapped by not having turbochargers, and they could not operate successfully above 15,000 feet. With its 37mm cannon, it later became an excellent ground support aircraft. The P-40, although it had some success with the Flying Tigers in China, was far inferior to Japanese fighters in a dogfight. American and Australian pilots tended to avoid these whenever possible and were usually successful because of luck or in some cases skill in catching the enemy at some disadvantage. Thus MacArthur's air force was lacking not only in numbers of planes but also in quality. During the early stage of the war, the Japanese held a dominant position from their two air bases at Rabaul.

Nevertheless, the U.S. and RAAF provided MacArthur with his only offense against the Japanese. Before there could be continuing effective strikes, however, it was necessary to refurbish the old airstrips in the Northern Territories and at Port Moresby and to construct new ones. New airfields were built principally north of Townsville along the Cape York Peninsula at Mareeba, Cooktown, and Coln. These enabled the air units to provide cover for the Torres Straits and also for staging attacks on Japanese bases on New Guinea and New Britain.

In late April, the first U.S. engineer troops, including two Negro units, were sent to Port Moresby, where they were utilized in constructing new air facilities as well as helping to improve the harbor in order to accommodate the projected buildup of men and supplies. At the same time the 8th Service Group, which consisted of fifty officers and a thousand enlisted men, arrived to man Jackson airdrome, one of three principal fields in the Moresby area. This unit, as with all other air service units, worked in heat and humidity under the most primitive conditions and at the end of a tenuous supply line. Not until December 1942 when an air depot group arrived was the pressure on the men of the service group eased. During this crucial period of the buildup of MacArthur's forces, the men of all U.S. and RAAF ground units worked around the clock to keep the planes flying; many of them had sustained serious battle damage.[9]

The difficulty faced by pilots and crews in taking the war to the enemy is well illustrated by the actions of the 22d Bombardment Group. The group first was based at Garbutt Field, near Townsville. Flying B-26s, it launched the first medium bomber strike at Rabaul on 5 April and continued the harassment of the Japanese during the rest of the year. To do so, the planes, loaded with bombs, took off from Garbutt and landed at Port Moresby for refueling and briefing. Each mission to New Britain was 2,600 miles long, much of it over shark-infested waters. Over land in New Guinea the aircraft flew above cloud-covered mountains more than 10,000 feet high. The terrain below was generally heavy jungle where, if a plane went down, the chance of survival was negligible. The bombers were unescorted, flying into an area dominated by Japanese fighters. The saving grace for the pilots of the B-26s was the speed of their difficult-to-handle planes. They could outrun any Japanese fighter, a luxury denied pilots of the slower Hudsons and Boeing B-17s. Planes of the 22d also struck at targets on the north coast of New Guinea and, to the best of their ability, supported the later action at Buna and Gona. During the first ten months of action, the 22d was credited with destroying ninety-four enemy planes in the air, ranking first of all U.S. Air Corps units by January 1943.[10] The improvement in the fortunes of the Allied air forces can be seen in the reequipping of this group in January 1943 with B-25s, which were to become the workhorse of the air corps in the Southwest Pacific.

From April through July 1942, the Allied air forces shot down eighty enemy planes and destroyed another twenty on the ground as well as damaging the fixed facilities on New Britain and Bougainville. However, eighty-three planes were lost in combat and an additional seventy-seven in accidents. Replacements for the lost aircraft were slow in coming; not until the Lockheed P-38s arrived in August did the United States have pursuit planes that could challenge the Japanese fighters on roughly equal terms. Morale among the aircrews, operating from isolated bases in primitive living conditions and forced to make these dangerous daily missions, was low. The command structure was faulty. American squadrons were under the tactical command of Australians, which was resented by American commanders. A further problem for the U.S. air units was the confusion of command at the highest level. MacArthur did not like General Brett and tended to minimize the difficulties he faced in trying to build an adequate air presence practically from nothing. One reason for MacArthur's antipathy toward Brett was the attitude of his chief of staff, Sutherland, who undermined the air force chief; this helped to convince MacArthur of Brett's incompetence. By late June, MacArthur decided to replace Brett, and on 14 July informed him of that in a short, curt note.[11]

Brett's replacement was Maj. Gen. George Kenney, who reported to MacArthur on 30 July and was greeted by a long tirade against the air corps. MacArthur said that he had no use for anyone in that service, from Brett down to and including colonels; he considered them to be disloyal to his headquarters. Kenney pledged his loyalty and promised to immediately inspect the forward areas to determine what changes should be made.

After spending a few days in the northern areas and New Guinea, Kenney returned and laid out his plans to MacArthur, who agreed to them and gave Kenney carte blanche to do whatever was needed. Kenney dismissed five general officers in the first few weeks, and soon many on Brett's old staff were transferred. All were replaced by men considered more competent by the new commander of the Allied air forces. Kenney also confronted Sutherland and in a direct manner informed him that air operations was not a part of Sutherland's job. The ensuing quarrel over command responsibilities was ended by MacArthur supporting Kenney.[12]

One of the complaints against Brett had been that he bowed too much to Australian wishes. If this was a problem, it was largely solved by the creation on 3 September of the Fifth U.S. Air Force. Kenney retained command of the Allied air forces while assuming command of the new organization, which was shortly to become the principal air striking force, although Australian units would continue to be active during 1942. With the new command structure, combined with the supply of more and better aircraft, MacArthur's problems—real and imagined—with his air support, although not completely solved, had improved immeasurably.[13]

MacArthur would fight a losing battle with Washington for direct permanent control of a large naval force. Admiral Ernest King, the chief of naval operations, was openly hostile toward the idea of shifting more of the Pacific Fleet to MacArthur's area. He had been the most vocal in opposing MacArthur's requests for added naval support in May. The decision to block Japanese expansion in the Solomon Islands by invading Guadalcanal in August meant that the bulk of MacArthur's small naval force, commanded by Australian rear admiral V. A. C. Crutchley, would be used to support the invasion. MacArthur would not be happy with his senior U.S. naval commanders until much later, but these ill feelings never reached the same levels as with his air forces.

One major problem that directly impacted MacArthur's plans for offensive action in northern Papua was the lack of suitable charts of the coastal areas from Milne Bay westward. Until adequate surveys could be made, Admiral Leary and his successor, Vice Adm. Arthur Carpender, refused to take capital ships into those regions. This meant that any attempted invasion of the Buna-Gona area had to be undertaken with minimal fire support from the navy.[14]

Much of MacArthur's and the Australian staffs' time was consumed by technical details of how the Allies could defend Australia with inadequate forces. This was purely a defensive mentality forced on them by Japanese superiority. The strategic question of how best to do this had been answered earlier by the Australian High Command. They would send minimal reinforcements north and hold the bulk of their forces farther south behind the Brisbane Line. MacArthur disagreed with this plan. He claimed later that almost immediately after arriving in Australia, he decided to abandon that plan and to "stop the Japanese on the rough mountains of the Owen Stanley Range in New Guinea . . . to make the fight for Australia beyond its borders."[15]

MacArthur did not announce publicly until early 1943 that he had concluded this strategy immediately on viewing Australia's plight. Prime Minister Curtin remembered this differently and believed that the decision was made much later. To this MacArthur replied in November 1943 that it was never his intention to defend Australia on the mainland, because he believed it would take at least twenty-five divisions and a huge naval and air commitment and would mean abandoning a large section of the country.[16] It is possible that MacArthur was indulging in unnecessary self-promotion in his claim. Nevertheless, the decision originated with him, and he convinced the Australian leaders of its correctness. The question during the spring of 1942 was how to implement his strategy.

Part of the answer was to build up Allied air strength in the Townsville area and at Port Moresby. This necessitated the construction of many airfields in the north and at Port Moresby. If Port Moresby was to be the key to controlling New Guinea, as stated in the joint estimate of 14 April made by the Australian chiefs of staff and MacArthur's headquarters, the garrison there had to be greatly increased. The number of troops at Port Moresby at the end of January was only 5,500, far fewer than would be needed to fend off the expected Japanese landings.

These were steadily augmented, with the largest reinforcement being the 14th Australian Infantry Brigade, with 4,100 men, which arrived on 15 May. Although this was after the crucial Coral Sea battle, the fear of a further Japanese invasion attempt still remained. By October there would be 60,000 troops at Port Moresby, which would be the main staging base for the first major Allied offensive in New Guinea.[17]

Further reinforcements were also sent to Milne Bay. Despite the potential threat to that crucial area, in June there were only two companies and a machine-gun platoon of the 14th Australian Brigade stationed there. However, the following month the 7th Infantry Brigade was ordered to Milne Bay from Townsville. A company of U.S. engineers was also dispatched, with orders to build an airfield. By the end of the month, a squadron of P-40s was operating from it.

Reinforcements were also sent into the Bulolo Valley, in central Papua. The Australian 5th Independent Company arrived at Wau on 26 May. The troops there were code named Kanga Force, and in late June they began an offensive against the Japanese garrison at Salamaua, causing considerable damage and killing more than a hundred Japanese. The Australian Force was too small to hold the gains and was forced to withdraw when Japanese troops were sent from Lae.[18]

Despite the antipathy between MacArthur and Admiral King, it appears in retrospect that the navy, with its depleted surface fleet, was doing everything possible to aid in the defense of Australia. The first priority was to secure the bases that guarded the supply route. This spawned the hit-and-run attacks by Vice Adm. William F. Halsey's and Vice Adm. Wilson Brown's small task forces in the early months of the war. One of these was an attack on Rabaul planned by Brown when in February he was temporarily assigned to Admiral Leary's ANZAC Force. It was a daring proposal, given the danger of bringing the *Lexington,* one of the few carriers operating in the Pacific, close in to land-based airpower. Despite the danger, Brown moved directly westward from New Caledonia, hoping to surprise the Japanese. Unfortunately, 350 miles east of the target, the task force was detected on 20 February by a Japanese flying boat, which alerted Rabaul. That afternoon the task force was attacked by eighteen planes; they were intercepted by *Lexington*'s fighters, which destroyed most of them. However, with surprise lost, Brown called off the raid. Without the element of surprise, his force was no match for the Japanese 25th Air Flotilla at Rabaul.[19]

Admiral Brown did not give up on his desire to strike at Rabaul, but he advised Admiral Nimitz that any future attack should be made with two carriers. In early March his proposed attack was approved, and Rear Adm. Frank Jack Fletcher was ordered to take the *Yorktown* Task Force and join Brown's *Lexington* Force. Brown did not want to move his carriers into the virtually uncharted areas of the Bismarck Sea close to the bases of the 25th Air Flotilla. The choice of target also changed when the Japanese occupied Lae and Salamaua on 8 March. Brown then decided to strike the ships there before the beachheads could be consolidated.

On 10 March he launched his planes from a position forty-five miles off the southern coast of Papua. A scout bomber was sent ahead to orbit above the chosen pass at 7,500 feet in the Owen Stanley Range. From there the planes were vectored to Lae. All 104 planes from the two carriers took part. The attackers achieved complete surprise; there was no air resistance and there were a number of ships off the coast of Lae. Given the unusual air superiority, the results were meager, primarily because the Japanese had room to maneuver their ships. Nevertheless, a large minesweeper, a 6,000-ton transport, and the 6,500-ton light cruiser *Kongo Maru* were sunk. The task force escaped unscathed. The raid, however important in showing the Japanese that their positions could be attacked by naval air strikes, could not halt the planned Japanese offensives any more than could the continued raids by MacArthur's land-based aircraft.[20]

The event that more than any other caused the Japanese to alter their plans to secure Port Moresby was the battle of the Coral Sea, the first major naval engagement of the Pacific war. The early, stunning Japanese victories had given them what one of their commanders later called the "Victory Disease." Nowhere was this more noticeable than in the disposition of the fast carriers of Admiral Nagumo's battle force, the main element of the Japanese navy. Instead of employing them directly to smash the remnants of the American fleet in Hawaii or support operations against the supply routes to Australia, he was directed into the Indian Ocean. There he succeeded in driving the Royal Navy into the westward reaches and as far south as Madagascar. His return to Japanese home waters was timely, because Admiral Yamamoto was belatedly preparing for his assault on Midway, where he hoped to lure the remnants of the U.S. fleet and destroy them. This proposed action took priority over the secondary plan to occupy Port Moresby.

Yamamoto's plan for the Port Moresby operation, code named MO, would thus not have the full weight of the combined fleet behind it. Nevertheless, the high command believed that they would have sufficient force to deal with the weakened Allied navy, which might be encountered. As would be true of all Japanese naval planning, the plan was extremely complex; it consisted of five parts. At the heart of the plan were the naval transports, which were loaded at Rabaul. Five of these carried the 3d Naval Landing Force and six more held the South Seas Detachment. The main support for the transports would come from two different forces. A cruiser force would protect the landing while a carrier striking force assembling at Truk would give long-range support. This was built around two big carriers, the *Zuikaku* and *Shokaku,* both veterans of the Pearl Harbor attack. A secondary goal in the MO plan was for another smaller landing force to occupy Tulagi, in the southern Solomons, to build a seaplane base. Its operation would be covered by another small task force of four heavy cruisers and the light carrier *Shoho.* The Japanese planners had concluded that the United States would have only one carrier available within striking distance of the landing parties. In this they were mistaken.[21]

MacArthur's headquarters was aware by mid-April of the heavy concentration of Japanese forces at Rabaul. All indications pointed to an attempt to take Port Moresby. Further projections were that the invasion flotilla would enter the Coral Sea in early May. To counter this threat, Nimitz reinforced Fletcher's *Yorktown* Task Force with that of the *Lexington,* now commanded by Rear Adm. Aubrey Fitch. Aside from the small screen of destroyers, the Allies had eight cruisers, including three from MacArthur's small naval contingent commanded by Australian rear admiral J. C. Crace. Fletcher's orders from Nimitz were very general. He was to bring his task force into the Coral Sea on 1 May to intercept the Japanese invasion flotilla. Tactical details were left up to Fletcher.

Fueling delays caused Fletcher to divide his force when informed by MacArthur's headquarters of the movement of the Japanese Port Moresby Force. He proceeded westward, hoping first to encounter the Japanese Tulagi landing force. However, the Japanese evaded him and safely landed troops on Tulagi. Fletcher then decided to attack the Japanese ships still present in the vicinity of Tulagi; he rushed northward, leaving Fitch far behind. The massive U.S. air attack of 4 May netted little; only two Japanese destroyers were damaged and four landing barges sunk. Fletcher then moved south and joined the *Lexington* Force the following day.[22]

The main Japanese carrier force was well within the Coral Sea by 5 May, and the Port Moresby invasion flotilla was moving toward the Jomard Passage in the Louisiade Archipelago, from where it would move westward toward Port Moresby. The two main carrier groups came together on 7 May, with the Japanese attacking Fletcher's screening ships and sinking two destroyers. Payback was soon in coming as planes from both U.S. carriers concentrated on the light carrier *Shoho,* which was sunk just before noon.

The main battle was contested the following day, with planes from both American carriers attacking the *Shokaku* and *Zuikaku.* The former was so seriously damaged that it was not available for action for months. At midday on the eighth, a massive Japanese air attack damaged the *Yorktown;* the *Lexington* took a series of torpedo hits and sank later that day. The main air action was over by midafternoon, with each task force moving away.

The tactical results of the engagement fought entirely by aircraft was, for the Allies, at best a draw. In the air battles the Japanese had lost forty-three planes; the United States had thirty-three destroyed. The loss of the *Lexington* and the damage to the *Yorktown* were serious blows to Nimitz's depleted fleet. This was hardly compensated for by the sinking of the *Shoho.* However, the Coral Sea engagement was a strategic victory for the Allies. Vice Admiral Shigyoshi Inoue, senior naval commander at Rabaul, early on the morning of 7 May, fearing for the safety of the Port Moresby Invasion Group, ordered it to turn away from the Jomard Passage and postponed the proposed landings by two days. With the sinking of the *Shoho,* the damage to *Shokaku,* and the loss of so many planes, Inoue recalled the transports.[23]

An even more momentous naval battle was being planned by Yamamoto, even as the last engagement in the Coral Sea was being fought. He finally had decided to attack Midway, which he assumed correctly would force Nimitz to commit the remnants of the U.S. fleet. Typically, his battle plan was overly complex, consisting of five separate attack groups. His main striking force, composed of four carriers—the *Akagi, Kaga, Hiryu,* and *Soryu,* with 272 planes—departed the Inland Sea on 26 May. Earlier that day a smaller attack group, the 2d Mobile Force, had left, hoping to provide a diversionary operation in the Aleutian Islands. The following day the Midway Occupation Force, consisting of twelve transports guarded by four heavy cruisers, left the Mariana Islands. Yamamoto himself was on board the world's largest battleship, the *Yamato,* with two other battleships and a destroyer screen. These ships departed on 28 May. That main force would shadow Nagumo's carriers, which remained hundreds of miles ahead.

The plan was that, once Midway had been neutralized and the U.S. naval force defeated, the main Japanese force would be available to cover the landings and occupy Midway. Although having superiority in ships, Yamamoto was ill served by his intelligence service, which underestimated the U.S. strength. More importantly, he believed that he would be able to surprise the defenders. The key to the defense of Midway and ultimately Hawaii was the U.S. code breakers, who had pinpointed the area and time of attack.

With this knowledge, Nimitz positioned his two task forces three hundred miles northeast of Midway, hoping to ambush the Japanese. Admiral Fletcher, with the hastily repaired *Yorktown,* was in overall command. The first action of the Midway battle was initiated on 3 June by Midway-based B-17s, which attacked the Japanese occupation force. No hits were scored. The main action occurred the following day when Nagumo, still believing that the U.S. carriers were in Hawaii, launched 108 planes in the early morning to strike Midway Island. The Marine pilots, in their outclassed Brewster Buffalo fighters, who intercepted the Japanese were shot from the sky by the Japanese fighters.

The attack on the island did considerable damage, and counterattacks by U.S. Navy and U.S. Army pilots against Nagumo's carriers were costly failures. The Japanese scout plane assigned to patrol the northeast quadrant was late in taking off, so Nagumo was oblivious of the U.S. carriers that were closing in on him as he prepared to receive his strike force. Rear Admiral Raymond Spruance had already launched all of his planes except for those needed to protect the carriers. Two hours later, Fletcher launched thirty-five planes from *Yorktown*.

In the midst of rearming his attack planes, Nagumo was informed of the presence of the U.S. fleet. In a quandary over whether to arm them with bombs or torpedoes, he procrastinated. Meanwhile, the dive-bombers and fighters from *Hornet* could not find the Japanese fleet, and many were forced to land on Midway; the entire group missed the battle. Meanwhile, *Hornet*'s Torpedo Squadron 8 had located the Japanese carriers and attacked with their slow Douglas Devastator bombers. The Japanese destroyed fourteen of fifteen planes; there was only one survivor. Soon after, Torpedo Squadron 6 from *Enterprise* met the same fate, as did *Yorktown*'s Squadron 3. Thus by midmorning, the Japanese had beaten off all attacks, destroying thirty-five of forty-one U.S. torpedo bombers.

Any elation that the Japanese might have had was short lived, because dive-bombers from the *Enterprise* and *Yorktown* found Nagumo's fleet shortly after the failure of the last torpedo attacks. Thirty-five planes attacked the *Akagi* and *Kaga*, whose fighter cover had been drawn down by the torpedo bomber attacks. Within minutes the two ships were ablaze. Shortly afterward, *Yorktown*'s dive-bombers hit the *Soryu*, with devastating results. All three carriers would be abandoned and later sunk. Planes from the *Hiryu*, the sole remaining Japanese carrier, found the *Yorktown* just before noon. The veteran of the Coral Sea was hit by a number of torpedoes and would later sink. Revenge for this attack was soon in coming, as dive-bombers from *Enterprise* struck the *Hiryu*. That carrier also was abandoned and sank the next day.[24]

Admiral Yamamoto on the *Yamato* was more than two hundred miles away, too far to affect the course of the carrier battles. On being informed of the loss of his carriers, he briefly contemplated further attacks on Midway but eventually decided that without air cover, such a maneuver would be disastrous. He ordered the massive combined fleet to retreat. The only positive result of his complex plan had been the occupation of Kiska and Attu, in the Aleutians, each of dubious value. When the Japanese losses at Midway are added to those of the Coral Sea, the results are staggering: In one month the Imperial Navy had five carriers sunk and one seriously damaged. The lost veteran aircrews could never be replaced. The balance of naval power in the Pacific was permanently altered.

The twin naval victories were not immediately appreciated by the Australians. Soon after the Coral Sea victory, the Australian War Cabinet was critical of the way the battle had been conducted and conveyed its criticism to Curtin, who passed it on to MacArthur. For all his differences with the navy, however, MacArthur was well aware of the importance of the Coral Sea victory. On 18 May he replied to Curtin, assuring him that he believed that the Coral Sea was "a brilliant effort which saved Australia from a definite and immediate threat."[25] That MacArthur realized how these two naval actions had reshaped the Pacific war is seen in the notes of a discussion he had with Curtin on the results of those battles. He indicated his belief that the battles had "resulted in the transformation of the position in the Southwest Pacific and the security of Australia had been assured."[26]

Although MacArthur was now convinced that Australia proper, even considering his inadequate force, was no longer in danger, he knew that despite the serious naval losses, the Japanese still had the local initiative. His immediate problem, therefore, was how to defend the Allied bases in Papua in order to be able to launch the offensives that would alter this negative balance.

Chapter III
Retreat to Ioribaiwa

In early June 1942, MacArthur reiterated his short-term plan for an offensive against the Japanese on New Britain. As with many of his early proposals, it is difficult to know whether he was serious or was simply using this as a means of alerting Washington to his needs. He had already been rebuffed in his requests for more naval and air support. If one believes the proposal he made to General Marshall on 8 June to reflect his understanding of the power situation in the Southwest Pacific, he was poorly informed as to Japanese strength concentrated around Rabaul. Nevertheless, he claimed that he could take the offensive aimed at capturing Rabaul if given a naval task force built around two carriers and a Marine division to augment the U.S. 32d and 41st Divisions and the Australian 7th Division, already in Australia. If successful, this would force the Japanese higher command to move seven hundred miles north, to Truk and bring an end to the threat to Australia.

It appears that Marshall was prepared to accept MacArthur's proposal and recommended this to Admiral King, who was not impressed. He argued against bringing carriers within range of land-based air, and on a nontactical level he was still not convinced that the division of command in the Pacific was the correct decision.[1]

Although the plan was not accepted, MacArthur's proposal to Marshall did spur the Joint Chiefs into serious consideration of the immediate Allied strategic goals in the Pacific. On 2 July they issued a directive that established those objectives. The proposed offensive was divided into three tasks. For Task One, Vice Adm. Robert

Ghormley, commanding the South Pacific area, was directed to seize Tulagi and the Santa Cruz Islands. Tasks Two and Three were to be achieved by MacArthur's forces. Of most immediate concern to MacArthur was Task Two, which ordered the taking of the northern Solomon Islands and clearing the Japanese from northern Papua. The final task was the occupation of Rabaul and adjacent territory on New Ireland. The seizure of Tulagi was set for 1 August. Admiral King, fearful for the naval supply line to Australia, pressed on with Task One despite objections from Ghormley that there were not enough ships or men to carry it out if the Japanese decided to resist. Carrying out Task One would lead to the key Guadalcanal campaign.[2]

Even before the directive, MacArthur had planned a limited action in the Buna region to establish an airfield from which Allied planes could threaten Lae and Salamaua. He decided to move his headquarters to Brisbane, eight hundred miles closer to the combat area, a move completed by 20 July. He also replaced the commander of U.S. ground forces, Maj. Gen. Julian Barnes, whom he had inherited when he took command. Major General Robert Richardson, who had earlier made an inspection of the Australian situation for General Marshall, was offered the position as commander of I Corps, which consisted basically of the 32d and 41st Divisions. He declined, giving as his reason that he would be uncomfortable serving under an Australian commander. He would ultimately command all U.S. Army units in the Pacific theater. The second choice was Maj. Gen. Robert Eichelberger, who had been a West Point classmate of both Maj. Gen. Edwin Harding, commander of the 32d Division, and Maj. Gen. Horace Fuller, commander of the 41st Division. Eichelberger later became MacArthur's choice to rescue what were considered difficult situations at Buna and Biak. Preparatory for action in New Guinea, the 41st Division on 12 July was moved north from the Melbourne area to Rockhampton. The next day, the 32d began its move from Adelaide to the Brisbane area.

The objectives on the north coast of Papua were three small native villages—Gona, Sanananda, and Buna. Before the war, Gona, located between the beach and the jungle, was described as a garden spot. Aside from the native village, the chief buildings there in

1942 belonged to the Gona Mission, which had been established in 1900. It consisted of a church of woven sago leaf, a mission house, and a school. The mission was headed by a Church of England priest, James Barton. Two nuns helped maintain the station. The parish was huge, and most parishioners were Orokaivas, who in the early part of the century were renowned as warriors and cannibals. Although some had been converted, many were still hostile to whites; some later would cooperate with the Japanese. Until July 1942 the small community had not been touched by the war. The second village, Sanananda, was located down the coast halfway to Buna. It was the shipping point for the Sangara Rubber Plantation. The company had built a corduroy road that ran inland for fifteen miles. Both the Allies and the Japanese were aware of this, and Sanananda would become a prime objective for both sides.[3]

The small village of Buna, which would become a major target, was located near the southern end of the coastal plain. The region from Sanananda to Buna was flat and low lying. In the Buna region the average elevation was only three feet above sea level, and it was only slightly higher as far as ten miles inland. In addition to the native village, Buna was the site of a government station, which was served by a few Australian officials. The area around Buna was dominated by the Girua River, which emptied into the bay through several channels. One of these, Entrance Creek, wound its way between the village and the government station. To the east was a huge swamp formed by the backup of the river over the low-lying ground. These natural obstacles alone would make it difficult for troops moving toward Buna from the interior. Buna and the other villages were important only because they were the northern terminal points for a series of native trails, the most important being the one connecting with the interior village of Kokoda, the site of another government station. Located there were officers' houses, a police station, a native hospital, a rubber plantation, and the only landing strip in the region.

The Kokoda Trail, or, as the Australians called it, the Track, began at Buna, fifty miles from Kokoda. From there a reasonable climb terminated at Wairopi (native for wire rope), where a wire rope bridge spanned a huge gorge over the Kumusi River. After that

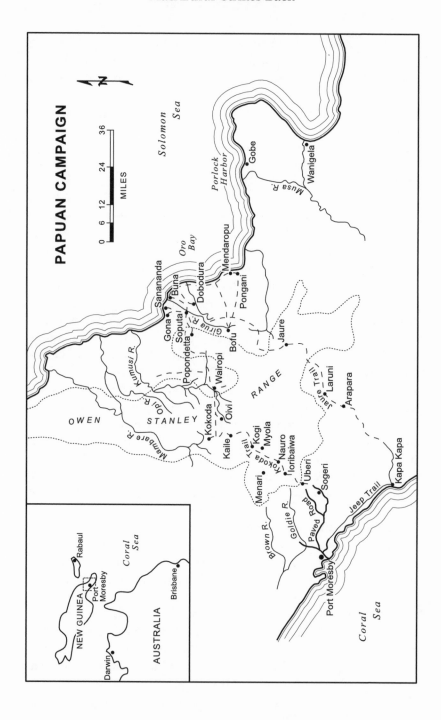

the trail became steeper all the way to Kokoda, which was located at an elevation of 1,200 feet on a small plateau between the foothills of two mountain ranges. Turning southward, the trail clung to the western side of a deep gorge as it passed through the villages of Deniki and Isurava and onward to Alola, where another trail from the northeast joined the main trail. This secondary trail made it possible to bypass Kokoda. From Alola, the trail continued south to Templeton's Crossing, at an elevation of 7,000 feet. A few miles south, the trail entered the misnamed Gap, which was really only a saddle between the ranges, approximately five miles wide and six miles long. Further on the trail narrowed even more so that troops had to move through it in single file. This area was plagued by excessive rainfall—more than three hundred inches a year. From the Gap, the trail descended to the native villages of Myola, Efogi, Menari, Nauro, Ioribaiwa, and Weeri—crossing east-west ridges as high as 6,000 feet—thirty hard miles distant by road from Port Moresby.[4]

MacArthur was fully aware of the importance of the Buna area. Allied monitoring of the Japanese radio traffic at Rabaul in June suggested that the Japanese might be preparing to take Buna preparatory to an advance on Port Moresby. MacArthur was handicapped, because he did not directly command the Australian forces in New Guinea and had to preserve the chain of command. Thus any concerns or orders had to pass through General Blamey's headquarters. In early June he learned that the commander in the Port Moresby area, Brig. Basil Morris, had taken no steps to guard the 6,000-foot-deep gap over the mountains. He communicated his concerns to Blamey and pressed for immediate action to send troops to reinforce the small contingent at Kokoda, far on the north side of the Owen Stanley Range.

One fault of MacArthur's headquarters throughout the early months of the campaign was ignorance of the conditions in New Guinea, due in part to being so far removed from the scene of action. However, his staff should have taken steps to discover the conditions of the troops who would carry out the operations as well as the condition of the route they would traverse. The Australian 39th Battalion, which would spearhead the operation, was a militia organization, composed largely of men under twenty years of age with no combat experience, even in theaters where the environment was better than in Papua. With only a few troops available, Brigadier Morris in early January had placed them in what was considered the best locations—facing the sea, with their backs to the mountains.[5] There had been considerable tension among all ranks prior to the Coral Sea engagement, because even with reinforcements it is questionable whether a serious Japanese landing could have been contained. A worried General Blamey had alerted New Guinea Force headquarters to prepare for a "serious attack." Brigadier Selwyn Porter, a veteran of the Syrian campaign, in immediate tactical command in case of an enemy attack, planned, as had his predecessors, to defend the beaches before falling back to a defense line near the Seven Mile Airfield, the largest and best airdrome in the Port Moresby area. The movement of troops preparatory to the presumed Japanese attack caused serious problems. There was a communications breakdown, and the control of moving troops was poor, causing traffic jams on the roads. The defense forces returned from their alert on 11 May. The lesson of early May showed clearly how much training was still needed for all combat troops.

On his arrival on 17 April, Porter had been taken aback by the conditions at Port Moresby. The village was shattered by bombs as a result of the daily Japanese air raids. He discovered that the troops were scattered along twenty miles of coast, a most unsound disposition of his force. He immediately set to work to reorganize his command, concentrating the units to be able to respond better to any threat. In the midst of this preparation, the news came of the probability of a Japanese landing. Porter and his superior, Brigadier Morris, had barely a month for reorganization before MacArthur's query about the Kokoda Trail. It seems obvious, in retrospect, that Morris had been dilatory in reinforcing Kokoda, but given the conditions of his troops and the fears of a seaborne invasion, it is understandable.[6]

Morris was slow to react even after MacArthur's query, but after prodding from Blamey, he finally acted. On 25 June he established the Maroubra Force, built up chiefly around the 39th Battalion (less one company). The 39th, a militia unit, was ill trained for such a mission. Before being sent to New Guinea, the men had spent most of their time unloading ships; even after arriving, they had been mainly occupied with doing labor work in Port Moresby. The little training they had received had been in dry scrub country in northern Australia.

The battalion was supported by a Papuan Infantry Battalion (PIB) composed of 280 natives and 20 whites. In addition, there were 600 native bearers—organized by Capt. Herbert Kienzle, a former gold miner and planter who knew the area well—to carry the extra gear of the force. Organization of the force was leisurely.

Company B, chosen by Brigadier Morris to reinforce the small garrison at Kokoda, left Port Moresby on 7 July. The men, dressed in light khaki uniforms and carrying sixty-five-pound packs in addition to their rifles, were totally unprepared for the long, difficult march. After a relatively easy trek from Port Moresby to Ilolo, they encountered ever more difficult sections of the trail. After Ioribaiwa, they confronted what was facetiously called the Golden Stairs, composed of logs anchored into the steep sides of the hills by wooden pegs. The 2,000 steps were covered with slime and mud, thus making footing treacherous, and led over steep ridges.

To the troops it appeared that the climb would never end. Overburdened with packs and soaked with sweat, many of the novice soldiers collapsed before reaching the top. At the end of the climb, most of the troops were exhausted, with many already having serious foot problems.[7] Afterward they entered an area of heavy jungle on the trail to the village of Menari. From there to the village of Efogi, the trail was surrounded by seven-foot-tall kunai grass. The march was made possible by the work of Captain Kienzle, who was responsible for dealing with the native bearers. They, moving ahead, established staging points at Ioribaiwa, Nauro, Efogi, Kogi, Eora Creek, and Deniki.

Despite such heroic work by the limited number of native carriers, they alone could not maintain sufficient supplies. Kienzle in his first report to headquarters made clear the absolute necessity of large-scale supply by air. Due to his foresight, the advance company had an easier time traversing the trail to Kokoda than the later units of the 39th. Nevertheless, after eight days, many of the men who reached Kokoda were hardly fit for combat.[8] Company B's commander, Capt. Samuel Templeton, led a platoon to Buna, where on 19 July he picked up supplies and machine guns brought in by a small schooner. Upon returning to Kokoda, he learned that the Japanese had landed.

Before the 2 July directive, MacArthur had planned to occupy the Buna area only in order to build an airfield from which his air force could attack Lae and Salamaua. However, with the Joint Chiefs specifying the seizure of these Japanese-held posts, it was necessary to modify the plan in order to occupy Buna in force. An airfield in the vicinity would still be necessary, so a reconnaissance party of seven officers, led by Lt. Col. William Pitt, was flown by a Short Sunderland flying boat to Buna on 10 July. They found the small airstrip there to be useless, but they reported that an airfield on the plains near the village of Dobodura, a few miles inland, would be excellent for large-scale military use. They passed on their positive findings to New Guinea Force headquarters.

On 13 July a high-level conference accepted the report, and two days later a general plan for the occupation of Buna was adopted.[9] The plan was given the code name Providence, and a special Buna Force was authorized. Brigadier General Robert Van Volkenburgh, commander of the 40th Artillery Brigade at Port Moresby, was chosen to lead. Providence called for the occupation in four stages, all under the protection of Allied aircraft from Milne Bay. D day for the occupation was set for 10 August, two days after the projected landings at Guadalcanal, which were expected to draw the majority of Japanese air and naval forces from Rabaul.

The first stage called for four Australian infantry companies accompanied by a few U.S. engineers to leave Port Moresby on D – 11 and cross over the Kokoda Trail to Buna. Radar and communications personnel and an antiaircraft battery would be brought to Buna by small boats during phase two. Phase three projected that the main force of an Australian infantry battalion, further communications personnel, and aircraft ground crews would arrive on D + 1 and the command of the operation would pass to Australian control. The final phase would see an engineer company and more air corps personnel moving in on D + 14.[10]

Intelligence reached Van Volkenburgh on 17 July that twenty-four Japanese ships had been spotted at Rabaul and a number of trawlers were seen at Talesa. Van Volkenburgh and Col. David Larr, the representative of headquarters G-2 at Port Moresby, concluded that this might indicate that the Japanese were preparing to seize Buna. MacArthur's headquarters was notified of the buildup, and Larr recommended that phase one of Providence be accelerated. Amazingly, MacArthur's chief of staff, General Sutherland, dismissed the warnings. He had his assistant, Brig. Gen. Stephen Chamberlin, reply, downplaying Van Volkenburgh's fears and claiming that there was no clear evidence that the Japanese intended to occupy Buna. Thus there was no need to radically alter the established time schedule for Providence. Chamberlin argued that to fly troops to Buna just might alert the Japanese to move before a sufficient Allied force could arrive to defeat them. The original plan would largely be adhered to.

In retrospect this was one of the more questionable decisions by any of MacArthur's subordinates. As early as 9 June, MacArthur had communicated his worries to Blamey concerning Buna and the security of the Kokoda Trail. Events would show how costly Sutherland's decision was, combined with the leisurely way that phase one of Providence was put into effect.[11]

Although the Japanese intended to occupy the Buna area, perhaps blinded by their early superiority, they also moved in a leisurely fashion. Imperial General Headquarters in Tokyo on 18 May issued an order to the Seventeenth Army, commanded by Lt. Gen. Haruyoshi Hyakutake, defining the strategic goals for the coming months. Units of his command, supported by the Second Fleet and the 25th Air Regiment, were to take key positions in New Caledonia, Fiji, Samoa, and Port Moresby. The target date for the assault on New Caledonia was 14 June.

The twin naval battles of the Coral Sea and Midway changed Japanese strategy. Operations against New Caledonia were canceled in early July. The new mission was to occupy the key positions near Buna preparatory to an attack on Port Moresby by army units crossing the mountains, using the Kokoda Trail. While General Hyakutake was in the Philippines in June, he was specifically cautioned against committing major forces to New Guinea until the trail was thoroughly scouted. The 15th Engineer Regiment, then at Davao, was selected for the reconnaissance, supported by a battalion from the South Seas Detachment.[12]

Major General Tomitaro Horii, commanding the South Seas Detachment *(Nankai Shitai)*, was chosen to command the operation, and Hyakutake was given approval to begin the operation on 11 July. The initial orders to Col. Yosuke Yokoyama were to seize a bridgehead, construct a road east of Kokoda, and report trail conditions to his superiors. If all was well, the major part of the invasion force would land. Lieutenant Colonel Toyanari Tanaka, staff officer in Horii's headquarters, made a detailed study of the problems of supplying troops with food and ammunition if a full-scale land operation directed at Port Moresby were attempted. He concluded that the projected campaign was impossible without the effective use of mechanical power. He reported his findings to Imperial Headquarters, but his warnings were ignored, and the operation was ordered to be carried out at any cost.[13] Thus before Yokoyama's small force could leave Rabaul, the plans had been changed. The Japanese would land the full force committed to the Port Moresby operation without complete information about the trail.

Yokoyama's force was augmented to 1,800 troops supported by 1,200 laborers from New Britain. The combat arm of the force was the 1st Battalion of the 144th Regiment, which had the task of securing the Buna area and pushing on toward Kokoda. They were supported by a naval landing force and artillery units. The 15th Independent Engineer Regiment would build depots and clear the roads. The Yokoyama Force would land and seize a foothold for the full South Seas Detachment, supported by the Yazawa Detachment, veterans of Malaya. Using the roads constructed by the engineers, they then would move across the mountains and take Port Moresby. Before the expedition left for Buna, the Japanese landed considerable forces on the islands of Tenimber, Aru, Kai, and Bunda in the Arafura Sea, pushing their potential bomber line to within 350 miles of Darwin.

The Yokoyama Force left Rabaul on 20 July in three transports. Their movement was unhampered by Allied air attacks. Inexplicably, General Brett, still commanding MacArthur's air force until General Kenney arrived, had suspended all bombing operations on the eighteenth. His excuse was that his crews were exhausted. On the twentieth, a B-17 sighted two naval squadrons. One of these contained the transports from Rabaul, but bad weather hid the Japanese from attack. The invasion force, now augmented by a cruiser and five destroyers, was again located the next morning. That afternoon it was attacked by a B-17 and five B-26s but sustained no losses. After bombarding Gona, the Japanese landed at Basabua, between Buna and Gona, late on the afternoon of the twenty-first and immediately began to consolidate their position. The following day, Allied aircraft flying through a heavy haze made a number of bombing and strafing runs on the beachhead but with few concrete results. One transport, the *Agatu Maru*, was hit and sunk; in addition, a landing barge with its personnel was sunk, and the Japanese shore installations were repeatedly strafed. However, the Japanese soon cleared their vital supplies from the shore into the jungle area. The Japanese advance force was firmly ashore and moved rapidly inland.[14]

Colonel Yokoyama lost no time in sending his forward elements onto the trail, and by the twenty-third they were within half a mile of Awala. Each man carried a load of approximately a hundred pounds of food and ammunition, although each carried only thirteen pounds of rice, enough for thirteen days of normal operations. However, they were ordered to stretch this to twenty days.[15] They encountered a patrol of the Papuan Infantry Battalion (PIB), but with mortars and machine guns they quickly drove the native soldiers back toward Wairopi. A platoon of the 39th soon arrived and made a brief stand before destroying the wire bridge across the Kumusi River. By early afternoon of the following day, the Japanese had crossed the river to the east side and forced the outnumbered Australians to fall back to a position near Gorari.

General Headquarters (GHQ) on this date ordered Brigadier Morris to immediately concentrate a battalion at Kokoda. Such an order showed clearly how out of touch the rear echelons were with the actual conditions on the trail and how difficult and time consuming it was to move troops forward. This inexplicable ignorance of the problems in Papua by both American and Australian staffs would continue throughout the entirety of the campaign for Buna.

In part, the complacency of higher headquarters was because of faulty intelligence of the terrain and general conditions in New Guinea despite the availability of hundreds of men who had lived and worked on the plantations and in the mines. Compounding such general ignorance was a faulty appreciation of the goals of the Japanese. Brigadier General Charles Willoughby, MacArthur's G-2, in an estimate of the situation in late July, stated emphatically that the Japanese would not attempt to cross the Owen Stanley Range. He believed that the seizure of the Buna area was merely to build airfields in order to make easier the bombing of Port Moresby and the Cape York Peninsula. He reiterated this conclusion on 12 August after the Japanese had landed and were pressing inland and threatening Deniki. Even when the main Japanese attack force, the South Seas Detachment, was landing, his appreciation of the situation remained the same. He believed to be vindicated in his conclusion when air reconnaissance discovered the Japanese to be lengthening the airstrip at Buna. Thus on 21 August, when General Horii left the beachhead to take direct charge of the offensive, General Headquarters still believed the trail to be too difficult for the Japanese to mount an overland attack on Port Moresby. The prevailing attitude toward the Japanese objectives obviously affected the response to the threat that allowed only company-strength units composed of green troops to bear the burden of halting the Yokoyama Detachment.[16]

The early phases of the Australian defense were marked by the insertion of small units of the 39th into the most forward areas.[17] Lieutenant Colonel William Owen was sent forward by air to Kokoda to take command, and on 26 August a platoon of the 39th was airlifted there; it was one of the few units to be brought forward by air. The problem of reinforcing the front lines by air was the lack of transport aircraft at Port Moresby. At this time there were available only two DC-3 Dakota transports with a maximum load capacity of twenty men each. Soon after arriving at Kokoda, Owen joined Captain Templeton and went forward to meet his men at Gorari. He ordered a few of the men available to set an ambush in hopes of delaying the Japanese advance. After inflicting a few casualties, this small group fell back to Oivi village. By the afternoon of the twenty-sixth, these troops and a few PIBs were surrounded. Templeton was killed while checking on the rear defenses, which left Maj. W. T. Watson as commander of the PIBs in charge. The Australians were saved from destruction by Lance Corporal Sanopa, a Papuan policeman who led them on a harrowing night march through the jungle to Deniki, bypassing Kokoda.[18] Here they found Owen with most of the survivors. He had earlier determined that with only eighty men, he could not hold Kokoda.

As was the case with most of the defensive operations, the weather was vile. Heavy rains were a daily occurrence, and the temperature varied from steaming hot at the lower elevations to extreme cold at the higher points along the trail. Despite adverse weather, and with only a few tired, hungry men, Owen, after being informed that the Japanese had not yet reached Kokoda, decided on 28 August to reoccupy the village. He moved his troops into Kokoda, set up a perimeter defense, and waited for the Japanese attack. He contacted Port Moresby with the information "Reoccupied Kokoda. Fly in reinforcements, including 2 Platoon and four detachments of mortars. Drome opened."[19]

Headquarters of New Guinea Force at Port Moresby was aware of the need for more planes. As early as 3 August, they sent a message marked "Most Urgent" to General Headquarters, noting: "Supply situation Maroubra and Kanga most serious. Must have transport planes with parachutes stationed here immediately. Failing this, operations will be jeopardized and forward troops liable to starvation."[20]

In response to Owen's request, two transport planes with supplies were sent to Kokoda. However, the pilots of the planes sent to deliver reinforcements, believing that the airfield was held by the Japanese, merely circled and flew back to Port Moresby. After regrouping, the Japanese launched a major night attack in the early-morning hours of the twenty-ninth. The defenders, after exacting a heavy toll on the attackers, were forced out of the village and were fortunate to be able to reach Deniki. During the melee, Owen was shot and killed.[21] His replacement, Maj. Allan Cameron, soon arrived with a few reinforcements. Even then he had only 480 men available in varying degrees of exhaustion. Perhaps reflecting the general attitude of the higher echelons, Cameron was bitter toward the survivors of the Kokoda venture. He certainly did not endear himself to his troops by calling them cowards.[22]

As if to further display his arrogance and ignorance of the situation, Cameron planned to retake Kokoda. On 5 August he sent out three patrols to locate the main Japanese force, none of which were successful. Nevertheless, on the basis of information from the patrols, he planned a three-pronged attack on Kokoda. His subordinates questioned the wisdom of such an action, pointing to the lack of information of the number and disposition of the Japanese. He persisted, and on 8 August sent Company D to set up an ambush for any enemy moving to reinforce Kokoda. A Company was to advance directly down the old trail to take Kokoda and the airstrip while C Company moved up the main trail.

C Company had moved only a few hundred yards when it confronted the main Japanese force, which the earlier patrols had not located. After a heavy firefight, the numerically superior Japanese forced a retreat. A further attempt to advance was also blunted, and the company retired to Deniki. Meanwhile, A Company had found few Japanese at Kokoda and reoccupied the village. However, Cameron, with his few reserves, was not aware of this until the morning of 9 August.

D Company had initially been successful in springing its ambush. After being briefly halted, the Japanese recovered and threatened to surround the Australians, who then retreated back to their jump-off point. It was apparent by evening that Cameron's plan had been thwarted. The only successful unit at Kokoda, meanwhile, was under constant pressure, and during the next twenty-four hours fought off a series of attacks. The company commander, Capt. Noel Symington, faced with a shortage of food and ammunition, concluded that he could not hold without reinforcements. After sustaining a heavy Japanese attack at dusk on the tenth, he began his withdrawal during a heavy rainstorm. Some of the troops became lost and did not rejoin the company at Deniki until the thirteenth.[23]

Lieutenant Colonel Hatsuo Tsukamoto, in charge of the forward area attack force, did not continue the offensive immediately, perhaps because his units had suffered severe casualties. This enabled the four Australian companies to improve their defense at Deniki. Finally, on the morning of the thirteenth, Tsukamoto attacked in the pouring rain. The Japanese were held during the rest of the day and night. On the fourteenth, he committed fresh troops, which finally got behind C Company. This forced Cameron to order a withdrawal to Isurava, where his men, weakened by lack of food, sleep, and shelter, and pelted by torrential rains, dug in to await further attacks.

The position at Isurava was reasonably defensible. The advancing Japanese infantry could be seen from the northern and southern positions. In addition, the eastward-flowing creeks could impede the attackers. To the east was the Eora Valley. Any direct attack of the Australian positions would be costly, but it was the most logical choice for the Japanese. On 16 August, Lt. Col. Ralph Honner took over command of the defense and, with only a few changes, approved the disposition of by now five companies.

Meanwhile, General Horii had brought forward five battalions of infantry, supported by a mountain artillery company and an engineer regiment. After concentrating his force, he began his attack on Isurava on 26 August. Despite the Japanese superiority in numbers of infantry, more mortars, and a field gun, their attacks were contained. However, members of the 39th Battalion, as one company commander noted, were on "their last bloody legs" and could not last another day.

Fortunately, that afternoon, elements of the 2/14 Battalion of the 21st Brigade began to arrive at Isurava. They were part of what the brigade commander, Brig. Arnold Potts, had planned to be an offensive to drive the Japanese back to Kokoda. To this end he had ordered men of what was considered an elite brigade to carry only enough supplies for the trek as far as Myola. He expected to find sufficient supplies there, air-dropped by the DC-3 "biscuit bombers."

These veteran troops of the Syrian campaign faced the same problems as had all the preceding units in the trek along the trail. Arriving at Myola, they discovered only five days' worth of rations instead of the planned twenty-five. The failure to deliver the supplies was due to a large-scale Japanese air raid on Seven Mile Airfield on the seventeenth, which destroyed three DC-3s and three B-17s and damaged ten other planes.[24] With his supply system in shambles, Potts gave up any idea of a major offensive and instead had to concentrate on holding Isurava.

The sad condition of the 39th Battalion, which had borne the brunt of the four-week defense, forced Potts to send its members back into reserve, and the 2/14 was brought in to take its place. He positioned the 53d Battalion at Myola to protect the right flank of the trail there. In total, Potts had approximately 550 men with which to halt Horii's five battalions, and some of these were still wandering about trying to retreat to Alola. Potts had requested reinforcements, but his superiors, fearing that the 2/27 would be needed to support the forces at Milne Bay, refused to release them. Potts placed only a company of the 2/14 at Isurava, but he knew that the rest of the battalion would have to be committed there as soon as the action started. Troops of the 2/16 would be given the task of protecting the right flank.

Partly because of the nature of the terrain, both the Japanese and Australians concentrated primarily on dominating the trail. Thus it was difficult to mount successful flanking movements. Horii's plan to capture Isurava was basically the same as in previous attacks. His main attack would be a frontal assault, thus pinning down the defenders. Australian correspondent Chester Wilmot, an observer of Japanese operations, noted the way that many Japanese attacks materialized. He wrote: "Before they attack they frequently can be heard chanting either their battle instructions or some semi-religious inspirational song. When they attack they often shriek or howl like savages and blaze away wildly with their machine guns in the hope of making the enemy panic and retreat. Like Gideon they build countless fires at night on the hillsides and fire off their weapons idly in the air to give an impression of overwhelming numbers of troops being in unsuspected places."[25]

The Japanese were tenacious in their direct attacks, continuing despite heavy losses. The chanting and screaming did not phase the Australians, who exacted a heavy toll on the attackers in all the engagements along the trail. Once an action had been broken off, the Japanese would retire to burn their dead.

In addition to the main frontal attack at Isurava, Horii would attempt to flank the Australians at the same time, however difficult it might be. If successful, this would threaten the Australians' line of supply and force a rapid retreat. Fortunately for the defenders, Horii did not put his plan into effect immediately, giving the Australians more time to dig in.

Not until 28 August did Horii begin his massed infantry attacks, and these continued throughout the day. But they were not able to dislodge the defenders. The Japanese suffered at least five hundred casualties during the assault. However, Potts believed that his position was increasingly untenable and decided to withdraw the 2/14, with the 39th covering this retreat. The 2/16 counterattacked on the thirtieth, which frustrated the Japanese attempt to cut the trail to Alola. In some cases the withdrawal was not orderly; some units, in order to escape, had to take to the bush, and many soldiers spent days in the jungle before being able to rejoin the main force. The 2/16 defended Isurava Rest House, to the south of the village, as long as possible, but the Japanese forced their way through and captured Alola by late afternoon. Potts pulled back his two AIF battalions to prepare a delaying position while the 39th and 52d were ordered to Eora Creek.[26]

The 39th Battalion had been in constant combat since the start of the campaign. The men's boots had fallen apart and their uniforms were in tatters. The survivors in all the companies had been afflicted with dysentery, and almost all had contracted malaria. Their condition was made worse by the lack of food, and the men were reduced to walking skeletons. The 52d had been badly shot up at Isurava. Potts sent the remainder back to a less dangerous locale, and the 39th was moved even farther back to Kogi.[27] Thus it continued to be extremely difficult even to keep the few tired, battered troops from being annihilated, let alone halt the Japanese advance, as Potts's superiors in Port Moresby wanted.

Two continuing problems for the Australians were how to keep the forward combat elements supplied and how to deliver even the most rudimentary health care to the combatants. Intestinal disorders and skin diseases were epidemic. Severe diarrhea and dysentery could not be treated adequately, given the conditions along the trail and the primitive medical system forced on the Australians by the Japanese assaults. Malaria was a scourge, and the hard-pressed medical officers, faced with an increasing number of battle casualties, could do little to aid those who had the debilitating disease. Even men with temperatures over 102 degrees Fahrenheit simply had to continue on. Under the stringent fighting conditions in Papua, the traditional Australian medical system broke down.

At the beginning of the campaign, the chief medical officer in the forward areas, Maj. Rupert Magarey, assigned ten medical orderlies to the villages at Uberi, Ioribaiwa, Nauro, Menari, and Efogi. The largest numbers of medical personnel were left at Myola, where most of his supplies were located. Had Kokoda been held, there could have been air evacuation of the most seriously wounded. Its loss was a severe blow to Magarey and his team.

The lack of available transport aircraft meant that the burden of carrying supplies forward fell on the native carriers. Early in the campaign it became obvious that combat troops could not be expected to carry the necessary supplies over the trail and still be in condition to fight. Captain Kienzle was at first responsible for recruiting carriers and establishing supply depots up the trail. With scant rewards, these unsung heroes of the war carried loads that would have exhausted the regular soldiers. Unfortunately, the care of these carriers was not adequate. The medical officer, Captain Vernon, reported in July that he found the carriers at Myola in bad shape. They had been subsisting for weeks on a meager diet of rice and no meat. Most had malaria, and they suffered from the cold at the higher altitudes because many did not even have a blanket.[28]

The native carriers proved during the entirety of the Papuan campaign to be indispensable not only for carrying supplies but also evacuating the wounded. They had to carry their wounded charges over terrain that taxed the infantrymen who carried nothing more than their packs. It took twenty-seven hours of continuous marching to carry either stretchers or loads of supplies from Kokoda to Myola, where the best medical facilities were, until Myola was lost. However, it was necessary to provide staging areas where the carriers and their patients could rest. Even so, it was a tedious journey of six hours from Alola to Eora Creek and from there another six hours to Templeton's Crossing.[29] Colonel Kingsley Norris described the work of the native carriers:

> With improvised stretchers—one or two blankets lashed with native string to two long poles spread by stout traverse bars— as many as eight or ten native bearers would carry day after day. To watch them descend steep slippery spurs into a mountain stream, along the bed and up the steep ascent, was an object lesson in stretcher bearing. They carry stretchers over seemingly impassable barriers, with the patient reasonably comfortable. The care which they show to the patient is magnificent. Every need which they can fulfill is tendered. If night finds the stretcher still on the track, they will find a level spot and build a shelter over the patient. They will make him as comfortable as possible, fetch him water and feed him if food is available—regardless of their own needs. They sleep four on each side of the stretcher and if the patient moves or requires any attention during the night, this is given instantly.[30]

Only the seriously wounded who had a chance of surviving were carried. All others had to walk and in some cases crawl over the most difficult parts of the trail as the Australians retreated from one village to another. They were not permitted the luxury of much rest at the staging areas but were pushed on to the next station as rapidly as possible. Before Alola was lost, all surgeries where success was deemed possible were performed. Later, the care of the very seriously wounded normally amounted to stopping bleeding. As Magarey later noted, any abdominal wound generally meant death, because there were no facilities for major surgery. Thus, in addition to the terrible terrain and continual rain, there was for the Australian infantrymen always the fear of receiving wounds that could not be treated.[31] It was no comfort to the Australian sick and wounded to reflect on the fact that the Japanese medical system was much worse than theirs. However, the poor Japanese standards would be one of the factors that doomed Horii's campaign.

Brigadier Morris was acutely aware of the problems of supply and how important the carriers were. However, he complained to higher headquarters about the lack of an alternative to the carriers. He stated:

> It is a journey of twelve days to Maroubra Force and there is no other surface means of transport. With 2,000 carriers working continuously, we should deliver just 3,000 lb. of supplies a day at Deniki—about half the amount needed there. I don't think we can keep 2,000 carriers working continuously, but with one freight plane, we can have dropped 4,000 lb. of supplies to the forward troops.[32]

The supply situation remained critical, but by early August it was possible to maintain four battalions at Isurava with a combination of carriers and airdrops by "biscuit bombers." Supply would be a continuing concern of Morris's successor, Lt. Gen. Sydney Rowell, and his field commander, Brigadier Potts. The loss of Myola, which had become the key forward depot, on 4 September was a major setback. Japanese successes did have one positive effect: They shortened the distance between Port Moresby and the front line.

The actions after Isurava followed a deadly monotonous pattern. The Japanese, with their superior force and firepower, would directly attack Australian positions situated along the trail while other units would flank the defenders, ultimately forcing a retreat. The Australians prepared ambush positions and exacted a terrible toll on the attackers before withdrawing. This fact was confirmed by a Japanese war correspondent who reported on the skill of the Australian snipers. In each engagement the Japanese would lose twice as many casualties as did the Australians.[33]

Constantly outnumbered, Potts utilized his troops brilliantly, allowing front units to withdraw to positions prepared by others to the rear. He had no choice but to play for time, waiting for the 2/27 to come up and hope that the fresh 25th Brigade, then on its way to Port Moresby, would allow for an eventual counteroffensive. The supply situation was still difficult. However, the closer they came to Port Moresby, the easier it was to get the necessary food and ammunition. Conversely, with all his success, General Horii's supply situation worsened.

Brigadier Potts had decided at Eora Creek to retreat through the Gap farther south to his main supply base at Myola. The Gap itself was not defensible, despite the idea held by MacArthur's headquarters to the contrary. General Sutherland earlier had expressed his view that the Gap could be readily blocked by using explosives. He obviously believed that instead of being a wide expanse, it was a narrow pass. General Rowell, whose patience must have been tried by such suggestions, pointed out that even if the Gap had been narrow, there was not enough time for the native porters to bring up the necessary quantity of explosives, and, further, they could be utilized much better elsewhere in the campaign.[34]

Such naive suggestions from MacArthur's headquarters had little effect on Potts, but those from his superior, Maj. Gen. S. F. Allen commanding the 7th Division, caused him considerable trouble. Having little concept of the actual conditions, Allen ordered that Myola be held at all costs. With the forces that Potts had available, this was out of the question. The exhausted troops did have a few hot meals, took baths, and had new uniforms issued before Potts ordered them to evacuate Myola on 4 September. He ordered that all supplies that could not be carried be destroyed. The Australians then fell back to Efogi village.[35]

Reinforced by the 2/27, Potts's men took up a defensible position south of Efogi on the high ground called Mission Ridge. Horii had also received reinforcements. The 3d Battalion of the Yazawa Detachment had landed at Gona on 2 September and moved quickly to the front. Thus Horii had an estimated 5,000 men for his assault on the ridge. From his brigade headquarters, Potts watched the Japanese columns moving down the trail and into position. He sent a message to New Guinea Force headquarters to "turn on all you've got from the air on Efogi and Myola at earliest tomorrow morning."[36]

He was not disappointed. A succession of bombing and strafing attacks on the village and Japanese positions on 6 September disrupted the Japanese attack plans and caused an estimated hundred casualties. However, these only postponed, but did not halt, the

Japanese offensive. In the early-morning hours of 8 September, Horii's mountain guns and mortars opened the attack by four battalions of infantry. Under such pressure, the Australian perimeter on the ridge collapsed. Potts and his headquarters personnel were briefly cut off from the main body and were fortunate to escape. The survivors of the Japanese assault retreated south to Menari, with many being forced off the trail and into the bush. There was no good defensive position at Menari, so the retreat continued on to Ioribaiwa. The newly arrived 2/27 had been shattered by its defense of Mission Ridge. Most of the battalion was forced off the trail; after trekking through uncharted jungle for fourteen days, the men managed to rejoin Potts's main body on 23 September. By 29 September, Potts had only three hundred men to continue the fighting.[37]

The abandonment of Myola and the retreat to Ioribaiwa shook the complacency of higher headquarters, who now realized how close the Japanese were to Port Moresby. Although the under-strength units of the greatly outnumbered 21st Brigade had fought a series of brilliant delaying actions, MacArthur and the Australian command had been slow to reinforce the battered units along the trail. MacArthur's headquarters and particularly his G-2 section had little grasp of what was occurring. MacArthur, in his unwarranted criticism of the Australian troops, at one time indicated his belief that they outnumbered the Japanese.[38]

It was in this atmosphere that Brigadier Potts, whose defensive tactics had so decimated the Japanese, was recalled to Port Moresby on 10 September. His replacement, Brig. Selwyn Porter, went forward to take temporary command, pending the arrival of Brig. Kenneth Eather, of the newly arrived 25th Brigade. Given the nature of the terrain, Porter could do little more than try to find the most defensible positions. The losses to the 2/14 and 2/16 had been so severe that he grouped the survivors together into a composite company. This unit, in conjunction with the 3d Battalion, held a spur just north of Ioribaiwa.

On 12 September the Japanese infantry, with heavy machine guns and mortar preparation, attacked the position. Despite heavy losses, the Australians held the ground. By this time Brigadier

Eather had arrived with the 2/31 and 2/33 Battalions of the 25th Brigade. He also had two field guns, which had laboriously been manhandled up the trail. He decided to counterattack but found that the Japanese could not be dislodged from their positions. One of his battalions during the course of the fighting became lost and another was routed by the Japanese. Fearing that he was about to be outflanked, Eather, on the morning of the sixteenth, informed General Allen that he had to pull back to Imita Ridge, a day's march from Ioribaiwa and a scant twenty miles from Port Moresby. Allen reluctantly agreed, then informed Rowell, who prophetically said, "Our heads will be in a basket over this."[39]

At Imita Ridge, Eather was in a good defensible locale, with a supply system that could provide him with the necessary materiel to beat back the Japanese. He now had the 25th Brigade and the remnants of the 21st Brigade, which would soon be joined by the 16th Brigade of the 6th Division. He also had continual support from U.S. and RAAF air units stationed at Port Moresby.

On 15 September, advance elements of the U.S. 126th Regiment reached Port Moresby, and Major General Vasey had also arrived with the headquarters of the 6th Division. The movement to Imita Ridge caused a flurry of excitement at General Headquarters in Brisbane, which resulted in unfortunate recriminations and transfers of some of the competent men responsible for the successful delaying operations. Imita Ridge was not only defensible, but Eather now had the means to seriously consider taking the offensive.

Conversely, Horii's situation was increasingly desperate. His troops had suffered heavy casualties in their direct attacks on the Australian defenses at each village. His medical system, rudimentary at best, had all but broken down. His men suffered even more than did the Australians from intestinal disorders, dengue, malaria, and scrub typhus. The Japanese supply system was stretched to the limits, and many of his soldiers were without food. Japanese correspondent Okada estimated that by the time they had reached Ioribaiwa, their losses had been 80 percent killed, wounded, and disabled by disease. Nevertheless, their morale was high. On one of the hills before Imita Ridge, they could see the goal of their torturous journey. Okada reported that he "saw through the trees a wide expanse of green wood gradually sloping away before us, and beyond that a sheet of misty light." The men rushed forward and shouted, "The Sea! Look! It's the sea of Port Moresby."[40]

The Japanese would get no closer. General Horii halted his offensive and ordered his men to prepare defenses and wait for the reinforcements promised him. Instead, he soon received orders from Imperial Headquarters to withdraw.

Chapter IV
Milne Bay

As General Horii's bedraggled columns closed in on their objective, the Japanese planners at Rabaul decided to launch a new campaign in Papua despite the continuing demands of their Guadalcanal operations. Their reason was that if the proposed operation succeeded, it would give them key airfields less than two hundred miles from Port Moresby. These were being constructed by the Allies at Milne Bay who had belatedly understood the importance of controlling the areas adjacent to the bay that prior to the war had been only sparsely settled.

The Japanese were almost completely ignorant of the terrain and climatic conditions. Even the Australians who administered the area did not fully comprehend the difficulty of carrying on military operations there. The bay itself was a deep cleft in the lizard's tail of extreme southeast Papua; it extended approximately twenty miles inland and was between four and five miles wide. On either side were mountains rising as high as 4,000 feet and dropping almost to the shoreline, leaving only a narrow strip of land between them and the sea. Much of this was covered by jungle. Because the region received more than two hundred inches of rain annually, the many streams overflowed, creating coastal swamps. At the head of the bay was a wide alluvial plain on which Lever Brothers had planted a large coconut plantation. The company headquarters and service buildings were located at Gili Gili. The dock there consisted of two large barges placed side by side with a ramp leading to a small jetty. The plantation area was serviced by only a few roads, most of them in varying states of disrepair. They were constructed of crushed coral rock covering coconut logs and by 1942 were in terrible condition. One road led to the jetty at Gili Gili. The coast road on the north side of the bay ran through the villages of Kilabo and Rabi to the station of the Kristian Bruder (K.B.) Mission, then beyond to Waga Waga, Wandala, and Ahioma villages.[1]

As early as May, Milne Bay had been selected by the Australian planners as the site for airfields, which could guard the approaches from the Solomon Islands to the Coral Sea. Instructions were given on 12 June for the immediate construction of a fighter strip and later a bomber field there, both with appropriate facilities. A company of the U.S. 46th Engineers and a company of Australian infantry were immediately dispatched to begin the construction.

They found little of permanence to aid them. There were no wharves and no ships, and at first there was general chaos. The commander of these first units, Col. Frank Burns, of the U.S. Army, reported that his main problem was supply. There were few ships available to bring in the necessary food, ammunition, and construction materials. From the beginning the workers were on a two-thirds ration of bully beef and biscuits. The supply situation had become even more serious; almost all the food was consumed before the arrival of the first Dutch freighter in July. After that, a continuous supply link was maintained, with Dutch, Australian, and U.S. ships bringing cargo and reinforcements to the bay.[2]

Despite the hardships, the construction crews finished Airstrip No. 1, located in the center of the plantation area, by mid-July. The 46th Engineers had been joined by the 43d, and work had begun on two other airstrips. The 46th Engineers were working on Airstrip No. 2, located one and a half miles west of Airstrip No. 1. By the time of the Japanese invasion, the 43d had bulldozed a strip 2,000 feet long, although Airstrip No. 3 would not be finished by then. It was located just west of the village of Kitabo, its eastern end within two hundred yards of the sea.

As soon as Airstrip No. 1 was completed, three RAAF squadrons were moved in. One was a reconnaissance squadron equipped with Hudson bombers. The others were the 75th and 76th Fighter Squadrons, which had done so well earlier in protecting Port

Moresby. Airstrip No. 1 was hastily constructed of open-mesh steel mats over a poorly drained base. In the continuing rain the runway became muddy, and it was extremely dangerous for planes to take off and land. Despite this hazard, the pilots in the P-40s did yeoman service supporting the infantry units in the upcoming battle. In addition they would destroy twenty-three Japanese aircraft.[3]

Reinforcement of the small garrison was speeded up in July. A militia unit, the 7th Infantry Brigade, commanded by Brig. John Field, arrived and began to establish a defensive force in the plantation area. Later, light and heavy antiaircraft units and a 25-pound artillery battery from the 2/25 Field Regiment were sent to aid the defenses. In addition, the U.S. 709th Airborne Antiaircraft Battery, with its .50-caliber machine guns, was flown in.

On 8 August, Field had a total of 6,212 men under his command. On 21 August, the AIF 18th Brigade, veterans of the Libyan campaign, commanded by Brig. George Wootten, completed its movement to the bay. The next day a new commander, Maj. Gen. Cyril Clowes, arrived with orders to protect the airfields and deny the Japanese access to the bay. He had only a few days to assess the general situation and make any changes in the defenses. He approved the disposition of forces made by Field and Wootten and waited for a possible Japanese invasion. There were certain deficiencies in the equipment available to him. He did not have any coastal artillery, searchlights, or landing craft. Nevertheless, he had available a force considerably larger than what had defended the Kokoda Trail. His command totaled 8,824 men, of whom 1,365 were U.S. troops. Of this number, 4,500 were infantry and the rest were construction troops and RAAF personnel.[4]

The Japanese organized the Milne Bay operation very late. Not until 22 August did Adm. Gun'ichi Mikawa, commander of the Eighth Fleet, order it to proceed. The objective was the three airfields then under construction. If captured, they would bring Japanese planes within easy flying distance of Port Moresby and would aid immeasurably in General Horii's attack then closing in on that vital base.

The Japanese intelligence reports were faulty, perhaps because of the bad weather, which continued to hamper aerial reconnaissance. Mikawa believed that the Australians had only three infantry companies at Milne Bay and perhaps as few as twenty aircraft. Thus he believed that there was no reason to wait for the army's Aoba Detachment, which had been designated for the invasion. It was still at Davao. Headquarters therefore decided to use only the naval troops then available. The Kure 5th Special Landing Force, the 362d Naval Pioneer Unit, and a few men from the Sasebo Special Landing Force were ordered to Milne Bay from Kavieng, a total of 1,171 men to make the main landing. In addition, 353 men of the 5th Special Landing Force would come from Buna, land at Taupota, on the north coast, and march overland to Gili Gili. Commander Shojiro Hayashi, in charge of the expedition, planned to land at the village of Rabi, located approximately three miles east of the wharf at Gili Gili. The first echelon of the attacking force left Kavieng on 24 August. At the same time, the troops from Buna were loaded onto seven power barges.[5]

A coast watcher sighted the barges of the Buna attack force on the afternoon of the twenty-fourth and notified headquarters. Although the weather continued to be foul, reconnaissance planes from Milne Bay located the barges on the twenty-fifth. They had put into a presumably safe harbor on the southwestern shore of Goodenough Island in the D'Entrecasteaux Group to allow the troops to eat and rest. Twelve RAAF P-40s from the almost completed Airstrip No. 1 took off, and shortly before noon the Australian pilots discovered the beached barges. They made run after strafing run on the stationary targets. When it was over, all the landing craft had been destroyed along with most of the stores and ammunition. Japanese troops were left stranded on the beach.[6] This part of the Japanese plan to attack Milne Bay from the north had been foiled. There would be no attack on Taupota. The success of the Japanese plan now rested totally on the detachments from Kavieng.

The convoy from Kavieng, escorted by destroyers, was more fortunate. It was also sighted early on the twenty-fifth, but then weather closed in, preventing the B-17s from Cape York airfields and the B-26s from Townsville from doing any damage in spite of a number of attempts. A break in the weather in the early afternoon allowed the RAAF P-40s to strafe the convoy, but this caused only minimal damage. By late afternoon the weather had closed in almost completely. The Japanese could safely begin unloading in the evening on the north shore near the village of Waga Waga. Prior to landing, Commander Hayashi had exhorted his men to kill without remorse.[7] The Japanese advance elements quickly established Hayashi's headquarters and supply dumps.

The following day, despite continuing bad weather, Allied planes attempted to attack the beachhead. Although most of the planes had to turn back, some managed to take advantage of breaks in the weather. The B-17s seriously damaged a large transport, the *Nankai Maru*, and drove others out to sea. The RAAF P-40s sank some landing barges and managed to destroy most of the supplies that the Japanese had brought with them.[8]

To compound the Japanese problems, they discovered on the twenty-sixth that they had landed in the wrong place. Instead of Rabi, the landings had been made at two points five miles farther east. Thus they were more than ten miles from their prime objective, caught on a narrow shelf between the mountains and the sea. Their way west lay through jungle and in some areas swamps. In addition, the mountain streams had become torrents because of the continuing rain. The coastal trail, hardly a road, had been washed away in a number of places.

Despite the weather and terrible terrain conditions, the Japanese pushed out lead patrols toward K.B. Mission almost immediately after landing. The first contact with the Australians was made early on the morning of the twenty-sixth when their patrols encountered elements of Company B of the 61st at K.B. Mission. After a firefight that lasted a few hours, the Japanese pulled back, and General Clowes sent another company forward to the mission.

General Clowes did not have a good idea of Japanese intentions. Although he would later be criticized by MacArthur for his caution, he proceeded in the appropriate manner until he could gain a clear picture of the situation. He knew that a significant number of Japanese had landed and were moving west, but he could not know whether this was the main force. Perhaps another landing would occur on the south shore or, even closer, in the Gili Gili area. Clowes therefore continued his main concentration in the plantation area

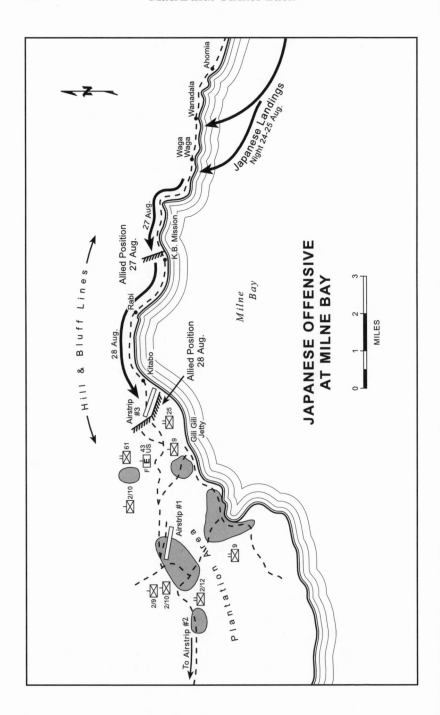

JAPANESE OFFENSIVE
AT MILNE BAY

at the head of the bay. Two companies of the 18th were posted directly at Airstrip No. 1 and the 9th Battalion of the 7th Brigade was placed in a potentially vulnerable coastal area at the Gili Gili jetty, to the west. Clowes maintained the 2/12 Battalion in reserve along the road between Airstrip No. 1 and Airstrip No. 2. The bulk of the American engineers were working at Airstrip No. 3, just east of the jetty, and were guarded by the 25th Battalion of the 7th Brigade. One company of the 61st of this brigade was located at Ahioma, east of where the Japanese had landed. The other company guarded K.B. Mission. It was this unit that first encountered the Japanese.[9] A platoon of the 61st was on the north coast to guard against an overland attack, and a reinforced company of the 25th was northwest, on Goodenough Bay.

Just at the time of the Japanese landings, two platoons of the company of the 61st at Ahioma tried to join the main elements farther west by taking to boats. They encountered the Japanese who were then in the process of landing. In the confusion, one of the ketches was sunk. However, most of the Australians made it to shore and later infiltrated back to the main Australian lines. The other ketch turned back to Ahioma. Later, the men of the two platoons evacuated their position and marched overland to Taupota, then back over the mountains before rejoining the battalion after several days' march.[10]

During the night of the twenty-sixth, the Japanese once again attacked the mission in much greater force and drove out the Australians. They retreated to the Gona River defenses just west of Rabi. However, the Japanese did not take advantage of this retreat, and the next morning the lightly armed 2/10 reoccupied the positions. General Clowes, still without definite knowledge of Japanese intentions, hoped that the 2/10 could provide him with more information as to the enemy's troop strength. The Japanese, meanwhile, had received reinforcements of more troops from Kavieng during the evening of the twenty-sixth. That convoy, too, had been fortunate. Although it had been sighted earlier, the weather had prevented Allied air attacks. With these added infantry supported by two tanks during the evening of the twenty-seventh, the Japanese once again attacked K.B. Mission. The tanks, equipped with brilliant lights, illuminated the Australian positions. The Japanese attack split the battalion and caused heavy casualties. Headquarters and two companies were forced into the jungle and did not reach the plantation area for three days. The rest of the 61st made its way directly back to the main staging area within a few hours. Now almost unopposed, the Japanese moved quickly ahead, and by the morning of the twenty-eighth had reached the Australian defenses at Airstrip No. 3.[11]

Brigadier Field, in command of the eastern defenses, had deployed two battalions, the 25th and what was left of the 61st, to defend the partially completed airstrip. The 2,000-foot runway running roughly west to east, which had been graded, provided a part of the defense. Its eastern end was only a few yards from the sea. Field had his troops positioned on the south side of the airstrip. The Japanese would thus be forced to attack frontally, because the sea protected Field's right flank. He placed the American antiaircraft battery, with its .50-caliber machine guns, at the eastern end of his defenses. The two companies of the 43d Engineers, with their .50-caliber machine guns and 37mm antitank weapons, were sited in the center of the line and were covered by Australian troops on either side. This was a critical position, because the trail from Rabi crossed the strip at that point.

The Japanese attacked the airstrips' defenses four times during the day but without their tanks, which had been so important to their victory at K.B. Mission. The tanks were bogged down in the mud and had been abandoned. Each Japanese assault was beaten off, and they sustained heavy losses. Despite the continuing heavy fog and rain, the RAAF P-40s of 75 and 76 Squadrons flew in low and strafed the Japanese positions throughout the fight. The squadrons had a number of selected infantry and artillery officers, who briefed the pilots on enemy targets and friendly dispositions. Oil drums, landing barges, and vehicles, particularly the tanks, were favorite targets.[12] With casualties mounting, the Japanese called off their attack and took refuge in the jungle areas.

By now satisfied that the defenses at Airstrip No. 3 would hold, General Clowes ordered the 7th Brigade to push forward against the Japanese positions. On the twenty-ninth its patrols met with stiff resistance. He then ordered the 18th Brigade to join in the advance toward K.B. Mission. By the afternoon of the twenty-ninth, he received a message from MacArthur's headquarters to take immediate action to repel a land attack on the key airfield. This never happened, but Clowes learned of the approach of another Japanese convoy and therefore canceled the orders to the 18th, fearing that a landing near the head of the bay was imminent.[13] However, that convoy, consisting of a cruiser and nine destroyers, was simply bringing reinforcements. In heavy fog during the evening of the twenty-ninth, 770 troops of the Yakusuka and Kure special naval landing forces were landed. Outranking Hayashi, Comdr. Minoru Yano, of the recently arrived reinforcements from Kure, took command of the operation. During the day of the thirtieth, the reinforcements moved up to take positions in the jungle alongside the battered veterans of the previous attacks.[14]

Brigadier Field had made few changes in the disposition of his forces. The major one was the relocation of the guns of the American antiaircraft battery to each end of the airstrip. In addition, the defensive firepower was bolstered by the mortars of the two Australian battalions and the 25-pound howitzers a half mile to the rear. He could also count on continuing fire support from the RAAF squadrons from Airstrip No. 1.

The expected Japanese attack began during the night of 30 August. First they illuminated the area with flares as they directed mortar fire at the Australians. Then came the infantry attacks. Troops of the 7th Brigade, bolstered by U.S. firepower, met the onslaught with automatic weapons in what an official army report described as a "wall of fire." In the manner of earlier Japanese attacks elsewhere, the ordinary soldiers, despite their physical condition and having sustained heavy casualties, repeated their attacks throughout the night. An Australian observer noted with some surprise that the morale of the Japanese soldiers was "particularly high throughout despite continued reverses and shocking supply conditions." There was no hesitation for some small units to attack larger Australian forces and willingly sacrifice themselves to secure only a few casualties.[15] In this case the Japanese had spent themselves by morning and were in full retreat. Not one Japanese soldier was able to cross the airstrip alive. At dawn the Australians counted 160 Japanese dead.[16]

Without pause, Clowes ordered the 2/12, supported by a company of the 2/9, to take up the pursuit of the retreating Japanese. At first there was no concerted opposition, only fire from snipers who had tied themselves into trees. Units of the battalion were posted at the Gama River and the village of Motieau. The main force advancing along the trail, which had become a quagmire due to the continuous rain, reached K.B. Mission by the evening of the thirty-first. By the next day the road to the mission was impassable. Small boats had to be used to get supplies and reinforcements to the front and to evacuate the wounded.[17] Many Japanese had moved into the jungle alongside the trail, allowing the Australians to pass. In the rear of the advancing Australians, the Japanese mounted a major attack on the Australian perimeter at Rabi. The attack was unsuccessful, the Japanese losing more than a hundred men in the course of the fighting. An attack on the units at Motieau was also repulsed, with the Japanese suffering heavy casualties. As the Australians pushed eastward, the problem of supply increased. However, a few small boats were used to bring rations and ammunition to the forward elements.

The medical problems throughout the campaign were similar to those encountered during the Kokoda retreat but not as extreme. One reason was that the distance from the front line to aid stations was much shorter, and despite the terrible conditions of the trail, the wounded could be transported much more easily. The medical facilities were good, and the staff provided excellent treatment in spite of the difficulties. A casualty clearing station was located in the plantation area between Airstrips No. 1 and 2, and two medical battalions, named "field ambulances" by the Australians, were sited in various locations between the main staging area and Airstrip No. 3. The casualty clearing station was actually a small general hospital; each company of the field ambulances was provided with staff and equipment to deal with the first stage of treating the wounded. In addition to the wounded, the medical staff also treated those who had malaria, typhus, or any of the many skin diseases encountered in such a wet, tropical environment.

The first casualties arrived at the 11th Field Ambulance by noon of the twenty-seventh, and soon all of its eighty beds were occupied.

As the fighting intensified, the problem of transportation increased and accommodations for the patients became more difficult. In some cases, cots were set up in native huts. By the thirty-first, surgeons of the casualty clearing station had performed ninety-six operations in seven days.

Ultimately the facilities at Milne Bay could no longer handle the numbers of sick and wounded. By 2 September there were 365 sick and 164 battle casualties held in all the facilities. The hospital ship *Manunda* left Brisbane on that date and arrived at Milne Bay four days later. Despite difficulties in transferring patients to the hospital ship, eventually 182 were taken aboard.[18]

The advance of Australians continued, with the 2/9 passing through the 2/12 to push forward against stiffening opposition to reach Goroni village, two miles east of K.B. Mission, by 3 September. The Australian position west of the village was shelled that evening by a Japanese cruiser and three destroyers, but damage was minimal.

By now the Japanese situation was desperate. Commander Yano, himself wounded, reflected this when he radioed Rabaul that "everyone resolved to fight bravely to the last." They fought a stubborn rear-guard action. Manning a series of machine guns at Goroni, the Japanese blocked the advance on the fourth until Cpl. John French, a veteran of the North African campaign, charged them. Within minutes he had destroyed the three machine-gun positions before being mortally wounded. For this action he was posthumously awarded the British Empire's highest decoration, the Victoria Cross.[19] Another desperate stand was made by the Japanese the following day; it didn't halt the Australians, who captured Waga Waga, one of the original landing points for the Japanese.

Admiral Mikawa, commander of the Eighth Fleet at Rabaul, still hoped to salvage the situation. The army's Aoba Detachment had finally arrived, and Mikawa believed that this thousand-man unit and a few men from the Yokosuka Special Landing Force could reverse the losses and still capture the airfields. Preparations were made to send the naval troops immediately and land the Aoba Detachment on 12 September. Mikawa appointed a new commander, Capt. Yoshitatsu Yasuda, to take command of all Japanese forces at Milne Bay. However, Commander Yano informed headquarters that his

troops were not capable of fighting much further.[20] With this information, Mikawa canceled the relief expedition and arranged for
the evacuation of the remaining Japanese from the Waga Waga
area. He sent three patrol craft and a light cruiser, which arrived
during the evening of 4 September. The wounded were evacuated
that night, and the following evening the ships returned to take off
the bulk of the landing force, leaving behind only scattered small
groups of soldiers.

The Japanese were fortunate. The Australians arrived at Waga
Waga only a few hours later. The cruiser illuminated the shoreline,
shelled the wharf and airstrip, and took the 3,500-ton cargo ship
Anshun under fire. Within twenty minutes the *Anshun* took six shells
and rolled over half submerged. The hospital ship *Manunda,* anchored in the bay with all its lights on, was not fired upon. The *Anshun* blocked the entrance of the *Manunda* into the wharf area,
forcing the wounded Australians to be transported by lifeboat, then
hoisted with difficulty to the deck of the hospital ship.[21]

The organized campaign concluded with the evacuation of the
bulk of the surviving Japanese from Waga Waga, but the Australians
pursued the stragglers beyond Ahioma. Some, exhausted and without food, were found wandering in the lower foothills of the mountains. Many were wounded and almost all were sick with a variety of
tropical diseases. Scattered parties of Japanese attempted to reach
Buna by crossing the mountains. Some were killed near Taupota and
others simply died of starvation along the north coast. The last of the
stragglers from the ill-fated invasion were captured in December.

The Milne Bay invasion was a minor disaster for the Japanese. It
cost them an estimated six hundred killed. The climate and terrain
coupled with the inadequate Japanese medical services had also
claimed a terrible toll of those survivors who were evacuated to
Rabaul. Most were suffering from trench foot, tropical ulcers, and
jungle rot; malaria was epidemic. Virtually none was in any condition to fight. The Australian infantrymen who were fighting their
first jungle engagement had sustained only moderate casualties—
161 killed in action or missing and 212 wounded. The U.S. units
that had helped defend Airstrip No. 3 had only one man killed and
two wounded.[22]

There was a strong belief at MacArthur's headquarters that the Japanese would not concede Milne Bay so easily and would attempt another invasion, only with additional force. More troops were sent, along with heavier artillery. The return of Task Force 44 from the Solomons made it possible for the Allied naval force to protect the approaches to the bay. Heavy construction equipment was brought in, and crews labored to carve out new camp areas for permanent establishments. Good roads were constructed, linking all areas of the north and south shores. Landing stages and jetties were run out to accommodate the unloading of large cargo ships. Airstrip No. 1 was lengthened and No. 3 was completed. Within a few months of the victory, new squadrons of P-40s, Beaufighters, and Hudson bombers were utilizing the airfields.[23] The fears of another invasion eased as the Japanese became more and more committed to their flagging campaign in Guadalcanal and the necessity of defending their holdings on the north shore of Papua.

The Australian victory at Milne Bay, small though it was in the larger arena of the war, was very important. Strategically it blunted the Japanese attempt to gain airfields within easy range of Port Moresby. It also showed clearly that the Japanese soldier was not invincible in jungle fighting and that the Australians, with proper leadership, could defeat them. Despite unwarranted criticism by MacArthur and Blamey of the way Clowes conducted the campaign, the victory provided a great morale booster for both the Australian military and civilians, in part wiping out the memories of the failure in Malaya and the East Indies.

Some of the participants in the defense of Milne Bay understood its importance, as shown by a memorial inscription, a piece of tin nailed to a coconut tree stump. The inscription read, "This marks the spot of the first land defeat of the Japanese Army in the Pacific."[24]

Tactically the victory provided the Allies with a secure set of airfields from which bombers could operate against Japanese bases in Papua and the northern Solomons without crossing the treacherous Owen Stanley Range. The retention of Milne Bay set the stage for the attempts to secure the northern coast of Papua from East Cape to Buna.

Chapter V
Changing Commands

The victory over the Japanese at Milne Bay, combined with the slowing of the offensive along the Kokoda Trail, should have reassured MacArthur's headquarters. There was every indication that the tide was turning, however slowly, against the Japanese. Their deepening involvement at Guadalcanal had meant a major shifting of their air force and naval units away from New Guinea. MacArthur now had an air corps commander whom he trusted implicitly. General Kenney and his able lieutenant, Brig. Gen. Ennis Whitehead, were receiving more and better aircraft. Planes of the newly formed Fifth Air Force, combined with RAAF units, all but ruled the skies over Papua—striking almost on a daily basis at targets along the trail—at Lae and Salamaua, and at Rabaul. MacArthur also had a competent commander of the U.S. I Corps, General Eichelberger, whom he could lean on heavily in the coming months to carry out his plans for an American offensive in New Guinea. Why, then, was the mood at General Headquarters in Brisbane in early September so negative?

One reason for MacArthur's attitude was the still unresolved question of command responsibilities in the Pacific. In Washington, Admiral King was not reconciled to the idea of dual command and had not given up hope of having Admiral Nimitz appointed as supreme commander. MacArthur was fully aware of King's actions and believed that this antipathy was one reason why he could not get the naval support he believed he needed. As the situation on Guadalcanal worsened, he found that his requests, not only for

73

more warships but for shallow-draft cargo vessels and landing craft, were simply put aside. General Marshall explained that preparations for action in the European theater demanded most of these. Further he was ordered to send the bulk of his small fleet to assist the Guadalcanal operation. In addition, Marshall requested a step-up in air activity against New Britain and the northern Solomons and ordered MacArthur to send a squadron of P-39s to Guadalcanal. Admiral Ghormley had wanted the P-38s, a far superior aircraft, but MacArthur successfully warded off sending them until early November.[1]

MacArthur was convinced, with some justification, that whether because of ignorance or malice, the concerns of the Southwest Pacific were being downplayed in Washington and London. He was told that he would have to look to Australia to provide more cargo ships. His repeated requests for more troops were turned aside with reminders of the overriding importance of the European commitments and the importance of the Solomons operation. On 30 August, when the situation in Papua appeared bleak, MacArthur warned the Joint Chiefs that unless changes were made in priorities, a "disastrous outcome is bound to result shortly." He pessimistically predicted that unless more naval and land forces were made available, a situation would arise "similar to those that have successfully overwhelmed our forces in the Pacific since the beginning of the war."[2]

Prime Minister Curtin, obviously influenced by MacArthur, communicated to President Roosevelt his continuing concerns that Australia, which had committed so much to the war effort, would not be able to defend itself. These communications, similar to those of April and May, did not result in any change of attitude in Roosevelt, Churchill, or the Combined Chiefs. The Southwest Pacific remained low on the priority list, one of the reasons for MacArthur's frustration.

On 25 September, Gen. Henry H. "Hap" Arnold, chief of the air corps and a member of the Joint Chiefs, arrived in Brisbane on an inspection tour. He spent a day with MacArthur and Kenney before flying off to Port Moresby, then to Noumea. He recorded in his diary his impressions of the situation in the Southwest Pacific. He praised Kenney for his work in reviving the air units, noting how successful the U.S. Army Air Forces had been in gaining air supremacy. He listened to MacArthur expound on his ideas about not only his own theater but global strategy. Arnold recorded at the end of the day his impressions of MacArthur: "MacArthur's two hour talk gives me the impression of a brilliant mind—obsessed by a plan he can't carry out—frustrated—dramatic to the extreme—much more nervous than when I formerly knew him. Hands twitch and tremble—shell shocked."[3]

After his visit to Port Moresby, Arnold recorded his negative feelings toward the Australians as fighters. He obviously had been influenced by MacArthur, Sutherland, and others at General Headquarters. In his brief visit he could not have had any logical basis for his pronouncements about the quality of the Australian troops then engaged only a few miles from Port Moresby.

It was obvious from his earliest actions in Australia that MacArthur was not satisfied with the command structure that had been created for the Southwest Pacific theater. The directive of 30 March establishing the details of command in that theater had specifically stated: "As Supreme Commander you are not eligible to command directly any national force."[4] His role was supposed to be strategic and political and his headquarters a coordinating body.

He chafed under this restriction, because he had to depend upon Australian commanders to carry out the operations in New Guinea. Because those operations were almost totally defensive, the role of his headquarters in the fighting was largely suggestive. The actual command of the Allied land forces (ALF) was exercised by Gen. Sir Thomas Blamey, who also had been placed in command of the Australian Military Force (AMF). There is some evidence to indicate that MacArthur did not support Blamey.

In early September, MacArthur probably was concerned about his own position if Port Moresby were lost. Later, when the situation had improved, his chief of staff, Sutherland, told Kenney, "If anything went wrong General MacArthur would be sent home."[5] However, there is little doubt that the reverses in Papua were being blamed not on MacArthur but on Blamey. The Australian general was not held in high esteem by senior American officers and some members of the Australian government. Major General Richard-son, after his inspection tour, reported negatively about Blamey and the Australian army. One of the reasons he gave for not accepting command of I Corps was that he did not want to serve under such a disreputable officer. General Arnold noted: "Blamey has no inten-tion of attacking unless he is forced into it."[6] Sutherland was openly contemptuous of the Australian commanders. Many of the Aus-tralian senior officers did not like Blamey and considered him a po-litical general.

It would have been strange if MacArthur did not share some of these ideas. In addition to his frustration with the awkward system of command and the necessity of depending almost totally on the Australian army, he was nervous. To the extent possible, MacArthur shunned the Australian senior commanders. He did not include any of them on his General Headquarters staff, despite suggestions from General Marshall and President Roosevelt to do so. General Eichelberger confirmed MacArthur's antipathy when he recalled:

Shortly after I arrived in Australia, General MacArthur or-dered me to pay my respects to the Australians and then have nothing further to do with them. This order I carried out to a very large extent throughout my service in or near Australia. I imagine General Krueger, when he took command of Sixth Army in May 1943, was given similar orders because he was conspicuous in his avoidance of the Australians, either mili-tarily or socially.[7]

MacArthur did have one great advantage in this early stage of the war. He had direct access to Prime Minister Curtin, who deeply ad-mired him and would act aggressively on his suggestions. This con-fidence allowed MacArthur to affect the Australian command sys-tem directly. He was increasingly critical of the Australian retreat along the trail, largely because his intelligence of the situation in New Guinea was poor. Sutherland's ill-timed suggestion about blow-ing up the Gap is an example of the profound ignorance of the cli-mate and terrain of the area. MacArthur also believed that the Aus-tralians had numerical superiority over Horii's forces. Seemingly without knowledge of the narrowness of the trail, he believed that the Australians retreated unnecessarily when they should have been attacking the Japanese flanks. Major General George Vasey, deputy chief of staff of the Australian General Staff, informed General Rowell that "GHQ is like a bloody barometer in a cyclone—up and down every two minutes."[8]

The Japanese landings at Milne Bay caused MacArthur a great deal of anxiety. General Vasey communicated this to Rowell: "Sutherland stated that MacArthur was very concerned about the apparent lack of activity on Cyril's [Clowes] part." Vasey noted that this was General Headquarters' first battle, and they were nervous because of a lack of continuing messages.[9] Once again betraying a lack of knowledge of the conditions facing General Clowes, MacArthur had Sutherland communicate with General Blamey on 28 August, noting:

> The Commander-in-Chief requests that you instruct Major General Clowes at once to clear the north side of Milne Bay without delay and that you direct him to submit a report to reach General Headquarters by 0800 K/29 [29 August] of the action taken together with the enemy's strength in the area.[10]

Clowes was unmoved by this peremptory request and continued his cautious operation before knowing the full extent of the Japanese commitment.

General Rowell came to the defense of Clowes, noting: "I am sure he was right. Inability to move except at a crawl, together with the constant threat of further landings, made it difficult for him to go fast or far."[11] However commendable his defense of his subordinate, it was another example to GHQ of the lack of enthusiasm, if not outright incompetence, of the Australian commanders. MacArthur had sent Sutherland and Kenney to Port Moresby to assess the situation there. On his return, Kenney, on 12 September, informed his chief that he believed that unless something changed, the Japanese would be in Port Moresby. He faulted Rowell and his staff for their defensive preparations and stated his opinion that he couldn't see why "12,000 white men should have to let two or three thousand

Japs chase them behind barbed wire." He charged that Rowell's de-
featist attitude had permeated the whole Australian New Guinea
Force.[12]

The pessimism at MacArthur's headquarters infected the Australian War Cabinet, which pressured Prime Minister Curtin to ask
Blamey to go to New Guinea, confer with Rowell, and report back
the conditions he found there. The general manager of the Melbourne *Herald* wrote soon afterward that Curtin, in an off-the-
record statement, indicated that the government was not satisfied
with Blamey, and there had already been a canvas of names to find
his replacement.[13] When ordered to New Guinea, Blamey was aware
of the criticism and knew that he had to prove himself a tough, able
commander. He flew to Port Moresby, inspected troops of the 7th
Division, and discussed the situation with Rowell. His report to the
war cabinet on 17 September, although containing many factual er-
rors in reporting the actions of the 39th Battalion, was in the main
supportive of Rowell and the Australian troops in Papua and was optimistic about future operations.[14]

MacArthur's concerns over the situation in Papua as he and his
closest subordinates saw it climaxed on the same evening after
Blamey made his report. MacArthur contacted Prime Minister
Curtin on the secrophone (secret telephone) and suggested that
the situation in New Guinea was such that Blamey should be ordered to New Guinea to take personal command. Once again he
displayed his rancor and lack of knowledge by claiming that General Eather's withdrawal to Imita Ridge, despite outnumbering the
Japanese, was caused by "lack of efficiency."[15] On the following day,
Curtin informed Blamey that he was to proceed to New Guinea and
take personal command of the situation there. It appears that at this
juncture Blamey considered the order to be militarily unnecessary.
His director general of medical services asked him directly if he was
worried about New Guinea. Blamey replied, "No, but Canberra has
lost it!"[16] He would not contest the order, because he was aware that
his career was at stake.

A further indication that Blamey was uncomfortable with the order and was concerned that Rowell might not understand and
would resent his presence at Port Moresby was the warning letter he

sent to Port Moresby. In this conciliatory note he expressed the hope that Rowell would not be too upset with the new arrangement.

Blamey arrived at Port Moresby on 23 September, a week after the troops under Rowell's command had halted the Japanese south of Ioribaiwa, and immediately informed the prime minister that he had assumed command. Rowell, although not openly hostile to his chief, was frank in his opinion that the action by the government was a vote of no confidence in his abilities as a commander. In the long conversation during the evening of the twenty-third, Rowell pointed out that the situation was under control, that the withdrawal to Imita Ridge had been necessary, and that Eather was now preparing a counteroffensive. Rowell suggested that, in conformance with Curtin's order, Blamey remain at Port Moresby but establish his headquarters there and continue to operate as he had from his army headquarters on the mainland. He, Rowell, would remain in direct command of the operations. Blamey, who had suggested that Rowell would act as deputy field commander, demurred, arguing that the introduction of an army headquarters in New Guinea was unjustified at that critical stage in the operations. The conversation appears to have become rancorous, and no semblance of an agreement was reached that evening.[17]

Blamey asked Maj. Gen. Sir Samuel Burston, a close friend of Rowell's, to speak to him and convince him to accept Blamey's solution. After a long discussion, Burston left feeling that he had not been able to convince Rowell to accept the inevitable because Blamey was simply carrying out the wishes of the prime minister and the war cabinet.

A further division between the two generals resulted from Blamey's visit to Milne Bay on the twenty-fifth. There he inspected troop dispositions and conferred with General Clowes and Brigadier Wootten, who was commanding the 18th Brigade. General Headquarters had been interested in securing the area around Wanigela Mission, midway between the bay and Buna, where a flat valley appeared promising for the construction of an airfield. Blamey suggested to Clowes that a detachment be sent to secure the area in preparation for an eventual attack on Buna. Clowes notified Rowell of the substance of the meeting. Thus when Blamey returned, Rowell protested against Blamey issuing an order directly to Clowes instead of allowing Rowell to do so. Blamey maintained that he had not issued an order but merely made a suggestion.[18] This minor event over military etiquette indicated the deepening rancor between the two men.

Rowell composed a letter to Blamey noting the details of his authority as commander of New Guinea Force and stating that it seemed obvious that this authority should now officially pass to Blamey. This prompted Blamey, on the morning of the twenty-sixth, to issue a directive notifying Rowell that, in conformance with his orders, he proposed to exercise direct command of the forces in the New Guinea area through Rowell and his staff. He ordered that arrangements should be made immediately to provide him with all tactical information concerning location and disposition of troops. All messages for Allied land forces headquarters and Australian military headquarters were to be submitted to him before dispatch. After receiving this written order, Rowell, in instructions to his staff that evening, laid down the procedure to be followed. This should have convinced Blamey that Rowell had capitulated and was resolved to accept his new role.

The two-hour conference held on the morning of the twenty-seventh appeared to go well, although it is probable that Blamey had earlier decided to remove Rowell. The following morning he informed Rowell that he was relieving him from command and had sent an adverse report to the prime minister and General MacArthur.[19] The ostensible reason for Blamey's action was the lack of information at Rowell's headquarters on the disposition and activities of the troops defending Port Moresby. In reality it was due to the clash of personalities brought about by Blamey attempting to comply with orders from the prime minister and the war cabinet.

In the report to higher headquarters, Blamey stated that Rowell had proved difficult, as he charged Blamey with not protecting Rowell's interests, and that Rowell was being "forced to eat dirt." Blamey complained of not being given the full details of the situation in New Guinea, and having to search them out for himself. He believed that Rowell took his coming to New Guinea as a personal attack and that if Rowell were to remain, he would be a disruptive influence. He wrote that Rowell did not possess the "necessary energy, foresight, and drive" in certain activities. Blamey believed that his subordinate, although competent, had little command experience and was one who harbored "imaginary grievances." Before leaving Port Moresby, Rowell initialed the report and later filed his rebuttal, expressing regret over Blamey's actions and noting that he had received no written instructions on procedure until three days after Blamey's arrival.[20]

Blamey's decision to remove his subordinate created a minor rift in the government, because Rowell did not go quietly but protested against the way he was treated. Blamey, for his part, would use all his influence to destroy Rowell's career, at one point even recommending that he be reduced to the grade of colonel. Later, Blamey opposed Field Marshal Sir Claude Auchinleck's request for Rowell to serve in India. The matter of Rowell's fitness to command at Port Moresby became obscured by Blamey's personal vendetta. Ultimately, Field Marshal Alan Brooke, chief of the Imperial Staff, overrode Blamey's objections and secured Rowell's services in Britain as director of tactical investigations in the War Office, where he served with distinction. Further evidence of Rowell's abilities came when, soon after the war, he was selected to be Australia's chief of the General Staff.[21]

Blamey, partially prompted by MacArthur's worried inquiries even after the counteroffensive begun by Rowell's successor, Lt. Gen. Edmund Herring, continued the removal of senior officers who had been involved in the retreat and were considered to be Rowell's men. One of the first to go was Brigadier Potts, who in an earlier conversation with Rowell and Blamey at Port Moresby indicated his criticism of the way the men of his brigade had been treated and the negative assertions made concerning their bravery. Blamey asked Rowell his opinion of Potts and was assured that the brigadier had done a splendid job. Potts returned to his command then at Itiki on 23 September. Later, General Allen visited the 21st Brigade; after a parade, he delivered a personal message from the prime minister extending the nation's thanks to the brigade for saving Port Moresby.

By then the Australians had begun their forward movement along the Kokoda Trail, and Potts could imagine that all was well at higher headquarters. The facts were otherwise. MacArthur was bombarding Blamey with demands that the Australians make more rapid progress. On 23 October, Blamey paid an unexpected visit to 21st Brigade headquarters, conferred with Potts alone for some time, and accused the officers of the brigade of not performing adequately; he stated that failures such as the retreat could not be tolerated. He informed Potts that he was relieving him of command and ordered him to leave for Darwin immediately, without allowing him to remain to meet his successor, Brig. Ivan Dougherty, or to address the men of the brigade. Nevertheless, word of his relief and the apparent reasons for it spread rapidly, resulting in a flurry of requests for resignations from his officers; all the requests were denied. Blamey later stated that he had gone to New Guinea to energize the situation. The cashiering of Potts, one of the heroes of the desperate fighting along the trail, elicited the opposite response. The morale of the brigade hit a low level and remained so for some time.[22]

The Australian counteroffensive, which began on 26 September, encountered scant opposition at first from the Japanese, because General Horii, as ordered, had begun to pull back. This led MacArthur and Blamey to believe that the two Australian brigades would have an easy time recapturing Kokoda. Then, in connection with General Headquarters, they planned to cooperate with U.S. forces to capture the Buna region. However, the Japanese still had the ability when they wished to hold up any quick advance. This they did at Templeton's Crossing and Eora Creek. As during previous actions, MacArthur betrayed his lack of knowledge of New Guinea and the difficulties of supplying troops to keep them moving in a constricted area such as the trail, especially when the enemy could block the progress by skillful defensive actions.

At first Blamey defended General Allen by reminding MacArthur of the difficult terrain and the many problems of supply. This defense seemingly was lost on MacArthur, who on 11 October radioed Blamey demanding to know what was delaying the advance. The same day, Blamey signaled Allen: "In view of lack of serious opposition your advance appears much too slow." He added that if Allen was feeling too much strain, "relief will be arranged." Allen's reply on the twelfth assured Blamey that he had every intention of capturing Kokoda as soon as possible, but he pointed to the fact that the "country is much tougher than any previous theater," and the vigor of the offensive depended on the "physical endurance of the men and the availability of supplies." MacArthur telegraphed Blamey on the seventeenth: "Press General Allen's advance. His extremely light casualties indicate no serious effort yet made to displace enemy. It is essential that Kokoda airfield be taken."[23]

Four days later, Blamey, obviously influenced by MacArthur's attitude, accused Allen of further delays, because his troops had made "practically no advance against a weaker enemy." On the same day he relayed a further message from MacArthur that "the tactical handling of our troops in my opinion is faulty" in the face of inferior enemy numbers.[24]

Never one to stand up to MacArthur, Blamey abandoned his defense of Allen and on 27 October signaled him: "Consider that you have sufficiently prolonged tour of duty in forward area. General Vasey will arrive at Myola by air morning 28 October."[25] Just as Rowell had been relieved on the eve of beginning the offensive, Allen was to be deprived of being part of gaining the victory that MacArthur so desperately wanted. The day following Allen's relief, Brigadier Lloyd's troops smashed the major Japanese defenses, and the way to Kokoda was opened.

Kokoda was recaptured on 2 November. The Australians had taken only thirty-five days to advance from Ioribaiwa to Kokoda, sixteen days fewer than the Japanese had needed to move the same distance over the same terrain. It is worth noting that General Vasey was flown in to the airstrip at Myola without incident. Allen had repeatedly requested trial landings be made to the strip to deliver supplies and evacuate the more seriously wounded. Those requests had never been acted upon. Allen had throughout his command been given less than was required to do the tasks assigned him within the time frame established by his superiors. He, like Potts, deserved better than relief under questionable circumstances.

Blamey did not stop with the purge of what he considered Rowell's men. Chester Wilmot, a distinguished author and reporter for the Australian Broadcasting System, had accompanied Australian troops in their retreat along the trail. General Rowell had subsequently asked him to prepare an analysis of that campaign and was so impressed by it that he attached it as an appendix to a report on land operations. Some of the senior officers in Brisbane obviously did not agree with the various criticisms in Wilmot's analysis, but they reacted only by burying the report. Blamey, however, had a more personal antipathy toward Wilmot, who, in the controversy surrounding Rowell's removal, was a vocal advocate of Rowell. In addition, Wilmot had alleged that Blamey, while in the Middle East, had conducted some "profitable rackets."

Wilmot's continual presence in New Guinea was too much for Blamey. He canceled Wilmot's accreditation as a reporter, thus banning him from the New Guinea area and seriously damaging his career. After some difficulty, Wilmot and the Australian Broadcasting System negotiated a posting for him with the British Broadcasting System, where he continued his excellent reporting of the war in Europe. The Wilmot affair, although not directly related to the changes that Blamey had made in the military command system, further decreased Blamey's reputation with many of the more senior officers in his command.[26]

Further evidence of Blamey's failure to understand the reality of the long, difficult retreat was his address given to the officers and men of the 21st Brigade at Koitaki Plantation on 9 November. When informed that Blamey intended to speak to them, they imagined that this would be a further occasion for compliments on the performance of the brigade during the withdrawal. This was a logical conclusion, because General Allen earlier in similar circumstances had extended the thanks of the nation to the men of the brigade for their role in saving Port Moresby.

After a parade the officers and men were drawn up in battalion formation near the dais from which Blamey was to speak. What he said shocked and disappointed all, but particularly the veteran survivors of the Middle East conflicts as well as the many desperate firefights at Isurava, Eora Creek, Brigade Hill, and Ioribaiwa. Although long unmentioned, there is little doubt of Blamey's disparaging remarks. Reflecting the a priori opinions of MacArthur's staff and his own suspect conclusions, Blamey told members of the assembled brigade that they had been defeated by a numerically inferior enemy. He believed that Australian troops should be worth three of the enemy. In the future he expected no retirement but advancement no matter what the cost.

The rank and file became more restive as he continued, some even interrupting his address. Nevertheless, he continued and concluded with a most unfortunate phrase, reminding them that "it is the rabbit that runs that gets shot." Some of the brigade's officers were so outraged by Blamey's speech that they refused to attend an officers' call to hear more from their commanding general. In that meeting he told them that he doubted whether the brigade had the will to fight and accused them of not being worthy of their men, refusing to share the hardships and hazards of battle.[27]

It is difficult to understand what good Blamey thought would come from his diatribe. The removal of Rowell, Allen, and Potts could be excused in part by the pressure from MacArthur's headquarters, combined with a flawed understanding of the conditions in New Guinea. This open criticism of men who, with minimal support from the rear echelons, had bravely fought in a long, torturous campaign could have gained nothing. Combined with his removal of the commander of New Guinea Force, the divisional commander, and the brigade commander, and the banishment of a distinguished war correspondent, this speech was a further negation of his avowed aim of energizing the situation in New Guinea.

The saving grace of Blamey's purge was the caliber of men he chose to replace those he had relieved. General Herring, then fifty years old, had served in World War I and been a close associate of Blamey's in the Middle East, serving as the commander of the 6th Division. However, he was not by any measure Blamey's man. Earlier in 1942, he, along with Generals Vasey and Steele, had campaigned for another younger officer to be commander in chief of the Australian army. At the time of his appointment to command New Guinea Force, Herring was the commander of the Australian II Corps in northern Australia. He accepted the position secondary to Blamey in New Guinea, which Rowell had objected to. In the months following his appointment, Herring proved that he could make the awkward command situation work well.

General Vasey also had active combat command in Africa and Greece. Before being ordered to supplant Allen as commander of the 7th Division, he was the commander of the 6th Division in Australia. Brigadier Dougherty, a vetern of Cyrenaica, Greece, and Crete, was given command of the 23d Brigade before replacing Potts. He had the most difficult task. Potts had been extremely popular, regarded as a hero by his troops. Dougherty was at first not enthusiastically welcomed by the officers and men of the 21st. He overcame their suspicions and would gain their unqualified support for the next three years.[28] Thus, despite the high-level meddling with a successful command team, those who replaced them in the midst of an offensive performed well in the trying months ahead.

Chapter VI
On to Kokoda

In the defense of Australia, MacArthur was the beneficiary of a number of significant events that occurred outside his theater of operations. Two of these were the naval battles of the Coral Sea and Midway, the former ending a major threat to Port Moresby. His plans for the defeat of the Japanese in New Guinea might have been frustrated if the Japanese High Command had not been forced to defend its dominant position in the Solomon Islands. With total naval and air superiority in the early months of the war, the Japanese had not rushed to occupy this string of islands northeast of Australia. However, by midyear they had garrisoned most of the major ones and constructed airfields on New Ireland, New Georgia, and Bougainville. The decision to occupy Port Moresby caused a postponement of plans to take Fiji and New Caledonia, but earlier it was decided tentatively to move farther eastward by occupying the small island of Tulagi to build a seaplane base there.

Work on the base began in May. On the twenty-eighth, the local commander at Tulagi, acting on his own initiative, sent patrols across the Sealark Channel to Guadalcanal, twenty miles away. At this time no thought had been given to establishing a permanent base there. The patrols were simply searching for a source of meat for the Tulagi garrison. The patrols reported a flat area on the old Lunga Plantation that would be suitable for an airfield. A survey party was sent there on 19 June, and within three weeks almost 3,000 men were working on the airfield. American reaction to these events resulted in six months of air, sea, and land battles for control of the area adjacent to the airfield.

The Joint Chiefs had alerted both MacArthur's and Admiral Ghormley's headquarters of the need to seize Tulagi. On 2 July they planned for the eventual conquest of Rabaul in three "tasks." The first was the occupation of the Santa Cruz Islands and Tulagi, scheduled for 1 August. The second, the capture of Buna, Lae, and Salamaua, was circumvented by the Japanese capture of Buna and subsequent actions along the Kokoda Trail. MacArthur was not pleased with the decision to carry out Task One, because it meant that some of the men and materiel he had urgently requested would now be used for the Solomons venture and he would be required to share his scant naval force with Ghormley. However, after receiving Marshall's communiqué indicating that the plan would not be altered, he agreed to cooperate fully. He met with Ghormley in Melbourne on 8 July and found that the admiral was not keen on the operation either, even though the date for its implementation had been advanced to 7 August. MacArthur and Ghormley recommended that the seizure of Tulagi be postponed beyond that date. Their reasoning was based on the inadequacy of the ground, air, and naval units to carry out the assigned tasks. The Joint Chiefs rejected their arguments and ordered the occupation to proceed on the agreed-upon date.[1] The knowledge that the Japanese had begun construction of an airfield on Guadalcanal made it even more imperative to seize it as well as Tulagi.

Ghormley's and MacArthur's warning about the inadequacy of the means to carry out the directive was apparent from the beginning of the Solomons operation. The army's 37th Division was in Fiji, and elements of the Americal Division were scattered throughout New Caledonia, but these could not be used because it was believed that they were needed to ward off Japanese attacks. The only force readily available for the task was part of the 1st Marine Division, newly arrived in New Zealand. One of its regiments had been detached and was then providing the main defense of Samoa.

The air units available proved insufficient to take full advantage of the airfield. The entire operation was hastily put together, reflecting the fears of Admiral King and the Joint Chiefs that an airfield on Guadalcanal in enemy hands could seriously threaten the vital supply line to New Zealand. The importance given to the

Guadalcanal operation can be seen in the numbers and quality of the naval support that Nimitz committed. Admiral Fletcher, in overall command, had three aircraft carriers, a battleship, six cruisers, and sixteen destroyers. The amphibious force carrying the Marines left Wellington, New Zealand, escorted by eight cruisers. The seventy-six ships involved made up the largest naval force assembled since Pearl Harbor. The major flaw was that the force to take and hold Guadalcanal was pitifully small. This large naval armada would not be available for any length of time after the landings.[2]

The Marines landed on Florida Island, Tulagi, and Guadalcanal on 7 August, the same day the Australians in New Guinea were retreating past the key town of Kokoda. At first all went smoothly. By nightfall of the first day, the key objectives had been secured. The U.S. Marine commander, Maj. Gen. Alexander Vandegrift, then dispersed his troops to provide a perimeter around the airfield and awaited the expected Japanese counterattack.

The Japanese at Rabaul and Tokyo missed their best opportunity to dislodge the Marines during the few days following the landings. However, they attacked the beachhead repeatedly with air strikes, and their navy delivered a crushing blow to the United States by sinking four cruisers in the battle of Savo Island. On 10 August, Tokyo ordered Lt. Gen. Haruyoshi Hyakutake, commanding the Seventeenth Army, to send a brigade to recapture the islands. A small portion of this invasion force, full of confidence, on 19 August marched westward toward the airfield. The Marines blocking the route cut the invading force to pieces. This was but the first of many direct assaults on the Marine positions ordered by overconfident commanders.

A major assault on the perimeter was launched on 13 September by two battalions of infantry, exhausted by a long march in the heat and humidity of the island. From their dug-in positions, the Marines once again beat off the enemy, inflicting heavy losses. This defeat had major ramifications for the New Guinea campaign, because the Japanese High Command decided to commit the majority of its available air, sea, and land forces to Guadalcanal. What had been an almost accidental encounter had thus become an arena for the test of the wills of both sides.[3]

In the weeks that followed, the Japanese committed two additional divisions. In early November, General Hyakutake transferred his headquarters to Guadalcanal to take personal command. Admiral Yamamoto directed a major portion of the combined fleet in an attempt to destroy the U.S. naval forces guarding the enclave around the airfield. The Japanese air force, in the first two months of the campaign, maintained dominance although suffering heavy losses from marine and navy pilots. Before the campaign concluded in February 1943, there was a series of major naval battles, with Admiral Ghormley and his successor, Vice Adm. William F. Halsey, committing the bulk of the naval force available in the South Pacific to the defense of Guadalcanal. Although suffering heavy losses in these encounters, the U.S. Navy thwarted every effort to wipe out the Marine bridgehead.

The Japanese were not alone in increasing the size of the forces involved. In the beginning, only two regiments of the 1st Marine Division were committed, but on 18 September the third regiment was brought in and in early October a regiment of the army's Americal Division landed, bringing to 28,000 the number of troops available to Vandegrift. A major attack against the airfield from the south was shattered on 25 October. This was the high-water mark of the Japanese infantry. Soon the 1st Marines were reinforced by more of the Americal troops, elements of the army's 43d Division, and the 25th. Thus even before Vandegrift handed over command to Maj. Gen. Alexander Patch, the U.S. tactics had ceased to be purely defensive. A series of offensives expanded the area they controlled while inflicting heavy damage on the by now sick, hungry, and dispirited Japanese. Some senior enemy commanders as early as November were recommending that Japan cut its losses and retire from Guadalcanal.[4] The decision was postponed, but ultimately the order was given, and the remnants of the Japanese force were removed in early February 1943. Of the estimated 36,000 Japanese who fought on the island, more than 14,000 were killed and a further 9,000 perished from disease.[5] The Japanese navy had lost a number of capital ships and 600 planes. The planes could be replaced; not so the veteran pilots. Japanese expansion in the Pacific was halted. Japan would never fully recover from the Guadalcanal battles.

MacArthur's direct contribution to the Guadalcanal campaign was considerable. He dispatched most of the ships of what was referred to as "MacArthur's navy" under Rear Adm. V. A. C. Crutchley, of the Royal Navy. These took part in a number of actions, including the first battle of Savo Island, where the cruiser *Canberra* was sunk. Only after urgent appeals was MacArthur able to convince the higher command to allow Crutchley's force to be returned to the Southwest Pacific theater in early September in order to protect against the possibility of a further attack on Milne Bay.

The most important service given by MacArthur to the Guadalcanal campaign was the commitment of his still small air force in strategic and tactical attack on Japanese bases. The Fifth Air Force repeatedly attacked Rabaul as well as Japanese air bases in the Bismarck archipelago and in the northern Solomons. Kenney's major problem throughout this period was the lack of serviceable aircraft to carry out the dual role of supporting the Australian and U.S. attacks in Papua as well as striking Japanese concentrations in the South Pacific theater. General Marshall had approved the transfer to the navy of aircraft originally ordered to MacArthur. This included twenty-nine B-17s and sixty-one medium bombers as well as a number of transport aircraft. In addition, MacArthur sent a squadron of P-39s to bolster the defenses of the airfield.[6]

Later, Kenney complained of the difficulty of getting many of the transport planes back from Noumea. Some of the aircraft that arrived in Australia were defective. The earliest shipment of P-38s had serious leaks in the air intakes and cooling system. These had to undergo extensive modification before they could be flown safely. Although MacArthur and Kenney objected to the transfer of some of these superior fighters to Guadalcanal, they complied as soon as the necessary repairs had been made. The first B-24 heavy bombers that arrived in Australia were also found to have major flaws. Most were delivered with cracks in the antishimmy collars for the nose wheel. A rush order was put through to the machine shops in Brisbane to manufacture the new steel replacements.[7] Despite such technical problems, all of Kenney's available planes struck Japanese concentrations day after day whenever the weather permitted. The efficiency of Fifth Air Force and RAAF attacks in Papua and New

Britain was increased because of the shift of so many Japanese planes to the Solomons.

As the grim struggle continued on Guadalcanal and Japanese losses there mounted, General Hyakutake on 29 August ordered Horii to stop offensive operations after crossing the Owen Stanley Range and securing a defensible base. Therefore, after reaching Imita Ridge, he ordered his decimated troops to dig in at Ioribaiwa and await reinforcements. Despite the high morale of the remaining troops, as reported by Japanese observers, it was obvious that, because of combat losses combined with those due to disease, he could not take Port Moresby without more troops. He had been provided earlier with one regiment and had been promised another. Supply was a problem that he could not solve and that would, even under the best of circumstances, undermine any future Japanese offensive against Port Moresby. The Japanese supply system, which was poor even during the early stage of their offensive, had almost completely broken down. Distance from the main supply base on the north coast was one factor. However, the major reason for the stoppage of supply was the continued attacks by American and Australian planes. With little opposition from Japanese planes, U.S. fighters and bombers repeatedly attacked Japanese supply stations and troop concentrations along the trail. Particularly effective was the Douglas A-20 medium bomber, which had been modified with eight forward-firing machine guns. Flying low, they would strafe the trail and drop fragmentation bombs fitted with parachutes, which allowed the planes to fly out of harm's way before the bombs exploded. Kokoda, the bridge at Wairopi, and Buna were key targets. A Japanese war correspondent noted that there was little Japanese air activity and the Americans had the air entirely to themselves. He also reported that almost 80 percent of the Japanese force had either been killed, wounded, or disabled by illness.[8] By the time Horii's victorious troops arrived at Imita Ridge, there was no rice available for them. The Japanese there and all along the trail were tearing up the countryside and looting native villages in their search for food.

Although temporarily on the defensive, and despite the condition of his troops and the faulty supply system, General Horii had no intention of permanently abandoning the offensive. At Iori-baiwa, his main defense position, his men had constructed a connecting network of fire pits and command posts, trenches, and a high protective fence. Fields of fire had been cleared and obstacles erected, and his mountain gun, four machine guns, and mortars were sited to the best advantage. On 17 September his operations order was optimistic and indicated that he planned to continue the offensive. Three days later from his headquarters near Nauro, he issued an Address of Instruction, which clearly indicated that he planned to take the offensive. After relating the victories of his army in the face of a stubborn enemy and under the terrible conditions of the trail, he explained: "The reason we have halted is to regain our fighting strength before striking a decisive blow at Port Moresby. . . . Fortify your morale and make your preparations complete so that the Shitai is strong for our next operation."[9]

The destruction of the Kawaguchi Detachment on Guadalcanal on 13–14 September left the Japanese without any large forces on the island. Thus the Imperial General Staff faced a major problem. If Guadalcanal were to be held, all available resources had to be concentrated to that end. New orders were issued on 18 September emphasizing that all efforts had to be utilized to secure the island. A further cause of alarm to the Japanese was the fear that MacArthur planned a coordinated air and seaborne invasion of the Buna area. If successful, it would isolate Horii's troops on the south side of the Owen Stanley Range. Fearing this, Gen. Hitoshi Imamura, commander of the Eighth Area Army, sent a number of stop orders to Horii. The key wireless order, which was received by Horii on the twenty-fourth, commanded him to "withdraw from present position to some place in the Owen Stanley Range which you may consider best for strategic purposes."[10]

Japanese correspondent Okada reported General Horii's reaction to the order. Upon learning of the wireless message, Okada rushed to the general's tent to find him in conversation with his chief staff officer, Lt. Col. Toyanari Tanaka. Horii said, "I'm not going back, not a step! Are you going back Tanaka? How can we abandon this position after all the blood the soldiers have shed and the hardships they have endured? I cannot give such an order."[11]

At this juncture a signalman entered the tent with another wireless from Imamura ordering him to withdraw completely from the Owen Stanley Range and concentrate on defending the Buna-Gona beachhead. Soon another message from Imperial General Headquarters arrived confirming the order to withdraw. Horii considered this to be from the emperor, which left him no choice but to begin preparations for withdrawing.

General Horii announced the decision to withdraw in an operations order early on the morning of the twenty-fifth. He ordered the 1st and 3d Battalions of the 144th Infantry to put up only token resistance at Ioribaiwa before retiring northward to the Kokoda area. He had earlier sent the 2d Battalion of the 144th to Isurava to help move supplies forward. The 41st Infantry, led by Col. Kiyomi Yazawa, would move as quickly as possible to the Giruwa-Sanananda area, where he would take over command of all troops in that region and expedite the buildup of coastal defenses. In the early evening of the twenty-sixth, after sustaining an Australian artillery and probing infantry attack, the two battalions of the 144th left their fortified positions and moved back up the trail. Before leaving, the commander ordered the mountain battery to fire at Port Moresby at extreme range in order to "uplift our downcast spirits."[12] The main body of the 144th reached Kokoda on 4 October. Earlier, Horii had formed the Stanley Shitai from the 2d Battalion, commanded by Maj. Tadashi Horie. He also had an engineering company and a battery of mountain guns. The shitai was to act as a rear guard, fighting from prepared positions to cover the junction of two trails through the Gap from Kogi and Myola.[13]

Plans for the counteroffensive against the Japanese defenses had been made by General Allen, commanding the 7th Division, and General Rowell, before his removal as commander of New Guinea Force. Aggressive patrolling by fifty-man patrols of the 25th Brigade had located many of the Japanese key positions at Ioribaiwa. Then on 26 September, men of the 25th, dressed in new green uniforms, began an all-out assault after a short bombardment by two field guns of the 14th Field Regiment. Expecting to meet heavy resistance, the Australian units moved cautiously ahead. The 2/25 Battalion made the frontal attack while the 2/31 and 2/33 flanked the ridge. Reflecting the attitudes of the senior commanders, the troops were surprised to find no significant opposition; the Japanese had simply slipped away. The Japanese withdrawal was so fast that the Australians could not catch them. Nauro, located twelve miles north of Ioribaiwa, was entered on 30 September, and Eather's troops moved rapidly through heavy rain up a 3,500-foot ridge, then down through heavy jungle to Menari. On the way they encountered a large number of well-sited gun pits, from which the Japanese could have inflicted serious damage on their pursuers, had they so desired. The Australians, having learned from their retreat, now advanced with adequate flank protection. Still without serious opposition, men of the 25th Brigade entered Myola on 9 October.[14]

At Nauro, the Australians first discovered the extent of the misery suffered by the Japanese. Many bodies were recovered with no apparent wounds. As the advance continued, more bodies were found, showing further evidence of the twin scourges of disease and hunger. Scrub typhus, malaria, and dysentery spared neither side. However, the Australian medical support was far superior to that of the Japanese. Their men, once they had contracted the virulent form of any disease, could not expect treatment. A Lieutenant Sakamoto in early October wrote, "Our life is worse than a beggar's. I wish people at home could see us now." He estimated that two-thirds of his men were afflicted with beri-beri.[15] Starvation, which had been noticeable even before the retreat, now had become widespread. Some soldiers were reduced to eating roots, grass, wood, poisonous jungle berries, and fruits. Some troops died of eating rancid bully beef left behind by the Australians a month before. The hungry men fanned out from the trail to invade native villages, which they systematically looted. They mistreated the villagers just as they had the carriers who were brought over from Rabaul earlier.

A long record of the Japanese atrocities emerged as the Australians pushed forward. Natives related a litany of abuses, including the abduction and rape of their women, shootings, and bayonetings. Nor were the Australian soldiers safe from the almost casual executions committed by the Japanese. At Templeton's

Crossing, two Australians were found whose bodies showed clearly that some Japanese were guilty of cannibalism. The diary of Lieutenant Sakamoto, captured after his death at Gorari, related that some companies were eating Australian dead.[16]

After arriving at Mission Ridge, the advance elements of the 25th discovered grim evidence of the desperate fight that had occurred on 2 September. The bodies of Australians were still in place, unburied, in their weapon pits or on the open ground where they had died in their desperate counterattacks. The corpses were mute testimony that refuted General Blamey's allusion that he would make at Koitaki on 9 November, that men of the 21st Brigade had somehow run like rabbits before the enemy. In total, there were more than two hundred bodies, Japanese and Australian, in various states of decay that had to be buried.[17]

As planned, the Japanese had retreated quickly. General Horii had dispatched a large part of his force to the Eora Creek area and beyond to Kokoda. Advancing north from Myola, the 25th Brigade encountered only patrols in the fairly flat rain forest area in the Gap between Kogi and Templeton's Crossing. Horii had decided to make his first concerted defense at Eora Creek Valley, where the creek passed through a deep ravine. He entrusted defense of the entrance to the Eora Creek Gorge to the Stanley Shitai, whose members entrenched themselves along the high ground above the trail. From there they could fire down on the Australians. Despite the heroic efforts of Eather's men, they were not able to dislodge this Japanese battalion for a week. The remnants of the shitai then fell back to Eora Creek, where they joined the main body of the 144th Infantry. The Japanese had built a series of interlocking gun pits, log blockhouses, and trenches along the ridgeline above the ravine. General Horii traveled from his headquarters at Kokoda to inspect the forest fortification on 25 October while the battle for the ridge was in progress.[18]

On 20 October, General Allen replaced the weary troops of the 25th Brigade with the relatively fresh 16th Brigade. In the five weeks of campaigning, the brigade had suffered 203 casualties, and 771 had gone down due to various tropical diseases.[19] In the continuing rain, the 16th attacked the ridgeline but with little success at first.

The Japanese defenses, which had all but halted the advance, caused General MacArthur and his staff to pressure General Blamey to speed up the operation. At first both MacArthur and Blamey believed that the Japanese would make a determined stand at Ioribaiwa. When they did not, and seemingly were fleeing back up the trail, both headquarters began to believe that there would be little Japanese resistance and that Kokoda and its airfield would quickly fall to the Australians. MacArthur's impatience with the situation in New Guinea had already resulted in the dispatch of General Blamey to Port Moresby and the relief of General Rowell. Now, despite evidence from his field commanders, MacArthur came to believe that the Australians, greatly outnumbering the Japanese, were procrastinating against an enemy not capable of a spirited defense, thus delaying the implementation of his plans to secure Buna.

Against such charges from higher headquarters, General Allen, who had moved his headquarters forward to Myola, could only relate the difficulty of the terrain and the tenacious Japanese defenses. He also complained about the lack of supplies. As the Australians advanced, their supply problems became more acute. Airdrops of supplies had improved since the retreat but were still inadequate. Rations and ammunition were dropped regularly along the trail. Allen had complained a number of times to Blamey about the level of supplies delivered by air. On 17 October he went into considerable detail in a message to Blamey: "Under present system it would appear that air force cannot supply planes necessary to assure dropping of 50,000 pounds daily weather permitting."[20] He pointed out that 50,000 pounds covered maintenance only and did not allow for the buildup of any reserve. His calculations were based on a 30 percent wastage. He also pointed out that even with more than 3,000 native porters working, they could not keep pace with the advance. Therefore, much-needed supplies were delayed in getting to the frontline forces. The carrier shortage reached an acute stage on the twenty-fifth, when only a hundred of the three hundred carriers he had sent forward in the morning returned to Myola that evening. The remainder were still on the trail, returning with wounded, and would not be available for transporting supplies forward for two days.[21] Allen pointed out that the major obstacle to any rapid advance was the terrain; the second was lack of supplies.

The barometer of emotions at MacArthur's headquarters continued to fluctuate. He had put together a plan for coordinated attacks on the Japanese, utilizing U.S. troops in a flanking maneuver to secure Buna. An integral part of that plan was the swift capture of Kokoda. The rapid advance against Horii's retreating troops had supported the a priori conclusions made by MacArthur that the capture of Kokoda could be accomplished swiftly, despite communiqués from Allen to the contrary. He believed that the Australians were simply not doing the job properly. This mind-set was not new. He had earlier passed on to Washington his conclusion that the Australians were not good fighters. Now eager to put his plans into effect, he pressured Blamey for quicker results, and Blamey in turn passed on to Allen the dissatisfaction of General Headquarters about the slowness of movement forward. On 21 October, Blamey relayed to Allen MacArthur's summation. The message stated: "Operations reports show that progress on the trail is NOT, repeat NOT, satisfactory. The tactical handling of our troops in my opinion is faulty."[22] Despite Allen's reports of heavy fighting after Templeton's Crossing, Blamey bowed to MacArthur and relieved Allen, replacing him with General Vasey.

Aside from the official dispatches available to him, MacArthur had seen for himself at least the beginning part of the trail. On 2 October he had done something unusual. During the fighting on Bataan, he had not left his headquarters on Corregidor to visit the front, and for six months he had remained either in Melbourne or Brisbane. Now, accompanied by Kenney and Sutherland, he flew by B-17 to Port Moresby late in the afternoon. The following day, accompanied by Blamey, he began an inspection trip forward. There he saw battered Australian troops coming back from the trail. At a forward supply dump, MacArthur got out of his jeep and walked up the muddy path. Near the spot where the artillery had opened the counterattack on Ioribaiwa, he encountered a battalion of the 16th Brigade going forward. He talked to Brigadier Lloyd and in his best Olympian manner reminded him that "by some act of God," his brigade had been chosen and that the "eyes of the western world" were upon them.[23] Hyperbole aside, MacArthur, standing at the beginning of the trail, must have been aware of how difficult it would be to drive back the Japanese. Blamey surely knew that MacArthur's later comments about the Australian troops were unfair and his expectations unreasonable. Nevertheless, he removed Allen just at the time when the 16th Brigade was about to break through the Japanese defenses at Eora Creek.

One plan that appealed to the higher command was proposed by General Potts before his relief. He suggested organizing a special unit, formed from the veterans of the 21st Brigade, that would raid Japanese supply lines from Myola to the Kumusi River. The idea of harassing the enemy by living off the land and striking at his key positions was one that later became an integral part of the Burma campaign, when the Chindits were formed, led by Gen. Ord Wingate. The plan was approved on 7 October and the unit was formed quickly, with a total of 407 men under the command of Lt. Col. Hugh Challen. Named Chaforce, it was sent forward and reached Myola on the eighteenth.

The plan appeared to be feasible on paper, but it was never put into operation. One reason was that the men, after their long march, were exhausted and many were sick. At best the operation would have to be postponed. It was discovered that there were no maps of the area off the trail east of the Kumusi, where Chaforce was to operate, and the aerial photography of the region was unclear. Allen then made the decision to keep Chaforce as a reserve and suggested to higher headquarters an alternate area where Chaforce could operate.

Permission to use this alternate plan was refused. Challen was ordered back to Port Moresby, and his men were utilized for general labor and supply service in the Myola area.[24] Eventually, Vasey would assign one battalion of Chaforce to each of Eather's three battalions to make up for losses suffered by the 25th Brigade. When the 21st Brigade was ordered into action later, the men of Chaforce rejoined their old unit.

General Horii had committed the entire 144th Regiment to defend the Templeton's Crossing and Eora Creek region on 21 October. Although the battalions were down to only half strength, they controlled the high ridgelines, where they had dug in with some large, strong fortifications and a number of interlockiing gun pits.[25]

The battle for these ridges, lasting a week, was confused, with the Australians forced to clamber up steep, muddy slopes against those positions, from which the Japanese could roll grenades down on them. Some of the Japanese strong points had to be taken by bayonet charges. An attempt was made to flank the Japanese by seizing two bridges across the swollen Eora Creek. The successful capture of these enabled an Australian company to force the withdrawal of a considerable enemy force. Throughout the daylight hours of the twenty-eighth, the Japanese poured a murderous fire on the Australians clinging to the muddy slopes. This fire was meant to cover the withdrawal of most of the remainder of the 144th, as Horii had earlier planned. That evening the Australians broke through the thinly held outpost line, and the Japanese rear guard fled toward Kokoda.[26]

Pushing rapidly ahead, men of the 22/3 Battalion of the 25th Brigade advanced down the main trail toward Kokoda. Vasey then turned the 16th Brigade eastward along a secondary trail toward Oivi. Notwithstanding its importance, Horii had decided not to defend Kokoda; rather he had ordered the next line of defense to be set up along the high ground near Oivi, five miles from Kokoda. The retreating Japanese on 1 November joined fresh troops of the 41st Division commanded by Col. Kiyomi Yazawa, which had arrived earlier to begin construction of the defensive positions. The Australians, moving down from the highlands toward the sunlit valley, were in good spirits, with food supplies much better. With no Japanese resistance to restrain them, they entered Kokoda on 2 November, two days after the Japanese had evacuated the destroyed village.[27] Large-scale airdrops began almost immediately, and the engineers began preparing the valuable airstrip for landings. MacArthur had his forward interior base, and for once he sent congratulations to the Australian commanders for the capture. This part of his overall plan to capture the Buna area finally had quieted his critics. He could now concentrate more fully on the other aspects of his plan for a three-pronged attack on the Buna-Gona-Sanananda beachhead.

Chapter VII
Enter the 32d Division

MacArthur's impatience with what he perceived to be the slow advance of the Australians toward Kokoda can be partially explained by his decision to commit U.S. troops. These, coordinated with the Australians, would clear the Japanese from the Buna-Gona beachhead. As the Australians would attack along the Kokoda Trail toward Wairopi, U.S. units would advance toward the same objective by means of secondary trail systems converging on the target area.

There was some confusion at higher headquarters as to who should be in command of the U.S. effort. On 14 September, at a meeting with MacArthur in Brisbane, General Eichelberger was told that he would be expected to go to New Guinea on about 1 October to be the task force commander. However, MacArthur's chief of staff, General Sutherland, protested this idea; he believed that the duty of the I Corps commander was not to lead troops but to provide for the training in Australia of U.S. ground forces. Obviously his arguments won the day, and Eichelberger remained at his headquarters in Rockhampton.[1]

In a manner that would typify many of the decisions made by MacArthur's staff in Brisbane on the basis of scant information, they had decided on which trails the U.S. units should follow. His staff had concluded that the trail from Port Moresby via Rouana Falls and the Mimani, Irua, Mugoni, and Kumusi Rivers would be the most suitable for his proposed turning movement. Brigadier General Hanford MacNider and a small number of senior officers of the

32d Division were sent to Port Moresby on 12 September to coordinate the arrival of the advance elements of that division as well as investigate the feasibility of using the route proposed by General Headquarters.

The choice of the 32d Division had nothing to do with its fighting efficiency or its training for jungle warfare. There were two U.S. divisions then in Australia—the 32d and the 41st. MacArthur left it to his newly arrived commander of I Corps, General Eichelberger, to select the one he believed should be utilized in the proposed offensive. The reason for the selection of the 32d was a housekeeping decision. The division was then stationed at Camp Cable, thirty miles south of Brisbane, and Eichelberger believed that the training camp there was inferior to that of the 41st, located near Rockhampton. The inadequate facilities at Camp Cable would necessitate the movement of the 32d to another site in the near future. Therefore, Eichelberger decided to simplify matters and chose the 32d for the Papuan venture. He consulted with Gen. Edwin Harding, the division commander, to decide which of the regiments should be chosen as the first to be transported to New Guinea. Harding indicated that the 126th was the best trained and best led; he informed the regimental commander, Col. Lawrence Quinn, to prepare for immediate transfer to Port Moresby.[2]

The fact that the 32d was even in Australia was due to the terrible shortage of trained personnel early in the war. In retrospect, its soldiers were unlucky to have been selected to operate in an environment for which none of their training prepared them. The 32d was a Wisconsin-Michigan National Guard unit—one of the earliest to be federalized. It was first ordered to Camp Beauregard, in Louisiana; then in February 1941 it was moved to Camp Livingstone, also in Louisiana. It was then still a square division organized into two brigades, with four regiments and attached artillery and engineering service units. It was not until early 1942 that it was reorganized into a triangular division with three regiments, the 126th, 127th, and 128th. The new commanding general, Edwin Harding, had been appointed in February and thus was responsible for the reorganization, which had not been fully completed when the division was ordered overseas. Harding was a West Point graduate, a classmate and friend of Eichelberger's in the class of 1909. He had an impeccable record, having performed ably in a series of responsible positions, the last being assistant division commander of the 6th Division before assuming command of the 32d.[3]

All the training given members of the 32d was pointed toward a conventional war in Europe. As an integral part of the Second Army, the 32d had participated in the most extensive mock campaigns in 1941, but as a square division it operated in terrain far removed from the kind of environment it would soon be in. As a long-time member of the division recalled: "All training in maneuvers was based on World War I fighting after we got to Louisiana. Then after moving into eastern Texas and western Louisiana for six weeks it was the same thing—the 2d Army against the 3d Army. After we went to North Carolina for training in October, it was still in the woods that we maneuvered for another month."[4]

In December 1941 the division was alerted for overseas duty. As a part of Force Magnet, it was to be moved to Northern Ireland as one of the first units to be deployed to Europe. The movement was scheduled to begin no later than July 1942. At that time the division was 4,700 enlisted men short of its authorized strength. There was, therefore, a hurried attempt to bring it up to strength by bringing in new inductees. In compliance with orders, the engineer battalion was sent ahead; the bulk of the division prepared to move to Fort Devens, in Massachusetts, prior to embarkation.

All this was changed by MacArthur's appeal for more troops to help defend Australia from the victorious Japanese, who appeared to be threatening an invasion in the near future. The War Department notified General Harding of a change of orders. He was informed that the division should plan on leaving San Francisco no later than 15 April. It was thus necessary to move the division from the East Coast to San Francisco in less than three weeks, a turn-around that normally would be scheduled for three months. Some of the troops still moving to Fort Devens never left the trains, which were simply rerouted west. A new engineer battalion was formed toward the end of March at Camp Edwards, in Massachusetts, from other units and assigned to the division. Thus the division, which had trained for the European theater and had in a manner been thrown together, was hardly a first-rate fighting machine when it arrived at Port Adelaide on 14 May.[5]

On the division's arrival in Australia, the movement from place to place and all the details of housekeeping cut into training time. The combat training that was done was accomplished in the outback in semiarid conditions where the temperatures were high but the humidity was low. This was a contradiction to MacArthur's later claims that from his earliest days in Australia, he had planned to halt the Japanese in New Guinea.

The rudimentary training afforded the 32d Division was by contrast predicated on the assumption that Australia would be invaded and the operative areas would be in the continent's interior. The troops were lectured to by the Australians on how to survive in the hostile outback conditions, particularly ways to find water in such desolate areas. How to operate against experienced Japanese jungle fighters was never stressed. To further complicate the problems of the division, there was the attempt at integration of American and Australian commanders. The Australian II Corps was responsible for defensive training and the U.S. I Corps handled offensive training.[6]

Despite General Harding's optimistic statements, Eichelberger was acutely aware of the shortcomings of the two divisions he had available. After an inspection where he gave the 32d Division a barely satisfactory rating, he informed MacArthur and Sutherland on 14 September that the division was "not sufficiently trained to meet the Japanese veterans on equal terms." He correctly attributed this to three factors: too many inexperienced replacements, lack of training, and, most important, lack of time.[7]

Despite the inadequacies of the 32d Division at that time, MacArthur had no choice but to use one of his poorly prepared divisions if he was to take the offensive against the Japanese. Eichelberger had chosen the 32d, and leading elements of the 126th had already been flown to Port Moresby. Company E had been selected to be the point unit. Before leaving Amberley Field, near Ipswich, the men had their uniforms sprayed with motley shades of green. The troops put them on while still wet, and they dried on the way. In addition, green burlap had been affixed to their helmets, presumably to assist in camouflage. General Harding visited the men before takeoff and gave an upbeat address in which he declared that the company was the "spearhead of the spearhead of the spearhead."[8]

The men of Company E, accompanied by four aidmen and Company A of the 114th Engineer Battalion, were loaded like sardines into the transport planes for the 1,400-mile flight to Port Moresby. There were no seats; the men simply lay down and tried to get comfortable for the long journey. Discussion centered on what kind of a reception they would receive. Many believed that they would be forced to fight immediately. One question was, should they fix bayonets before deplaning?

They arrived at Moresby's Seven Mile Airfield at six o'clock on the evening of the fifteenth. The temperature even at that hour was 115 degrees Fahrenheit. They did not need to fix bayonets, as they were escorted peacefully to trucks that took them to their first camp at Tupeselei. From there, along with the 91st Engineers, they labored from dawn to dusk to extend the road to Kapa Kapa, thirty miles from Port Moresby. From there they continued the road construction to the rubber plantation at Kalikodobu, called by them Kalamazoo. The road, constructed on steep grades, was a narrow path suitable for only one vehicle to move at a time. The path was pushed ahead to the village of Nepeana. Preliminary reconnaissance showed that from that point the terrain was so bad that it was not feasible to try to extend the road farther.[9]

Meanwhile, the rest of the combat team, without its artillery, a total of 3,610 enlisted men and 180 officers, left Brisbane harbor on 18 September. The regimental commander, Colonel Quinn, and two of his staff flew ahead to make final arrangements for the movement of the 126th into camp. On 28 September the convoy carrying the regiment reached Port Moresby, where they found that the 128th had already arrived. This was due to General Kenney, who was so pleased with the way the transport of Company E had gone that as soon as he had information of their safe landing, he rushed to MacArthur's office and asked permission to airlift the rest of the regiment. Informed that the 126th had already begun loading on ships in the harbor, Kenney said, "All right, give me the next regiment to go, the 128th, and I'll have them in Port Moresby ahead of this gang that goes by boat."[10]

His staff opposed the proposal, but MacArthur agreed to the air-lift. Kenney began preparations immediately. Twelve DC-2 transports, which he borrowed from the Australian civil airlines, were flown to Amberley Field by the seventh. All bombers overhauled anywhere in Australia would be used to haul troops to New Guinea until further notice. Kenney also ordered any airplanes coming from the United States to be commandeered along with their civilian ferry crews. With these added planes, six hundred troops a day could be delivered.

The flight, even with stops for refueling, was long and grueling for the men stretched out on the floor of the planes. A few of the bombers had holes in the fuselage from antiaircraft fire, some so large that a soldier could look out and see the stars. Some helpful crew members on damaged planes gave pieces of canvas to the men so they could plug the holes. Soon after takeoff the canvas patches simply blew away. Despite minor problems, the airlift was a resounding success, in part witnessed by MacArthur, who had, on the advice of Kenney, flown to Port Moresby to investigate for himself the situation in Papua.

On 1 October, responding to the surprise Japanese withdrawal from Ioribaiwa, General Headquarters issued a comprehensive plan for the attack on the Buna-Gona area. On 11 October a more detailed plan was issued. This called for the recapture of Goodenough Island and the movement of troops toward the Japanese positions along three axes—the Kokoda Trail, the Kapa Kapa–Jaure Trail, or the Abau-Jaure route. At the same time, a movement would be started up the north coast from Milne Bay. The attack on the Buna area would be in two stages. Moving overland, the American forces in conjunction with the Australians would secure the line of the Kumusi River from Owalama Divide, north of Jaure, to the crossing of the Kokoda Trail near Wairopi. The troops moving up the coast, after the capture of Goodenough Island, would secure the coastal areas as far north as Cape Nelson. After these objectives had been reached, all available forces would attack the Buna-Gona beachhead. This plan was dictated in part by the terrain and weather, but MacArthur was also concerned that the Marine venture on Guadalcanal might collapse, enabling the Japanese to concentrate more men in the target area. In such a case, he wanted to have a route of escape for the Allied troops operating north of the Owen Stanley Range.[11]

Brigadier General MacNider, who had been sent to Port Moresby on 12 September to arrange for the reception of the first troops of the 32d, dispatched two reconnaissance teams to ascertain the best overland route. He sent Capt. William Boice, the intelligence officer of the 126th, accompanied by seven men and forty native carriers, by luggers (small boats) to Kapa Kapa. Boice was to investigate the route from there to Jaure. Little was known of the route, because the natives avoided it and no European had traversed it for years. General Rowell had opposed using it despite the fact that troops could be supplied by sea one-third of the way. The major disadvantage was that a 9,000-foot pass had to be surmounted. Rowell suggested the route from Abau to Jaure. Colonel Lief Sverdrup and a small party were therefore dispatched to Abau, farther down the coast, to check on the feasibility of using that trail. Colonel Sverdrup had investigated the trail north of Abau and reported that it was difficult for marching and impossible for any pack animals. On 14 October, General Headquarters, which had planned to send the 127th over this trail, canceled all plans for its use as a route to the coast.[12] Boice had reported that the Kapa Kapa–Jaure Trail was a feasible route, and the decision was made to move the 126th over this trail.[13]

The bulk of the 2d Battalion of the 126th was moved up to Nepeana. On 6 October the advance elements—250 men from the Antitank and Cannon Companies with 100 carriers under the command of Capt. Alfred Medendorp—set out along the trail to Jaure. Medendorp's primary responsibility was to establish dropping zones at Larum and Jaure to enable airdrops of supplies for the main elements of the 2d Battalion. They found that Boice's account was misleading. It was possible for men to march and at times crawl up the steep grades, but it was slow, exhausting work as they moved up through cold, heavy forests to what was called Ghost Mountain, at 9,100 feet. Many of the men were exhausted after only a few days'

climb. To make matters worse, they encountered Capt. S. H. Buckler and the thirty-five Australian survivors who had left the Kokoda
Trail on 30 August to escape the Japanese. They had used little-
known native trails from Wairopi to Jaure and had barely survived
with food given them by the natives. The sight of these half-starved,
emaciated men, combined with the location, so frightened the native carriers that most of them deserted.[14] This meant that the bulk
of the supplies had to be left behind.

On 13 October, Medendorp's exhausted troops arrived at the
mountaintop village of Larum. The next day they began to clear the
dropping ground. After leaving a small detachment to take care of
the supplies there, Medendorp took the rest of his command to
Jaure. It took almost a week to cover the last sixteen miles to that village. They arrived there on 20 October.

On 14 October the rest of the 2d Battalion, accompanied by a
portable hospital unit and a platoon of the 114th Engineers—nine
hundred strong, accompanied by several hundred carriers—left Kalikodobu. The ordeal of the Medendorp command was multiplied
many times over. The men were strung out in companies, with each
man carrying six days' rations. The main food was hardtack, rice,
and bully beef, some of which was rancid and caused much illness.
Diarrhea and dysentery were epidemic. First Sergeant Paul Lutjens,
of Company E, recalled the ordeal:

It was one green hell to Jaure. We went up and down continuously; the company would be stretched over two or three
miles. We'd start at six every morning by cooking rice or trying
to. Two guys would work together. If they could start a fire
which was hard because the wood was wet even when you cut
deep into the center of the log, they'd mix a little bully beef
into a canteen cup with rice, to get the starchy taste out of it.
Sometimes we'd take turns blowing on sparks trying to start a
fire, and keep it up for two hours without success. I could
hardly describe the country. It would take five or six hours to
go a mile, edging along cliff walls, hanging on to vines, up and
down, up and down. The men got weaker; guys began to lag
back. . . . An officer stayed at the end of the line to keep dri-

ving the stragglers. There wasn't any way of evacuating to the rear. Men with sprained ankles hobbled along as well as they could, driven on by fear of being left behind. . . .[15]

The men early on had begun to discard raincoats, blankets, helmets, ammunition, and anything that added to the weight of their packs. The men of the mortar company threw away first the base plates, then the tubes, and finally the ammunition. Thus when they went into action later, they had no mortars.[16] They had to ford waist-deep streams and channels of mud. Half the time they could not see the sky, and it regularly rained hard from three o'clock each afternoon. A veteran of the march, then a nineteen-year-old lieutenant, recalled the ordeal:

I remember climbing those mountains and after 15 or 20 minutes of climbing, falling down beside the track and knowing then I couldn't go any further, but you knew if you didn't get up you were going to die right there. You would then find a little bit more strength to go a little bit further, and you got up. But I remember knowing that I was never going to get where ever we were going. I was completely exhausted and hungry. It was a matter of how was I going to keep living. Combat later was almost a relief. I didn't have to climb the mountains any more.[17]

Finally, on 25 October, the leading company arrived at Jaure. All the companies were concentrated there by the twenty-eighth, but the battalion commander, Lt. Col. Henry Geerds, had suffered a heart attack and had to be evacuated to Port Moresby. The ordeal of the 2d Battalion was not repeated. It was the only unit to cross the Owen Stanleys on foot.

MacArthur had ordered all available shallow-draft boats, fishing trawlers, and luggers with sails to concentrate on Milne Bay. Because he had no landing craft available, these would be needed to move troops past Cape Nelson and beyond. He requested a Marine regiment to be the leading element of the amphibious operation. At first Admiral King agreed to the deployment of the 8th Marines, but Nimitz and Ghormley protested and MacArthur was notified that he had to conduct any seaborne operations with the forces he already had. General Blamey objected to transporting troops by sea because of the danger from reefs, the slowness of travel, and the added danger of Japanese air attacks. The decision was thus made to move them by air. Nevertheless, the Australian ship *Paleima* continued to chart a safe channel to Cape Nelson. The first of the two-ton luggers, the *King John* and *Timoshenko,* arrived at Milne Bay; after taking on supplies and Col. Laurence McKenny, the 32d Division quartermaster, the small convoy left on 14 October. Two days later it arrived at Wanigela.

The task of capturing Goodenough Island was given to the 2/12 Battalion of the 18th Brigade, which was stationed at Milne Bay. The battalion was loaded on two destroyers, which then landed the troops on both sides of the island's southern tip on the night of 22 October. There were only 290 Japanese left on the island; the larger part of the 5th Naval Landing Force, which had been stranded there in August, had been evacuated by submarine. From their well-prepared positions, the Japanese held off the Australian attacks during the daylight hours of the twenty-third. That evening a submarine arrived and, shuttling back and forth during the night, removed most of the Japanese to nearby Fergusson Island. Later a cruiser was sent to pick up the survivors and take them to Rabaul.[18]

MacArthur's plans by the last week of October appeared to be on schedule, with the occupation of the island, combined with the planned concentration of the two regiments of the 32d Division in the Wanigela region and the clearing of the Japanese from much of the Kokoda Trail.

The problem of transferring the remainder of the 32d Division across the Owen Stanley Range was solved by General Kenney. As early as July, he had been fascinated with the prospect of moving enough men by air to a flat location near Wanigela Mission. However, transport aircraft were scarce. In early September his air transport section had only forty-one transports available, and fifteen of these were of little use except for parts. Even with the decision of higher authority to provide two additional transport squadrons, the Fifth Air Force did not receive its full quota of transports until mid-November.[19]

Nevertheless, Kenney persisted. He had learned that a Hudson bomber had been forced to land at the field near Wanigela. With native help, the tall grass had been cut, making the field usable by large transports. Kenney broached the idea to MacArthur of flying troops there in August, but Blamey and Rowell, faced with the dangers to Port Moresby, did not want to even consider such a project. It was not until the situation along the Kokoda Trail improved that General MacArthur, during his visit to Port Moresby, gave his approval after Kenney had assured him that from personal observation the field was adequate.[20] General Blamey concurred. One reason for the change in his attitude was the fear of having to shift troops by sea in the slow-moving craft available. Once decided, Australian troops, the 2/10 Battalion of the 18th Brigade, and a few American engineers were flown to Wanigela, where they immediately began to improve the landing field.[21]

Other airfields were later established in the vicinity of Pongani, which was slated to become a major base for the attack on Buna. Cecil Abel, a missionary who had resided in the Abau district, reported to Generals Harding and MacNider about a landing site near the village of Fasari, in the upper valley of the Musa River. From there a trail led directly to Pongani. If true, this welcome news meant that there would be another airfield for Kenney's transports to use.

Abel returned to Fasari and, with native labor using hand tools, soon had cleared the field; by 19 October, planes were using it. Three other sites were soon located in the vicinity of Abel's field. One field at Embesa was suitable only for emergency landings, but the one at Kinjaki Barige, twenty-five miles northwest, and another at Pongani itself could be used by the transports. By early November all these airstrips were in use.[22]

It was possible to consider seriously the transfer of most of the men of the 32d by air because the Allies controlled the skies over Papua despite the fact that there was a considerable concentration of Japanese planes based at Rabaul. The main concern of the Japanese during this period, however, was Guadalcanal. For five weeks there was no significant Japanese air activity over the crucial areas where the Allies were operating. Strikes at Rabaul by B-17s and PBYs of the 19th Group were commonplace throughout September and October, with varying degrees of success. Attacks against shipping were of questionable value. Only one Japanese ship was sunk during raids in October, although later records indicate that nineteen were damaged. Damage to the town was more extensive, and there was some indication that flights from Lakunai and Vunakanu to Guadalcanal were interrupted. Kenney's planes also attacked Japanese installations on New Georgia and Bougainville in support of the Guadalcanal operation. Planes of the Fifth Air Force, particularly the A-20s and B-25s modified with eight forward-firing machine guns, were more successful in strikes against Lae and Salamaua; along with the P-400s and Beaufighters of the RAAF, they played a major role in disrupting Japanese supply routes as they retreated along the Kokoda Trail. However, it was impossible with the planes available to stop the Japanese from reinforcing the Buna-Gona beachhead, although a number of barges were sunk. Many of the supplies for that enclave were landed by night from submarines.[23] There was no serious threat by the Japanese air units to the movement of the 128th Regiment.

The transport of the bulk of the 128th and the Australian Independent Company, a commando unit, in the operation that MacArthur's headquarters had given the code name Hatrack, began on 14 October. The flights continued for two days before bad weather briefly interrupted the air movement. However, by the eighteenth most of the 2d and 3d Battalions and the Australian 2/6 Battalion had been flown in. The full movement of the division was not completed until 4 November.

Everyone at higher headquarters was delighted with the success of the air transport, even those who at first had been skeptical. General Harding, congratulating Kenney and his deputy, Maj. Gen. Ennis Whitehead, at dinner on the nineteenth, joined his air colleagues in support of airpower when he said: "I'm drinking the stuff you guys are these days. I don't know what it is or what it's going to do to me, but it sure tastes good." Newly promoted Lieutenant General Eichelberger at this point was well satisfied with his old classmate and his ability to get things done. "You are doing a grand job, going places and doing things." Harding was so self-satisfied that he believed the campaign against Buna might be quickly ended.[24]

Except for the 2d Battalion of the 126th, most of the men of the division had not encountered the disease-ridden, near impossible terrain of Papua. The 128th was soon to discover how difficult even moving a few miles would be. Reconnaissance had indicated that a number of good trails branched from Wanigela. It was decided to move quickly overland the few miles to Pongani. The plan was for the 6th Australian Independent Company to lead the way, followed by the 3d Battalion and, soon after, the other two battalions of the 128th. The trail chosen crossed the Musa River at Totore village. It was discovered that the heavy rains had caused flooding and wiped out most of the trail, but the Australians managed to cross the river and reach Pongani.

The Americans, after traversing knee-deep swamps, had to stop at a miserable site at Guri Guri, near Totore. The engineers built a log raft and crossed the river, only to discover that they were on the wrong trail. They then decided to string a cable upstream from the camp. Fifteen hundred feet of cable was dropped by air, but the engineers had no special tools. All this proved fruitless when it was discovered that the trail ahead was under seven feet of water. Faced with this situation, it was decided to attempt to move the troops to Pongani by water. The 3d was ordered to march to Gobe village, just west of Porlock Harbor. From there they would be taken by ship around Cape Nelson to Pongani. The other battalions would wait at Wanigela until boats were available to transport them. The march of the 3d Battalion to Gobe took four days, with a large portion of the unit debilitated by malaria.[25]

Colonel McKenny had expected to unload the supplies from the *King John* and *Timoshenko* at Wanigela, then return to Milne Bay for more. However, General MacNider, who had flown in earlier, decided to use the small ships to carry supplies forward to Pongani for the units of the 128th then marching from Cape Nelson. In addition, he instructed McKenny to transport 102 men of a company of the 128th who had just arrived by air from Port Moresby. The men were loaded on the two small ships, which departed the next afternoon and made their way along the uncharted waters off Cape Nelson, taking care to avoid the coral reefs that dotted the route. They rounded the cape without incident by early morning. McKenny ordered the ships stopped until dawn, when they then proceeded slowly to Pongani, where they dropped anchor a quarter of a mile offshore and prepared to begin off-loading the men and stores.

Suddenly a twin-engine bomber made a pass over the ships, then returned, dropping two bombs, which missed the ships. A second attack was more successful, with its bombs striking the *King John*. Eighteen men were wounded, two fatally. The plane was an American B-25 whose pilot believed the two small ships to be Japanese.[26] This example of friendly fire would be duplicated many times and was the reason that, despite the positive work done by the air force, it was looked upon by infantrymen in the close confines of Papua as a mixed blessing.

No further action hampered the unloading of the rest of the 3d Battalion from the six trawlers ultimately operating from Wanigela. Colonel McKenny established his headquarters at Mendaropu, three miles up the coast. On 21 October the regimental commander, Col. J. Tracy Hale, arrived, and a few days later General MacNider landed. By 2 November the entire regiment less the small numbers still at Port Moresby was in the Pongani area, where supply dumps were rapidly growing.

The movement of the 126th to the Buna region was complicated by General MacArthur's fears of a Japanese victory at Guadalcanal. His headquarters had even prepared a plan for withdrawing all Allied forces from the north in case it was necessary. Although pleased with the air movement of the 32d troops, he did not want to concentrate two regiments near Pongani. He explained his reasoning to Blamey in a long communication on 20 October:

> The enemy can at will bring overwhelming forces to bear upon the north coast of New Guinea and it must be contemplated that any of our organizations engaged there must be ready and able to withdraw successfully across the mountains with only such supplies as can be made available by air and by native carriers.[27]

General Harding was informed on 19 October that Abel's field was ready for the landing of transport aircraft. He immediately requested that the 1st and 3d Battalions of the 126th be flown in. Once landed, the troops would march to Pongani. General Blamey turned down the request, because there was no evidence of good trails leading from the field to Pongani. Harding then requested that the two battalions be flown to Kinjaki Barige and Pongani. This time Blamey approved the request, but MacArthur, citing the situation on Guadalcanal, canceled the movement until the situation in the Solomons had been clarified. He continued to worry until the naval battle of Guadalcanal on 12 November destroyed the bulk of Japanese reserve troops.

Eager to begin an attack on Buna, General Harding saw the situation differently. Without really knowing what kind of defenses the Japanese had constructed there, and believing that only a battalion held Buna, he told Kenney that "things look pretty favorable now for a quick conquest." He and his staff believed that Blamey was at fault, not wanting the Americans to steal the glory, and therefore halting all U.S. forward movement until Vasey's men had proceeded farther toward Sanananda. Although MacArthur's and Blamey's reasons had little to do with ideas of glory, Harding's attitude, which was the same as Kenney's, demonstrated the friction that existed between the Australian commanders and their American counterparts.[28]

It was Blamey who changed MacArthur's mind about airlifting the remainder of the 126th by assuring him that he had no intention of leaving it at Pongani. The remaining battalions would be flown there and immediately marched inland to join the 2d Battalion, which was located in the vicinity of Bofu after its torturous climb over the mountains. From that region the 126th could easily cooperate with General Vasey's movement along the Kokoda Trail. If the situation became desperate and a withdrawal was necessary, it could be achieved using the interior trails.

MacArthur agreed on 2 November and, pending a buildup of supplies, authorized a coordinated offensive to begin on 15 November. The air movement of the 1st and 3d Battalions began on 8 November. Heavy rains had made the old field at Pongani unsafe, so most of the 1st Battalion was landed at Abel's field, then they marched to Pongani. A new airfield at Pongani was completed by the ninth, so the remainder of the 126th was landed there.[29]

As soon as troops of the 126th arrived at Pongani, they were sent immediately to the Natunga-Bofu area. By the fourteenth, the

126th, and even those troops who had been landed at Abel's field, had reached their assigned positions in the interior. Meanwhile, General MacNider was consolidating the 128th in the Oro Bay–Embogo-Embi area, farther up the coast from Pongani. The bulk of the 1st Battalion was at Embogo, the 2d was at Eroro Mission, and the 3d was near Embi. Patrols were actively probing northward and into the interior. Forward supply dumps had been established at Embogo and at Hariko, where MacNider's headquarters was located. Harding had arrived and established his divisional headquarters, and MacArthur had moved to Port Moresby to be closer to the final action to drive the Japanese from their enclaves at Buna, Gona, and Sanananda. The first serious offensive by an American division in the Southwest Pacific theater was about to begin, with optimism pervading every headquarters.

Chapter VIII
Sanananda-Gona Operation

The capture of Kokoda eased the supply situation that had plagued the Australians during their entire offensive. Repairs and renovation of the airfield were begun almost immediately in preparation for the landing of C-47 transport planes, the first of which arrived on the morning of 5 November. Soon, supplies of ammunition, clothing, medicine, and, especially, food were built up. This allowed troops who had subsisted largely on rations of bully beef and rice to enjoy such unheard of items as bread and even chocolate. The medical facilities also were greatly improved. The 2/4 Field Ambulance, a company-sized medical unit, set up a main dressing station, which allowed for reasonably comfortable care for battle casualties, although, as casualties mounted when the Australian units pushed toward Oivi, the tented station proved inadequate, and the sick were forced to build their own shelters.

For the first time, it was possible to evacuate seriously wounded and sick by air to the hospital at Port Moresby. More than a hundred patients had been flown out of Kokoda by 11 November, and the numbers increased in the following weeks. This was in contrast to the situation that prevailed at Myola. Of the five large planes that had attempted to land on the primitive airstrip there, two had crashed. Higher headquarters refused to allow the transports then available to be used in such a risky venture. Eventually a few smaller planes were found that could land and take off in relative safety. Nevertheless, only forty patients were evacuated by air from Myola. Native porters continued to be used extensively, although patients

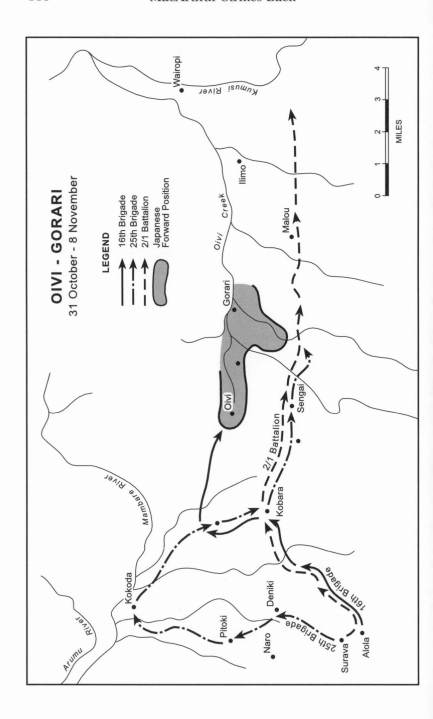

who had recovered sufficiently walked either to a medical station or to Port Moresby. The last of such patients from Myola, after being shut up there for two and a half months, arrived at Port Moresby just before Christmas. Meanwhile, the facilities at Kokoda had been expanded, and medical units had been sent ahead with the 16th Brigade as it began its offensive against the Japanese defending the village of Oivi, eight miles from Kokoda.[1]

The village of Oivi was just a collection of huts located in a rubber plantation on the right bank of a creek. It was protected by the high ground on either side of the trail. A number of spurs extended roughly parallel to the trail, each heavily wooded, as was the main highland area. In a questionable move, General Horii decided to contest the Australian advance here instead of retiring beyond the swift-moving Kumusi River. After the action at Eora Creek, he brought Colonel Yazawa back from the coast and established his force in strong, well-prepared positions on the high ground on either side of the main trail. He ordered Yazawa, with the bulk of the 144th Infantry, to hold Oivi as long as possible. The Japanese had enough food and ammunition for at least a week. They sited heavy and light machine guns with interlocking fields of fire to guard the approaches. Snipers screened the routes to the heights. The Japanese also placed mortars and two mountain guns zeroed in on the trail. Horii had also sent forward the 3d Battalion of the 144th with attached engineer troops to defend Gorari, six miles east of Oivi. He understood that a successful flanking movement by the Australians to occupy Gorari would threaten Yazawa's position at Oivi. He was correct. Gorari was to become the key to further advance along the trail.[2]

Brigadier Lloyd's 16th Brigade began its advance from Kokoda early on the morning of 5 November. His plan was to send his leading company down the main trail toward Oivi. Whenever it met serious opposition, it would pin down the enemy and begin a localized encirclement while a following company attempted a deeper encirclement that would thus cut off the route of retreat. By the end of the day, Lloyd had committed the 2/2 and 2/3 Battalions to the attack, but they had gained little ground. Attacks the following day resulted in no further advance. The stalemate before Oivi continued on the eighth, despite the use of mortars to try to dislodge the Japanese from the high ground. Counterbattery fire from the Japanese mortars and artillery forced the Australians to dig in at the positions they had gained.

One of the reasons for the stalemate was the condition of the men. From the time of the crossing of the mountains through 8 November, the brigade had suffered 107 killed in action and 278 wounded. Many more were suffering from illness; some were so sick they had to be evacuated to the medical aid stations.[3]

Meanwhile, General Vasey on 5 November had ordered the 2/1 Battalion forward to take advantage of a lower trail that paralleled the main one. A number of secondary trails led north from the lower trail to join the main trail. After some difficulty, one of the patrols discovered one of the side trails that led to Gorari. The main body of the 25th Brigade had by the eighth arrived just south of Gorari, and Vasey decided to commit both his brigades in order to crack the Japanese defenses. The 16th Brigade was ordered to continue to attack Oivi; Brigadier Eather's troops would move up the trail discovered by the 2/1 to seize Gorari and thus cut off the escape route of the Oivi defenders.

On the eighth, with air support from both U.S. and RAAF planes, the 2/31 and 2/25 Battalions had made considerable progress, forcing some Japanese units to retreat northwest in torrential rain. Nevertheless, the Japanese still controlled the part of the trail immediately south of Gorari. On the ninth, two other battalions, the 2/33 of the 25th Brigade and 2/1 of the 16th, swung around the 2/25 and moved north toward the village. In the afternoon the village was captured. By evening, three Australian battalions were spaced at intervals along the trail leading to Gorari, with the 2/31 at the lower end and 2/33 holding Gorari in the north. Within two days the Japanese along the main trail near Gorari were pushed into three enclaves and were surrounded by the Australians.

On 11 November the Japanese attempted to break out of the easternmost enclave, and the forest area became a killing ground. Two Australian battalions contained the Japanese attacks. Troops of the 2/31 forced their way into the Japanese defenses from the south as the 2/25 attacked from the north. By midmorning, Japanese resistance there had ended, with the Japanese suffering 143 killed. Australian losses were slight—only seven dead and eighteen wounded. By noon these battalions moved down the main trail to attack another enclave from which the Japanese had halted the advance of the 2/1 the previous day. Aided by the 2/31, the 2/1 was successful in surrounding the Japanese there. The Japanese made a desperate counterattack against two companies of the 2/1 but were cut to pieces by Australian riflemen. Ultimately only a few Japanese were able to escape, filtering through gaps in the attackers' line. After this action, the Australians counted 114 dead Japanese soldiers. By the end of the day, the entire Japanese defenses at Gorari had been breached.[4]

While the 25th Brigade was involved at Gorari, the 16th Brigade finally was able to move forward against the Japanese at Oivi. General Horii, with a number of members of his staff, had decided earlier to inspect the defenses at Oivi. He could see that the main positions there had been compromised. On 10 November he ordered a general retreat. Thus the Australians attacking later were surprised to find that the strong, well-camouflaged weapon pits had been abandoned. It became clear that many of the troops who put up such a desperate fight at Gorari were those who had abandoned the Oivi positions and were attempting to retreat along the trail but were caught by the successful Australian flanking movement. The dual actions at Oivi and Gorari had resulted in the destruction of the Japanese 144th Regiment, the unit that had been responsible for the massacre of Australian troops at the Tol Plantation on New Britain early in the war.

After losing an estimated six hundred men, the remnants of the Japanese force were in full retreat to the Kumusi River. Denied the use of the main trail, Colonel Yazawa led the remainder of his force in a stealthy night march on a little-known trail through the rugged jungle northeast of Oivi. The route would take them to the Kumusi at a point north of Wairopi. From there his men began their long march along the left bank of the Kumusi, which brought them to the mouth of the river twelve miles north of Gona. General Horii, impatient to reach the coast to take over directly the defenses there, decided to risk crossing the flooding river. When Yazawa's troops reached a point on the river opposite a trail on the other side, Horii had a log raft constructed, and he and four members of his staff boarded it on the nineteenth. The swirling waters soon upset the raft. A number of soldiers jumped into the river to try to save their general. According to Japanese sources, they were dissuaded by Horii, who, in keeping with the often destructive code of Bushido, told them to stop and save themselves instead. The raft was quickly swept away. With Horii's death, the Japanese lost one of their most talented leaders.[5]

After contact was lost with the general, Colonel Yokoyama, of the 15th Independent Engineers, assumed command of the largest group of retreating Japanese, numbering approximately 1,200 men, who had been held out of the battle while stationed in the Il-imo region. Yokoyama would also take charge of the defenses at Sanananda and Buna. They reached the Kumusi at Wairopi and began crossing the river under cover of darkness on 12 November. The wooden bridge, constructed by the Japanese after the Australians in their retreat had destroyed the older wire rope bridge, had been blown apart by Allied bombers. Thus the troops had to be ferried across in folding boats, then they marched toward the coast. They reached a coffee plantation at Soputa, seven miles inland, before daylight. A graphic account of the condition of the Japanese soldiers was left by the *Ashai Shimbun* newspaper correspondent Okada, who earlier had accompanied Horii's victorious troops, then shared the ignominious retreat. Okada wrote of the stragglers:

> They had shaggy hair and beards. Their uniforms were stained with blood and mud and sweat and torn to pieces. These were infantrymen without rifles, men walking barefoot, men wearing blankets or straw rice-bags instead of uniforms, men reduced to skin and bones plodding along with the help of a stick, men gasping and crawling on the ground. Stretcher-bearers, too weak to carry their stretchers, were staggering along in groups of fours, supporting the sick and wounded on their shoulders or carrying them on their backs or rather dragging them on the ground helping one another among themselves.[6]

Before being evacuated, Okada further described the conditions of the base hospital at Giruwa as being so overcrowded with sick and wounded that many simply lay out in the jungle. Even the stretcher bearers needed medical care. There was little food available for the men, who suffered from extreme malnutrition in their retreat along the trail. Some had been so hungry that they ate roots, grass, and even clumps of earth. Many died from damage to their digestive systems. Iodine was available only for the most seriously wounded.[7] These were the worst cases in the entire Buna-Gona area. However, in all areas there was a chronic shortage of food and medical supplies. In addition, many of the troops who had escaped after Oivi had lost their weapons, and for some time only the front-line units and those in immediate reserve had guns. Those without guns were ordered to tie bayonets to poles. If the soldier did not even have a bayonet, he was required at all times to carry a wood spear.

Despite their defeats and the extreme shortages, the Japanese position was not hopeless. They had a good supply of ammunition and had built up strong defenses with enough troops to man them. The commanders believed that they would not be abandoned and expected to be resupplied with food, equipment, and men from Rabaul.

General Vasey had decided to rest the bulk of his two brigades before resuming the all-out pursuit of the Japanese. He planned for the 25th to begin its general advance eastward on the fourteenth, followed the next day by the 16th Brigade. However, two battalions, the 2/25 and 2/31, moved ahead and reached the Kumusi on the thirteenth. The river at that point was approximately twelve feet deep and three hundred feet wide and was reported to be flowing at eight miles per hour. Although the Australians scoured the riverside, they encountered only snipers; the bulk of the Japanese rear guard had crossed the river in small boats and on rafts, having thrown away rifles, ammunition, and other supplies in their rush to escape.

Bridges across the river had all been destroyed, so before moving farther toward the coast, the Australians had to construct one. The air force dropped cables and tools on the fourteenth. Swimmers using a captured Japanese folding boat got the cable across, and one company was soon on the other side. The engineers then constructed a small suspension bridge and began another farther downstream. A diarist of the 16th Brigade recorded the scene as the Australians began crossing the Kumusi:

> The scene at the river bank was reminiscent of an old English fair or Irish market day. Battalions of heavy laden troops in their mud-stained jungle green shirts and slacks, carrier lines with the natives gaily comparisoned in bright colored lap laps, bedecked with flowers and sprigs of shrubs stuck jauntily in leather bracelets, all mingled as they waited their turn to cross. The means used for crossing were both hazardous and adventurous but were attempted in something of a carnival spirit. On the one hand an extremely flimsy suspension bridge that gave all users a bath at its sagging middle and on the other a high strung flying-fox that, whilst efficient, occasionally stopped with the occupant swinging helplessly above the stream.[8]

Once the Australians were safely across the river, the battle for the Kokoda Trail, which had begun with the first landings of the Japanese on 21 July, was finished, with the utter defeat of the invaders. A sense of jubilation was felt by everyone, from common soldiers to senior commanders. The latter believed that all that was needed was a quick push to the coast, with the American 32d Division concentrating on Buna and the Australians continuing their triumphal offensive aimed at Sanananda and Gona.

On 14 November, General MacArthur issued his plan of attack on the Japanese beachhead, specifying the objectives of both the Australian and American divisions and drawing the boundary between the two roughly along the Girua River, whose mouth was just west of Buna. The conquest of the Japanese defenses would rest solely on the land campaign. Admiral Carpender told MacArthur on 10 November that he would not endanger his ships in the shallow, reef-ridden waters south of Buna. MacArthur had also requested amphibious and engineer assault forces as well as landing craft, but none was available. An amphibious officer from Washington in December reported to the War Office his opinion that Buna could have been taken in November if one of the Allied units could have been landed from the sea.[9] Despite all the logistical problems, combined with the terribly difficult terrain, there was general optimism at higher headquarters.

The Japanese both at Rabaul and at the beachhead had not been idle. Whereas Carpender was afraid of committing his ships to the area, the Japanese navy, using a deepwater channel from Rabaul, was rapidly building up the strength of the depleted Japanese units in the enclave. Even before reinforcements reached Colonel Yokoyama, he had approximately 5,300 effective troops, although these were jumbled together. The army units consisted of the remnants of the 144th Infantry, the 15th Independent Engineers, the 3d Battalion of the 41st Infantry, and the 47th Antiaircraft Artillery Battalion. In addition, there were naval landing troops of the Yokosuka and Sasebo special landing forces and a number of naval laborers. Yokoyama had a few artillery batteries that had been left behind to guard the beach. Colonel Yazawa, from his position across the Kumusi, had available another 900 men. More than 1,800 men were in the hospital, some of whom might be released if the situation warranted their use. Reinforcements would soon arrive from Rabaul as the high command realized the importance of keeping the Allies from gaining the key positions in northern Papua. Three hundred replacements for the 144th and elements of the 229th Infantry of the 38th Division, a total of approximately 1,000 men, were landed at Basabua, bringing 6,500 effectives into the enclave. The new commander of the 144th, Col. Hiroshi Yamamoto, was ordered to Buna to take charge of the defenses there. He had approximately 2,500 men under his command, almost half of whom were newly arrived and freshly equipped troops from Rabaul.

Colonel Yokoyama dispatched approximately 800 troops under Maj. Tsume Yamamoto to Gona, because it guarded the all-important landing area at Basabua. Yokoyama retained control of the defense of the important Sanananda-Giruwa area. He ordered a large portion of his command, approximately 1,800 men plus a 700-man contingent of Korean laborers, to take up positions at the junction of the Sanananda and Killerton trails. This salient, South Giruwa, divided into three sectors, was commanded by Col. Hatsuo Tsukamoto, with a total of approximately 1,700 men. Backing these frontline troops at a second trail junction located half a mile to the north were a company of infantry and 300 men of the Independent Engineers. They also had a mountain gun battery. Yokoyama himself remained at Sanananda with a mixed command of naval landing construction troops, the rest of the 41st Infantry, a cavalry troop, and another mountain artillery battery. Thus when the Australians began what they believed would be a quick victory at Giruwa and Sanananda, they found instead a large force of Japanese intelligently led and well deployed to take advantage of every natural terrain feature, augmented by well-built defensive positions.[10]

An Australian report after the capture of Gona recalled just how well the Japanese engineers had prepared the defenses along the eleven-mile front from there to Cape Endaiadere. They had constructed hundreds of coconut log bunkers, some reinforced with iron plates, others with iron rails and oil drums filled with sand. In areas too wet for trenches and dugouts, bunkers were built seven to eight feet aboveground. They were carefully concealed with earth, blocks, and palm branches to blend with the surroundings. The bunkers, which could contain anywhere from three to five machine guns, were sited so that the guns were mutually supporting. The bunkers were normally protected by infantry in open pits located to the front, sides, and rear of the main emplacement. Some infantry would be concealed in holes dug under trees, or they would simply conceal themselves in the jungle and wait until the enemy troops had passed before attacking. Snipers located in trees or trenches were an integral part of the enemy defense system, both in the Australian and U.S. zones.[11]

Imperial General Headquarters in Tokyo, shaken by the reversals on Guadalcanal and the Australian advance along the trail, decided to reorganize their command structure in the southern Pacific region in order to secure victory both in Guadalcanal and Papua. On 16 November, the Eighth Area Army was created; it consisted of the Seventeenth and Eighteenth Armies. General Hyakutake, who initially had operational control of both Papua and the Solomons but had become primarily concerned with Guadalcanal, was appointed to head the Seventeenth Army there. The Papuan campaign was assigned to the Eighteenth Army, commanded by Lt. Gen. Hatazo Adachi, who was ordered from his post as chief of staff of the North China Area Army. Both generals were made subordinate to Lt. Gen. Hitoshi Imamura at Rabaul.

In a conference with Premier Tojo, it was made clear that Adachi was to stop the Allied advance in New Guinea at all costs. He arrived at Rabaul on 25 November to discover that fresh reinforcements, the 21st Independent Brigade, had arrived from Indochina. He immediately dispatched on four destroyers the first echelon, consisting of a battalion of infantry, a company of mountain guns, and the unit commander, Maj. Gen. Tsuyuo Yamagata. Adachi failed to provide air cover for the four destroyers, which were sighted by Allied bombers and damaged so badly that they had to return to Rabaul. He sent the second echelon of eight hundred men on board four destroyers on 30 November and provided a strong fighter plane escort, which beat off attacks by B-17s and B-25s. Before the troops could be unloaded at Basabua on 2 December, they were attacked by more planes, forcing the ships to move farther north, where five hundred men were landed by barge near the mouth of the Kumusi, despite continuing fierce Allied air attacks. General Yamagata's forces, joined with those of Colonel Yazawa, was a significant force, but they were located far away from the beachhead, with the Australians between them and Gona. Adachi would attempt a further reinforcement of the enclave in mid-December, but Kenney's planes, flying more than a hundred sorties, again forced the withdrawal of the ships before the majority of the troops were landed. These would be the last significant reinforcements received by the Japanese in the Buna area.[12]

The plan envisioned by Allied higher headquarters was for a general advance on 16 November by the Australian 7th Division and the U.S. 32d Division against the Buna-Gona beachhead. The U.S. troops were located on the right, with their objective Buna; General Vasey's two brigades were to capture Sanananda and Gona. The dividing line between the Australian and U.S. forces was roughly the Girua River. East of the river and immediately adjacent to the Aus-

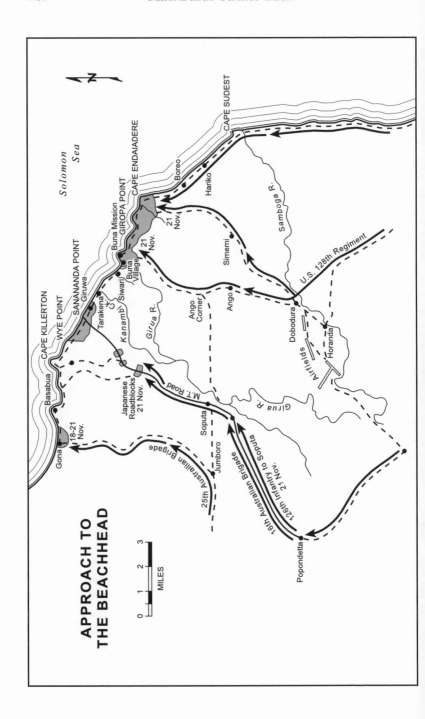

APPROACH TO
THE BEACHHEAD

MILES
0 1 2 3

tralians was the 126th Regiment, commanded by Col. Clarence Tomlinson. Based on Bofu, the 126th was to move on Buna village and Buna Mission by way of Inondo, Horanda, and Dobodura. At the same time, the 128th, commanded by Brigadier MacNider, would move along the coast in two columns to attack the Japanese at Buna from the east.

General Vasey selected two main generally parallel trails that ran from the Kumusi to the coast to advance on his twin objectives. He ordered Brigadier Eather's 25th Brigade to attack along the north-ernmost trail through Awala and Hagenahambo, over the Amboga River, and through Jumbora to Gona. Brigadier Lloyd was ordered to begin the advance of the 16th Brigade on 16 November, soon af-ter the 25th had left its base. Its objective was Sanananda via the vil-lages of Isivata, Sangara, Popondetta, and Soputa.[13]

The trail between Wairopi, where the main Australian troop ele-ments were located, and Gona, forty miles away, was little used. It traversed sections of bush, kunai grass, jungle, and swamp. Any rapid movement was out of the question. Undaunted, the leading Australian unit, the 2/33 Battalion, commanded by Lt. Col. A. W. Buttrose, moved out on schedule, and for the next two days there were no enemy contacts. Nevertheless, the march took its toll. Many men weakened by malaria and marching in the intense heat simply fell out before the battalion reached the village of Jumbora on the eighteenth. Scouts were then sent forward, and a dropping ground for airborne supplies was readied.

The scouts soon discovered the forward positions of Major Ya-mamoto's defenses. At that time he had, in addition to the eight hundred men originally posted to Gona, another hundred from units of the 41st Infantry and a number of walking wounded. His de-fense was centered on the mission, located at the head of the trail. In the period before the Japanese fallback, the entire area had been well prepared to resist and was honeycombed with bunkers, trenches, and firing pits. The Japanese position was bordered on the west by Gona Creek, which, although narrow, afforded consid-erable protection from attack from that direction. To the south was a heavily timbered area where a series of defensive positions had been established. Part of the area to the southeast was swampy, and farther east was a large number of concealed firing pits along the coast.[14]

The Australians had no idea of the nature of the defenses at Gona, and this ignorance dictated their tactics for the next two weeks. On the eighteenth, the leading companies of the 2/33 encountered the southernmost Japanese defenses about a thousand yards south of the mission. Lieutenant Colonel James Miller's 2/31 then took the lead, and he ordered a series of direct attacks on the Japanese positions during the day. By nightfall, little headway had been made, and the unit was pulled back after suffering thirty-six casualties.

Food and ammunition were in short supply, so until that situation was remedied by airdrops on the 21st, Brigadier Eather let his tired troops rest. By then the brigade had fewer than a thousand effectives from a normal complement of 1,900. Nevertheless, Eather resumed the attack in force on the twenty-second. His plan was for the 2/33 to attack frontally while the 2/31, the main force, was to move to the right toward the beach, then shift to strike the Japanese from the east. The 2/25 was positioned to act as a reserve.

These tactics appeared good as the offensive was planned. However, Eather had misjudged the Japanese strength. After having stealthily moved close to the forward Japanese position, the Australians charged with their bayonets fixed. They were met by withering fire from the entrenched Japanese and were driven back into the swamp. The brigade lost sixty-five men and gained nothing. On the twenty-third the assault was resumed, with the 2/25 attacking from the east. This, too, was repulsed after suffering sixty-four casualties.[15]

The Australian assaults had convinced Major Yamamoto to pull back his men from the forward positions and concentrate on holding Gona village and the mission. Before resuming the attack, Eather requested air strikes. The air force responded on the twenty-fourth by giving the Gona enclave a thorough bombing and strafing. The next day Eather resumed the attack. He had the four 25-pound howitzers, which had been flown in, fire more than two hundred rounds in preparation. Then he sent in the 3d Infantry Battalion, which had only recently come under his command.

The Australians this time penetrated fifty yards into the Japanese positions before heavily concentrated fire drove them back. Once again they had been stalemated by the discipline and near fanatical actions of the battle-wise Japanese troops. It was obvious to General Vasey that the 25th Brigade, whose total strength was now only 750 men, was in no condition to continue the offensive. The 25th was not called upon again in the assault on Gona. Vasey had requested the 21st Brigade, which had been resting at Port Moresby, and these troops began to arrive the last week of November and had, by 30 November, replaced the 25th on line. The 25th had been ordered into a reserve position south of Gona. Major Yamamoto had forced a stalemate on the southern trail and still retained his strong defenses around Gona village and the mission.[16]

Even before the Japanese halted the 25th in front of Gona, they had stopped the forward movement of the 16th Brigade in its offensive toward Sanananda. Here the 2/2, leading the brigade, had crossed the Kumusi River by means of a footbridge and two flying foxes before midnight on 15 November. By the next morning the entire brigade was across and began its advance. Heavy rains had made the trail a quagmire, and the troops had to ford a number of small streams in waist-deep water. By the evening of the seventeenth, fifty-seven men of the 2/2 had collapsed from exhaustion and heat prostration. The troops also had to suffer from hunger, because the food supply system had broken down. There were no airdrops until they were almost to Soputa. The 2/2 reached Popondetta by the evening of the eighteenth, but the men were so exhausted that they relinquished the lead to the 2/3. Fortunately there was no Japanese resistance until Soputa, where a small rear guard was encountered from the southernmost of Colonel Tsukamoto's outposts. Early on the twentieth, the 2/1, now leading, broke out of the jungle into a large plain covered with kunai grass and began to receive artillery fire.

This was the beginning of a series of attempts by the Australians to move on Sanananda. The process for the next three weeks was to attempt to flank the main Japanese position along the trail. There were well-constructed fire pits and trenches located at the junction of the Cape Killerton and Soputa-Sanananda trails, backed by a number of light and heavy machine guns and mortars. They also had mountain guns, which were used effectively.

The Australian plan, as initially begun on 20 November, was for the main element of the 2/1 to attack directly ahead against the southern defenses while a company under Capt. B. W. Catterns would swing wide, skirting the kunai grass to hit the Japanese right flank. Catterns had available only ten officers and eighty-one enlisted men, all that were left of two companies. The forward movement was contained, but Catterns's company broke through the first defenses and drove the Japanese back through a native village. In this engagement the Japanese lost an estimated eighty men, but the Australians also had taken a number of casualties.

Upon reaching the trail, Captain Catterns's men quickly set up defensive positions within the main Japanese perimeter just east of the trail. On the twenty-first the Japanese attacked from three sides. All these were beaten off, with the attackers sustaining further heavy losses. The other companies of the 2/1 moved ahead slightly, but the 2/2, taking advantage of Japanese preoccupation with Catterns's men, pushed around the Japanese left flank, and by the evening of the twenty-first had advanced 3,000 yards before being stopped by fierce Japanese counterattacks. They had also captured the Japanese fieldpieces that had given them so much trouble earlier. These were found buried along with a considerable amount of ammunition.

Unable to dislodge Catterns and now threatened on the left, the Japanese covering force pulled back to the junction. Catterns's understrength company had suffered sixty-seven casualties of the ninety-one men who had begun the attack, but it had forced the Japanese to move back to their main defenses.[17]

Despite the improvement in its position along the trail, it was obvious that the 16th Brigade was played out. The brigade had lost one-third of its strength in battle casualties since crossing the mountains. It was down to fewer than a thousand men from its original strength of 1,770. The remaining men were hungry and exhausted, and every day more were being hospitalized for malaria and other tropical diseases. The brigade could defend the positions gained but had little offensive potential. General Herring requested that the U.S. 126th Regiment be moved across the Girua River and take over the main responsibility for the attack on Sanananda. General MacArthur concurred, and the 126th was removed from General Harding's area.

Although strengthening the offensive potential in the Australian sector, the decision removed half of the U.S. troops then beginning the desperate fight for Buna. The decision was in keeping with MacArthur's and Blamey's earlier decision to view the Sanananda-Gona region as the main operational area, but it crippled the 32d Division. The situation by the twenty-fifth in the Australian and U.S. zones belied MacArthur's optimistic communiqué of 20 November in which he asserted, "Our ground forces have rapidly closed in now . . . and we are fighting on the outskirts of both places." The following day he ordered that "all columns" were to be driven through to objectives regardless of losses.[18] Such pressure from General Headquarters illustrated how little was known at MacArthur's new headquarters at Port Moresby of the actual problems facing the U.S. and Australian combat units. Such an attitude on MacArthur's part would result in an almost total misunderstanding of what the 32d Division was then facing in its attempt to take Buna.

General MacArthur and John Curtin, Prime Minister of Australia, at Mascot Airdrome, Sydney, Australia. (Australian War Memorial, Canberra)

General George C. Marshall, Chief of Staff, United States Army.

Admiral Ernest J. King,
United States Chief of Naval
Operations.

Admiral Chester W. Nimitz,
Commander in Chief,
Central Pacific Theater.

Major General Richard Sutherland, Chief of Staff, Southwest Pacific Theater.

Major General Robert Eichelberger, Commander I Corps and Advance New Guinea Area.

Major General Edwin Harding, Commander 32d Division.

Major General George Kenney, Commander Fifth United States Air Force.

General Sir Thomas Blamey, Commander Australian Army and all Allied ground forces in Southwest Pacific Theater.

Lt. General Sir Sydney F. Rowell, Commander New Guinea Force until September 28, 1942. (Australian War Memorial, Canberra)

Major General George Vasey, Commander of Australian 7th Division, New Guinea. (Australian War Memorial, Canberra)

Major General Cyril Clowes, Commander of Milne Bay operations. (Australian War Memorial, Canberra)

Major General Sir Edmund Herring, Commander New Guinea Force after replacing Rowell on September 28, 1942. (Australian War Memorial, Canberra)

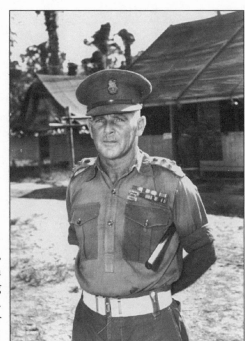

Brigadier Arnold Potts, Commander Australian 21st Brigade during Kokoda Trail defense. (Australian War Memorial, Canberra)

Japanese dugout and pillboxes, Warren Front southeast of Buna Village. (MacArthur Archives, Norfolk Virginia)

Disabled Bren gun carriers in Coconut Grove, Urbana Front. (MacArthur Archives, Norfolk, Virginia)

Lieutenant Colonel Herbert Smith and troops crossing stream in Urbana Front area.

Troops in assault boat carrying supplies, Warren Front.

U.S. troops crossing log footbridge surrounded by deep jungle in Urbana Front area.

Damaged tanks in Coconut Grove, Urbana Front.

U.S. troops carrying wounded on litters near Dobodura airfield.

Native stretcher bearers and wounded at an aid station.

Native bearers and U.S. troops on trail, November 15, 1942.

Australian troops loading 25 pounder artillery piece on lugger at Oro Bay.

Chapter IX

Buna Operations: First Phase

The commitment of the 32d Division revealed a host of inadequacies on all levels. Seldom in the history of American wars has a major unit been rushed into combat with such poor appreciation of the enemy's strength and without adequate fire support and even a rudimentary functioning supply system. It was programmed for failure from the outset.

There were a number of key reasons for the problems encountered by the division in its assault on Buna. Critics of the performance of the 32d at that time pointed to its being a National Guard unit with inadequate training. This was certainly the case, but the fault lay not so much with the division but with the fact that it was never trained for jungle warfare. As General Eichelberger noted, it was sent to New Guinea not because it was better prepared than the 41st Division but because it was easier to dispatch it than to resettle it in a better training area in Australia.

A further problem that hampered the projected offensive was the command structure and the attitude of the senior commanders. General MacArthur was frustrated by having to relay his orders through General Blamey's headquarters. From there the appropriate directives were issued through General Herring and finally to General Harding. Although generally concealed, there was an attitude held by both Americans and Australians of their allies' fitness and will to fight. However unjustified, General Harding believed that "the reason why the attack on Buna was delayed was because Blamey considered the Kokoda Trail action to be the most important."[1] This seemed to be confirmed when the bulk of the 126th

Regiment was ordered to that sector to replace the burned-out brigades in their offensive. Certainly Blamey had little confidence in the abilities of the 32d Division. His opinions about the American forces were similar to those earlier stated by Sutherland and Kenney about the Australians.

The Australian and U.S. troops, poised for what was believed would be the short, final offensive in the Buna-Gona area, were ill served by the intelligence sections of higher headquarters. It was generally believed that the Japanese defenses were manned largely by battered, disease-ridden troops; therefore, a feeling of optimism prevailed at all command levels. Such optimism was shown not only at the headquarters at Port Moresby but also by General Harding, who chafed at being held up from delivering what he imagined would be an easy final blow at Buna. His G-2 section on 6 November stated that, based on air reconnaissance, there were only 200 to 300 troops at Buna, Simemi, and Sanananda and a very small number at Gona. Despite contrary projections, General Willoughby and General Vasey placed the numbers at 1,500 to 2,000 men; the feeling persisted that Buna could easily be taken.[2]

The only maps available to the division were the Buna sheet of a strategic map series, a target map plan, and an uncontrolled mosaic photo map consisting of three sheets covering the area inland from Buna to Horanda. The first of these was known to be wholly inaccurate, the second was of only small value, and the third did not cover sufficient territory to be of use during the move forward. As a result of this inadequacy, most of the information available to the G-2 section was gained by attacks and patrolling. Patrolling became difficult due to the proximity of the enemy, and the information gained was suspect, because patrol leaders had no good maps. Therefore, it was difficult for them to vector the directions of their patrols and plot enemy dispositions accurately.

The complex nature of the Japanese defenses was not fully known to division headquarters until well into the initial campaign.[3] This ignorance was compounded at higher headquarters. Without knowledge of the actual situation confronting the troops, MacArthur and his staff could easily conclude that they were deficient in courage and that their commanders were negligent in not pushing them harder.

General MacArthur, whose problems with Washington had not ended, desperately wanted a victory, not only to defeat the Japanese but also to show what could be done if he were given more troops and particularly naval support. He became increasingly anxious as the first few days of the 32d Division's offensive failed to secure what he and his headquarters staff considered possible. Ultimately his concern would lead to what he believed would be the simple solution to the impasse—the removal of the division commander.

On a much lower level than General Headquarters, the projected offensive suffered from many inadequacies. Chief among them was the supply system. Many of the needed supplies were brought forward by a small fleet of luggers and fishing trawlers, which moved slowly up the coast between the coral outcroppings. The passage was slow and dangerous and subject to attack by Japanese planes, so much of the movement was done at night. These small vessels were unloaded onto smaller outriggers for transit to shore. Air transport became more important as the new airstrips at Dobodura were completed, but at first there were only three small fields available, and planes could bring in only limited supplies. Later, designated dropping areas were established in forward zones where ammunition and medical supplies were supplied by parachute. Unbreakable goods such as rations or clothing were even dropped without parachutes.[4]

In the early days of the attack on Buna, there was a chronic shortage of most supplies, including rations, which forced many troops to subsist on what could be scavenged from the jungle. Lack of such basic items as gun patches and oil resulted in rifles and machine guns jamming, and there was a constant shortage of mortar and artillery ammunition. The commander of the heavy weapons company of the 3d Battalion of the 128th Regiment recalled that at the beginning of the attack on 19 November he had only twenty-five rounds of 81mm mortar ammunition and was warned by the battalion commander to save as many rounds as possible.[5] Only with more and larger ships becoming available and a more regularized system for handling the increased flow of air traffic would the supply situation be eased.

MacArthur's relations with the navy were strained. Soon after arriving in Australia, he had requested a larger allotment of ships. He particularly wanted aircraft carriers assigned directly to the Southwest Pacific theater. Being denied this, he had to content himself with only a small fleet, of which the major complement was Australian. One can sense and appreciate his frustration as he observed the numbers of landing craft available for the invasion of North Africa while he had none. He would later be known for his strategy of using amphibious forces to bypass Japanese strongholds. He could not attempt an amphibious operation at Buna for the simple reason that he had no landing craft. Even if he had had a few, it would not have been possible to use them, because there was no safe channel from Cape Nelson onward through the coral reefs. Admiral Carpender, in sharp contrast to the attitude of Admiral Halsey at Guadalcanal, refused to risk any of his larger ships to assist the action in Papua. On 7 November, General Blamey had requested that the navy send destroyers to protect the supply ships from Milne Bay and their unloading near Buna. He reiterated his request in a communication to MacArthur on 19 November, arguing that the ships would be operating under the cover of land-based aircraft. He further noted:

> The bulk of the land forces in New Guinea have had to move into positions where it is impossible to support them and extremely difficult to give them the necessary ammunition and supplies to maintain them. They are facing the ordeal of battle where defeat may mean destruction. The attitude of the Navy in regard to the destroyers appears to be to avoid risk at a time when all services should give a maximum of cooperation to defeat the enemy.[6]

After a close study of the aerial photographs available, Blamey also recommended that a landing operation along the Buna coast be undertaken from destroyers. Upon receipt of this suggestion, MacArthur convened a meeting of his naval advisers on the twenty-seventh to consider the feasibility of such an operation. He reported that the considered opinion of the experts was that the employment of destroyers in such an operation was as yet not practical. The lack of charts was given as the major reason for their negative report. All that they could promise MacArthur was the use of two smaller armed ships to provide defense for the supply ships. As soon as motor torpedo boats arrived from the South Pacific, six to eight of them would be deployed off the Papuan coast.[7] Thus it became clear, even as the 32d Division was beginning to bog down in its assault on Buna, that it could expect no direct assistance from the navy. In contrast to the operations on Guadalcanal and later in attacks on other islands in the South Pacific, the 32d would have no big gun support from naval ships.

Not only could Harding not expect naval fire support, his division would be forced to operate against the Japanese defenses with almost no land-based artillery. Under normal operating conditions, a division at that time had four battalions assigned, with a total of thirty-six 105mm howitzers plus twelve 155mm howitzers. The supply system in October and early November was such that it was decided to commit the 32d without any such support. General Harding and his artillery commander, Brig. Gen. Samuel Waldron, finally convinced General Headquarters to break down one 105 and fly it to Pongani, where it would be moved to a firing position near Buna.

The difficulty of transporting the large, heavy artillery pieces was only one reason for the inadequacy of fire support for the infantry attacks. General Kenney was convinced that traditional artillery was unnecessary in a jungle environment, and his opinion carried great weight with MacArthur. In a letter to Gen. Hap Arnold, Kenney delivered his opinion succinctly:

> Tanks and heavy artillery can be reserved for the battlefields of Europe and Africa. They have no place in jungle warfare. The artillery in this theater flies, the light mortar and machine guns, the rifle, tommygun, grenade and knife are the weapons carried by men who fly to war, jump in parachutes, are carried in gliders and who land from air transports on grounds which air engineers have prepared.[8]

Such an attitude placed the responsibility for reduction of fixed defenses squarely upon the air force. The many air strikes later con-

ducted against the concealed bunkers and pillboxes at Buna failed
to be an adequate substitute for plunging fire from howitzers.

The need for artillery was apparent to all concerned with the beginning of the 32d Division attack. A partial fulfillment of Waldron's requests had been the delivery of two 25-pounders to Oro
Bay. These were loaded on a captured motor-driven barge and accompanied by the trawler *Minnemura* and the *Alacrity,* which was
towing a barge loaded with rations and ammunition left for Mac-
Nider's base, beyond Hariko Point. After issuing orders for the
movement of troops, General Harding decided to see what was happening forward and left his headquarters at Mendaropu in charge
of Col. John Mott to go on board the *Minnemura* for what was expected to be a routine inspection trip. The small flotilla stopped at
Embogo, where Col. Laurence McKenny, on board another small
craft, the *Bonwin,* joined them. A number of sightseers, including a
reporter and photographer and two visiting colonels from the
United States, also came along. Shortly after six o'clock, as the ships
passed Cape Sudest, they noticed a large flight of planes approach-
ing at a high level from the northwest. At first the planes, Japanese
Zeroes, passed the ships, but then they turned and began their low-
level strafing runs. The *Bonwin* and the barge on which the artillery
pieces were lashed down were hit first and set afire. Then the *Minnemura's* fuel tanks were hit and it, too, began to burn. The *Alacrity,*
which had stopped, was also sunk as the crew was transferring ammunition to a lighter ship.

The men who were not wounded began to jump overboard,
among them Generals Harding and Waldron. Harding refused to
get into the small dinghy; because the shore a mile distant was visi-
ble, he and most of the men began swimming while still under attack from the planes.

It was not until the following morning that the full extent of the
catastrophe was known. Twenty-four men had been killed, among
them Colonel McKenny. Nearly a hundred men were wounded,
many severely.[9] The two much-needed fieldpieces, almost all the
ammunition, and the important stores, including the heavy
weapons for the 128th, were lost. Even more important, the little
supply fleet had lost three luggers and the Japanese barge. The loss

of the barge was particularly unfortunate, because it was vital to the transport of heavy equipment up and down the coast. In a separate action the next day, Japanese planes hit two of the remaining luggers, one at Embogo and the other at Mendaropu. One was so badly damaged that it had to be beached; the other had to be removed to Milne Bay for extensive repairs.

These two attacks left only one small ship to supply Harding's troops east of the river. Fortunately, Generals Harding and Waldron and key members of the 32d Division survived, but they were for a time out of touch with all units except MacNider's. The arrival of the last lugger, the *Keltou*, allowed the wounded to be moved forward to Pongani for evacuation and General Harding to move to Embogo, where he established his headquarters.[10] This decision placed an added burden on the hard-pressed communications system.

All the planners from MacArthur's headquarters down to the regiments had minimized the problems posed by the terrain and the way the Japanese had taken advantage of it. The first of the problems was that there were few dependable trails. There were five that, under normal circumstances, could be used to move men and supplies forward. These were Jumbora to Gona, Soputa to Sanananda, Soputa to Buna village, Dobodura to Buna village, and the coastal track north through Cape Endaiadere. The swamps and jungle between these trails prevented cutting lateral trails. This meant that when the attacks were begun, the impassable, junglelike swamps prevented any quick shift of forces from the left flank near Buna village to the right near Cape Endaiadere. Such transfers took at least two days. Meanwhile the Japanese, who had placed their defenses on the only dry ground available, operated on interior lines and could swiftly move reinforcements to any threatened point.

The Japanese defenses between Buna village and Cape Endaiadere took full advantage of the terrain. They had the sea to their rear, which meant it was secure because of the lack of any amphibious threat from the Allies. Their right flank was anchored on Buna village, where the unfordable Girua River and Entrance Creek spilled into the sea. They further counted on the Soputa to Buna village trail, the only route to their right wing positions, being flooded during the rainy season. From Buna village the Japanese defenses followed Entrance Creek inland to where the Soputa trail forked to Buna village and Government Gardens. From here the perimeter was extended eastward across the swamp to the northeastern edge of the old airstrip, thence down the strip eastward along the new strip through the coconut plantation to the sea.[11]

Thus all Allied attacks were channelized into four narrow fronts. The first was through the swampy region in front of Buna village. Farther south was the fork of the Soputa-Buna trail, which came to be called the Triangle. A third front was the narrow bridge between the airstrips, and the last was through the coconut plantation. In all the defensive areas there were dozens of bunkers and firing trenches. The bunkers were generally of two types. In the more open areas they were larger, built of coconut logs, and reinforced with steel rails, iron plates, sheet steel, and oil drums filled with sand. Some of the larger fortifications could hold up to thirty troops. Where the terrain was overgrown, the Japanese had built smaller, less heavily reinforced bunkers. Near the airstrips they had built a few concrete and steel pillboxes.

Once a bunker had been constructed, it was covered with earth, on top of which were laid grass, palm fronds, and other materials to camouflage the structure and help to cushion explosions. Firing slits in the bunkers were narrow and thus were difficult to detect by attackers. Entrances, which were in the rear, were placed so they could be covered by fire from neighboring bunkers. In some cases the entrances led directly to firing trenches; in others, narrow tunnels led to them. Thus troops could move swiftly from bunker to trench and back with minimal detection. Given the time constraints and shortage of materials, the Japanese engineers had created a formidable defense that would have been difficult to penetrate even had the Allies possessed heavy-caliber guns.[12]

Before departing on the ill-fated trip to inspect the forward areas, General Harding had issued orders for the first all-out attack on Buna. There could be no flanking movements, due to the terrain, and because of the lack of landing craft, any amphibious operation was out of the question. Therefore, once the major objectives had been defined, the troops would have to attack straight ahead against the Japanese defenses.

Early on the morning of the sixteenth, the 128th began the forward movement on the right. Lieutenant Colonel McCoy's 1st Battalion moved up the coast from Embogo, crossing the Somboga River, and by evening had reached the mouth of Boreo Creek, a mile north of General MacNider's headquarters at Hariko, without opposition. Lieutenant Colonel Kelsie Miller's 3d Battalion left the Warisota Plantation, three miles west of Embogo, and, after a brief encounter with a Japanese patrol near Dobodura, proceeded toward Simemi. There it deployed, prior to the attack on its initial target, the bridge between the two airstrips. The 2d Battalion, commanded by Lt. Col. Herbert A. Smith, followed close behind and was to act as a reserve. On the seventeenth, Harding had ordered the other forces at Pongani, including the 1st Battalion of the 126th and the Australian Independent Company, to board the luggers bringing up supplies and be taken forward by sea. General Waldron had placed his puny artillery force of two 3.7-inch mountain howitzers near Ango.[13]

The loss of the luggers changed everything. For General Harding, all that occurred afterward seemed negative. The supply situation, never good, became threatening, and Harding ordered General MacNider not to begin his attack until the nineteenth so more supplies could be brought forward. The forces at Pongani, which he had planned to move by sea, now had to march to the front to join in the attack toward Cape Endaiadere. The Engineer Company, which could have been used in the reduction of the blockhouses, was instead sent to Dobodura to work on the airstrips. Farther to the west, Harding had planned for two battalions of the 126th to move past Ango to attack Buna village and Buna Mission. Until the troops from that regiment could arrive at Ango, the 2d Battalion of the 128th was ordered there to protect the vital trail juncture.

Before the 126th could arrive, Harding received orders to transfer it to General Vasey's area to take over the stalled offensive against Sanananda and Gona. This decision illustrated clearly the bias in favor of the Sanananda front, which would persist well into December. Generals Blamey and Herring naturally favored the Australian troops, which were in fact worn out. They believed that the addition of the bulk of an American regiment would restore the movement that was not possible by the decimated, exhausted Australian brigades. However justified from a strategic viewpoint, even discounting bias, the shift of the 126th troops while they were still marching to Ango did irreparable harm to Harding's offensive. Instead of having the better part of a regiment attacking Buna, he now had only Colonel Smith's 2d Battalion of the 128th in position for an attack ordered for the twentieth.[14]

Surprisingly, it took some time for higher headquarters to understand that a general unified attack along a contiguous line was impossible. Nevertheless, MacArthur, in his communiqué of 20 November, had called for a simultaneous movement forward to take the narrow coastal strip at Buna. In reality, the forces attacking toward Cape Endaiadere were separated by heavy undergrowth and swamps. Thus the fighting, until the final reduction of the Japanese strong points, would be divided into two separate and not necessarily supporting assaults. General Harding recognized the need for this geographical and operational division and gave the name Warren Force to those units under General MacNider operating east of the swamp. On the twenty-third he designated those operating against Buna village and Buna Mission as Urbana Force. The heaviest fighting during the first few days of the campaign would be in the area that would soon be the responsibility of Warren Force.

The first attack began at 0700 on the nineteenth as the 1st Battalion of the 128th in a column of companies crossed the creek near Boreo along a narrow path, with the goal being the cape two miles distant. They soon encountered a Japanese outpost line that Colonel Yamamoto had created in front of his main defenses. Those main defenses, 750 yards south of the cape, ran through Duropa Plantation to the east end of the new airstrip; they consisted of well-manned, concealed machine guns along the trail and in the plantation area. Heavy fire from these forced the troops to deploy off the trail. They attacked again but were confused by the Japanese fire, which seemed to come from all directions. Sniper fire kept the men pinned down. Jungle growth obscured the enemy's position and caused mortar fire and grenades to be ineffective. Torrential rains, which continued throughout the day, also hampered the attackers. Any optimism that the men of the 1st Battalion might have had was rudely shaken by the veteran Japanese defenders, who beat off every attack. Little progress had been made by late afternoon, and further attacks were called off because of a shortage of ammunition and lack of rations.

The situation in the 3d Battalion zone was no better. As the troops approached the trail between the old and new airstrips, they found that it narrowed to a causeway bordered on either side by swamps. Intense fire from prepared positions along the western end of the new strip in front of the trail junction halted the forward movement. The troops were hampered by a lack of mortar and artillery support and were plagued by the fact that many of the Australian Mills bomb grenades they had been issued failed to explode. Lieutenant Colonel Miller continued to order the advance, and the men at times were forced to attack through swampy terrain in waist-deep water. By the end of the day, after sustaining heavy casualties, the battalion was still at the edge of the clearing approximately three hundred yards south of the junction, and, like the 1st Battalion, was low on ammunition and nearly out of rations.

On the twentieth, having been resupplied, the 1st Battalion resumed the attack after the Japanese positions had been struck by air attacks and a few artillery salvos. These caused little damage to the Japanese defenses. Despite heavy fire, however, men of Company C on the extreme right managed to infiltrate the Japanese positions and destroy a number of machine-gun nests. This allowed the battalion to move forward a few hundred yards, but the main Japanese defenses remained relatively untouched. During this action, Lieutenant Colonel Carrier's 1st Battalion of the 126th and the Australian Independent Company arrived tired out from their twenty-five-mile march from Pongani. Harding planned to use them in a much larger attack the following morning.[15]

Meanwhile at Port Moresby, General MacArthur was beginning to show signs of the impatience he had exhibited before he pressured Blamey to remove Rowell and Allen. He had issued a communiqué on the twentieth in which he optimistically stated that "our ground forces have rapidly closed in now" and were fighting on the outskirts of Buna and Gona. He had set the next day for an all-out forward movement by all units and expected "all columns" to drive through to their objectives without regard to losses.

While McCoy's troops were beginning their assault on the Japanese left, Harding received a peremptory message from MacArthur: "Take Buna today at all costs."[16] Such an attitude betrayed not only a profound ignorance of the situation but was indicative of the mind-set of MacArthur as well as all the senior members of his staff, none of whom had visited the front. Their displeasure with the lack of movement would increase during the following days and lead to recriminations against Harding and allegations that the men of the 32d Division simply refused to fight.

Even without the peremptory messages from Port Moresby, General Harding had planned an attack in much greater strength for the twenty-second. It would be preceded by heavy air strikes. The plan called for Lieutenant Colonel McCoy's battalion on the right and Lieutenant Colonel Carrier's on the left to advance on a broad front toward Cape Endaiadere. The Australian company farther in the interior would infiltrate the Japanese positions along the new airstrip while the 3d Battalion of the 128th would capture the bridge between the two airstrips.

However well conceived, the plans were thrown awry by two unforeseen events. The first was the air attack. Although the planes arrived on schedule, they did minimal damage to enemy positions, and one plane dropped its bombs on the forward troops of the 3d Battalion, killing four men and wounding two. The other negative factor was the faulty communication between division and the battalions, which had not been advised of the projected bombardment nor given the hour for their attacks. The orders actually reached the battalions forty-five minutes after the air attack.

The planned assault was postponed until after General Harding had arranged for a second air attack. This was scheduled for 1245, with an artillery bombardment followed by the general attack at 1300. The air strike was canceled, perhaps because of fears of again hitting friendly troops. However, Harding convinced the air force to try again. This attack began just before 1600, eight hours after the initial plan was to have been implemented. Once again the pilots of the A-20s and B-25s became confused as to the target area. Some bombs were even dropped in the sea. One B-25 scored a direct hit on Lieutenant Colonel McCoy's lead companies, this time killing six, wounding twelve, and almost burying seventy others.[17] It is not surprising, therefore, that the morale of the men who began the attack at 1630 was severely shaken.

The support from the artillery was minimal and the mortar fire was ineffective. One reason was the near impossibility of determining the correct range to any target. The commander of the 128th's heavy weapons company remembered: "We had to crawl up in the jungle to try and get the accurate range to a target and then crawl back. I eventually put my guns out on the beach in hopes of getting better observation."[18] This was not the only problem. There was not enough ammunition for anything like saturation firing. Even the rounds that were fired were generally ineffective, because they were fused superquick, exploding on impact and doing little damage to the bunkers.

The troops of the 1st Battalion reached the Japanese line and fought valiantly but to little avail. On the left the 3d Battalion did not even reach the bridge, which was its objective. It did manage to cross the open fields and reach the trail junction before being met by a withering cross fire that forced the men back to a more defendable position south of the junction. The attack had cost forty-two casualties. Harding concluded that with the force he had, he was not likely to take the bridge, so he ordered Lieutenant Colonel Miller to leave one company to hold the territory won and move the rest of the battalion back to Simemi, where it would operate in conjunction with the 1st Battalion in the attack against the cape. By the evening of the twenty-second, Miller's troops had completed their move.

General Harding was acutely aware of his lack of firepower and the strength of the Japanese positions. He desperately needed more guns and ammunition. The supply situation had improved since the tragedy of 16 November. There were now five luggers available, and the airstrip at Dobodura was opened for air traffic. General Waldron had brought in two more 25-pounders and their Australian crews. Thus by the twenty-sixth, the artillery support, although still inadequate, was eight 25-pounders, two 3.7-inch mountain guns, and the single 105mm howitzer. Ammunition supply continued to limit the amount of fire to support the infantry attacks. There was no common firing chart, and observation of effectiveness was by forward observers whose range of vision was severely limited by the jungle. Aerial observation using RAAF Wirraways did not begin until early December.[19]

In search of more firepower, Harding determined that the area of the Duropa Plantation was suitable for tanks, so he placed an urgent request for some of the light Stuart tanks then at Milne Bay to be transported to Oro Bay. General Clowes was swift to try to oblige, but once again the inadequacy of naval transport became the major problem. The only craft available were captured Japanese barges. Even though these were not suitable, an attempt was made to load the tanks. This proved a failure—the barges sank, taking the tanks with them.[20] Harding thus had to be content to continue with only infantry attacks against what had already been proved to be formidable defenses.

As the attacks toward Cape Endaiadere stalled, Colonel Smith, with only the 2d Battalion of the 128th, attempted to take the junction of trails before Buna. Later called the Triangle by the Americans, this was a major Japanese defense position. It was later determined that Capt. Yoshitatsu Yasuda, the Japanese commander, had twice as many troops available as Smith had. Yasuda had positioned a number of machine guns south of the junction and had an elaborate system of mutually supporting bunkers in the Triangle. There also were machine-gun positions and fire trenches placed on either side of the trails leading to Buna village and the mission. Deep swamps on either side channeled any attack. It is not surprising that the first direct attack by the 2d Battalion, on the twenty-first, was halted. By early afternoon, Smith ordered his companies off the trail to try to flank the Japanese positions, but they found it nearly impossible to maneuver in the swamps. By evening it was apparent that without reinforcements, the attack would get nowhere.

Harding, however, had no reserves immediately available. Therefore, he sent an urgent request to General Herring for the return of one of the battalions of the 126th that had been shifted to the Australian sector. Herring agreed. General Vasey was utilizing the 3d

Battalion, so it was decided to dispatch Maj. Herbert Smith's 2d Battalion across the Girua River to reinforce Smith's attacks on the Triangle. (Some confusion arose over the names of the commanders, both of whom were Herbert Smith. This was solved by giving the code name "White" to Lieutenant Colonel Smith and "Red" to Major Smith.[21]) The river was flooding, so it took most of the night for the troops to get across by rafts and cable. Most were in position by the morning of the twenty-third. Now, with two-thirds of a regiment available, Harding gave the name Urbana Force to this sector of his front. Because he had designated those elements under MacNider as Warren Force, named for his native county, he now honored General Eichelberger's hometown with Urbana Force.

Colonel Smith realized that his Company G on the right had become stalled in waist-deep water. He proposed pulling it back and concentrating a full-scale attack on the left of the Triangle. Smith's request was not received at division headquarters until early on the afternoon of the twenty-third. Not receiving confirmation, he moved the company back from the swamp on his own. Orders finally arrived ordering him to begin the attack at 0800 the next morning. He was promised artillery and air support.

At the appointed time, twelve RAAF P-40s made one pass over the target and missed it completely. The infantry attack was held up until another air strike could be ordered. Smith was promised that twelve more fighters would strafe the Japanese positions just before 1400. No bombers were available, but fighters appeared—four, however, instead of twelve. And instead of strafing the Japanese positions in the Triangle, they strafed Smith's headquarters, wounding one man. Smith waited a few minutes to ascertain whether more planes would come, then ordered the attack to begin. A brief preparatory bombardment with 60mm mortars began the attack. Urbana Force had only two 81mm mortars and little ammunition for them. At about 1430, shortly after the two battalions began the attacks, the few artillery pieces at Ango opened up.[22]

As before, the Japanese stopped the advance on the left immediately. The center company, Company F of the 126th, encountered heavy barbed wire entanglements strung across the trail; having no wire cutters, the men were forced to dig in short of the main Japanese positions. On the right, Company E of the 128th marched through the swamp and reached a kunai grass flat while Company G attempted to flank the Japanese positions. Company G was held up just outside the Triangle, and the men of Company E on the kunai grass flat were subjected to withering Japanese fire from troops brought up from Government Gardens.

A major problem developed as the rifles and machine guns, full of dirt and water, jammed. Further, many of the mortar rounds fell short because the propelling charge in the ammunition was wet. Also, communications problems resulted in a complete pullback of the right-hand companies even though Smith wanted only a partial withdrawal. Thus on the twenty-fifth it appeared obvious to Smith that his tired, hungry troops were in no condition to resume the offensive immediately.

General Harding had lost confidence in Lieutenant Colonel Smith, believing that the attacks had not been pushed with enough vigor. He sent Col. John Mott, his chief of staff, to the Urbana front to take over command. Mott decided, and Harding agreed, that future attacks should be made on the left, aimed at Buna village, while holding the positions gained on the right. It was decided to give the nearly spent troops a brief rest but resume with a coordinated attack during the night of 29–30 November.

Despite the difficulties of moving the troops to their designated positions in the dark through swampy terrain, the attack to secure the grassy areas held by the Japanese began after a brief delay. After some initial success, the westernmost companies attacking toward the village were halted shortly after daylight by the Japanese bunker line three hundred yards short of the village. Despite reinforcements and heavy mortar support, the troops were unable to advance farther. However, Company F of the 128th, in a wide flanking movement, reached Siwori village, up the coast. They established a blocking position that denied the Japanese the route between the Buna and Sanananda fronts. This was the only genuine success. After ten days of fighting, the Japanese defenses in front of Urbana Force had only been dented. The most concentrated bunker and machine-gun emplacements before Buna village—the Coconut Grove and the Triangle—had not been touched.[23]

Meanwhile, on the Warren front, the planned-for attacks had not resulted in any substantial gain. On the twenty-second, Harding ordered Lt. Col. Alexander MacNab, the executive officer of the 128th, to be responsible for better coordination of attacks toward the cape. He and MacNider planned for an attack the following day. MacNab concentrated his mortars and tried to find better observation posts for them and the artillery. Although not as effective as MacNab believed, the fire, although still blind, enabled the 1st Battalions of the 126th and 128th to push the Japanese back upon their main defenses. The Australian company operating to the west also made slight gains. General MacNider was wounded by a rifle grenade during the attack as he came forward from his headquarters to observe the action. Harding replaced him as commander of Warren Force with Colonel Hale, and they decided to rest the troops while planning for a new offensive on the twenty-sixth.

The plan for that offensive was to open with a large-scale air attack and artillery bombardment. Then the 1st Battalion of the 126th, on the left, would attempt to advance northward along the coastal track. It would be followed by McCoy's 1st Battalion of the 128th. At the same time, one company of the 128th and the Australian company would try to take the new airstrip.

The aerial bombardment began as planned at 0730 on the twenty-sixth and lasted for almost an hour. RAAF Beaufighters and P-40s strafed the area, then A-20s dropped bombs. Once again the air attack did not seem to adversely affect the Japanese in their bunkers. As the men of Miller's battalion moved out, they were almost immediately pinned down by heavy fire. Later they were strafed by Japanese planes. The attack of the 126th was also contained after its lead companies got completely turned around as they were advancing through the swamp. Although maintaining a continuous front against the enemy, the attack had again proved the strength of the Japanese defenses. Harding decreed a two-day pause after the failures of the twenty-sixth. Nevertheless, the troops on both fronts sustained further losses on the twenty-seventh as once again Allied planes dropped bombs on them.[24]

General Harding sent his G-2, Maj. William Hawkins, to Port Moresby to straighten out the air force on the exact positions that the 32d occupied in order to minimize further damage from Allied planes. He once again pleaded for armor. He suggested that some of the captured barges at Goodenough Island be brought to Milne Bay so that the Stuart light tanks could be transported. Again he was informed that the barges were not big enough. However, he was promised that thirteen light armored Bren gun carriers would be dispatched to Porlock Bay, and four of them would be available by the thirtieth.

Harding made his plans for the attack on that date based upon utilization of the Bren gun vehicles. The plan was for an advance on a fairly wide front straight up the trail in a column of companies from the 1st Battalion of the 128th, with two Bren gun carriers leading the attack. Lieutenant Colonel Carrier's 1st Battalion of the 126th, with the other two Bren gun carriers, was to strike westward and attempt a breakthrough in the new strip area. Miller's battalion was to be held in reserve to take advantage of any gains made by either attacking battalion. The available artillery and mortars, as in other attacks, would attempt to soften up the defenses while the air force, then committed to attacking an enemy convoy, would give whatever assistance it could.

Given the circumstances of the Japanese defenses and the weakness of Harding's force, it was not a bad plan. However, it was compromised almost immediately by the failure of the supply system. The Bren gun carriers did not arrive in time to take part. The attack proceeded without them, with the artillery firing at the Japanese positions and the air force, after having successfully attacked the convoy, strafing the forward areas at midmorning and again in early afternoon.

Not surprisingly, the infantry, without satchel charges, flamethrowers, or direct heavy artillery support, failed to dislodge the Japanese. In McCoy's sector, the leading company, after an advance of only a hundred yards, encountered a huge log barricade that the Japanese had built across the trail. Heavy fire from in front and the flanks halted all forward movement.[25] A 37mm antitank gun was brought up but could not blast a way through the barricade. As one soldier remarked, "Coconut logs are strange. When you shoot into them, they close up and there is hardly any penetration."[26] In the stifling heat, the men of McCoy's battalion had no choice but to dig in and wait for another attack plan. In the meantime, Carrier's attack on the left also failed, although one company advanced as far as the center of the airstrip before heavy fire forced the men to dig in.

As the month ended, Warren Force, despite heroic efforts, had not penetrated the Japanese defenses. This would not happen for almost three more weeks, after the tanks that had been denied Harding were finally brought to the front. The same conditions prevailed on the Urbana front. The supply and communication systems had all but failed. The troops were half starved, generally subsisting on one-third of a C ration per day, a situation that had gone on for weeks. There was a critical need for shoes, socks, and new uniforms. Little tentage was available to protect the soldiers from the continual rain. General Eichelberger, on his first tour of the front on 2 December, confirmed the plight of the soldiers. He later wrote: "The troops were deplorable. They wore long dirty beards. Their clothing was in rags. Their shoes were uncared for or worn out. They were receiving far less than adequate rations and there was little discipline or military courtesy."[27]

A further problem that impacted on the 32d Division was a shortage of ammunition—particularly for the mortars and the few artillery pieces—as well as gun oil, patches, and other cleaning equipment for the rifles and machine guns. Malaria was epidemic. One survivor recalled that he did not know anyone at this juncture who did not have malaria.[28] The troops were also subjected to dengue, jungle rot, and dysentery. All types of medication for the sick were in short supply, even salt tablets and chlorination pellets. During the month the division had also suffered 492 battle casualties, with 82 killed and 325 wounded. It is therefore strange that those senior officers at Port Moresby seemed ignorant of the true state of affairs and instead heaped blame on the division for not living up to the early false optimism. This divergence between reality and the mythic beliefs of MacArthur and his advisers would result in the dismissal of General Harding.

Chapter X
Eichelberger Arrives, Harding Departs

As the situation in Papua became stalemated, General MacArthur had a number of other problems calling for action that limited his appreciation of the conditions confronting the 32d Division. He was still attempting to obtain more ships from the navy but found that Admirals King and Nimitz were no more willing than before to allow a substantial MacArthur navy. He also supported Prime Minister Curtin and General Blamey in their appeals to London for the return of the Australian 9th Division from the Middle East. In the Pacific area he watched with dismay as the Guadalcanal operation continued to demand more support from Kenney's still small air force. He had to protest what he considered an attempt to divert the 1st Marine Division from Australia. Then once it was decided to allow the Marines to be withdrawn to Australia, there was the problem of locating the division in a suitable location. The relationship with the Marine command was strained when it was discovered that the site for deployment of the division was in a notoriously high malaria area.

There were a number of embarrassing problems caused by the influx of American troops. Australia had an all-white immigration policy. MacArthur had more than twice the percentage of black troops than in the European theater. The employment of these soldiers rankled many Australians and caused some friction. However, the most vexing of all was the relations between off-duty American and Australian servicemen in the cities. Contrary to the myths that developed in the years after the war, they did not like one another.

The latent hostility exploded on 26 November when U.S. Military Police and Australian soldiers clashed outside a post exchange in Brisbane. The result was one Australian soldier killed and nine wounded. The following day, Australian troops roamed the city, attacking Amercian soldiers randomly. Twenty-one were injured. General Blamey suggested restructuring the military police by assigning officers from both services to single units. MacArthur, who was committed to the integrity of U.S. forces, vetoed the idea. An increase in the number of military police in critical areas kept violence among the troops at a minimum, but the hostility remained.[1]

The command structure that MacArthur had put together was also a source of problems. The blending together of U.S. and Australian systems did not work well. The antipathy felt by individual soldiers extended to the senior commanders. Worse still was the cumbersome command structure in Papua after General Blamey had removed Rowell and moved his headquarters to Port Moresby, to be joined later by MacArthur and much of his headquarters. Present in New Guinea to control the actions of the equivalent of two infantry divisions was the commander of the Southwest Pacific theater, the head of the Australian army, and the commander of New Guinea Force. All were capable of issuing orders to Generals Vasey and Harding. A typical U.S. military organization would have had another officer, a corps commander in this chain of command, but Eichelberger had been sent to Rockhampton and had been expressly informed by Sutherland that he had no role in the Buna campaign; rather he was only to supervise the training of the 41st Division.[2]

Concern with basically nonmilitary events can excuse in part MacArthur's understanding of the problems at Buna. However cumbersome the command system was, it did serve to protect MacArthur from an accurate picture of what was happening there. He depended for information to a large extent on men whom he trusted. Foremost among these was his chief of staff, Richard Sutherland, who had been with him in the Philippines. By all accounts Sutherland was hard working, extremely intelligent, and very loyal. Many who served with him also remembered him as overbearing, with a tendency to interfere in areas of which he had scant knowledge. General Kenney had discovered this soon after arriving in Australia. Only by facing down Sutherland was he able to operate without the interference that had plagued his predecessor. Sutherland's ignorance of the geography and situation on the Kokoda Trail and at Milne Bay had earlier proved only an embarrassment. By this time General Kenney had become one of MacArthur's closest confidants. Although an excellent air force commander, he knew little about infantry operations. However much it may have annoyed MacArthur to have Blamey in charge of Allied ground forces, he did bow to his combat experience and tended wherever possible to agree with Blamey and his senior commanders. When MacArthur became seriously concerned about the stalemate at Buna, he turned for information to Sutherland, Kenney, and, particularly, Blamey and Herring.

MacArthur and the others at General Headquarters had presumed, as had Harding, that the campaign against the Japanese in the Sanananda-Buna corridor could be concluded quickly. Even the Australian leaders whose brigades were worn out in the Kokoda fighting had judged the Japanese troops to be hungry, tired, and disease ridden and thought that the defenses would soon collapse. MacArthur had issued an extremely optimistic communiqué on the eve of Harding's first attack. This attitude contributed to the decision to remove two-thirds of the 126th Regiment from Harding's command and shift them to the Australian sector. Despite the appeals made for more artillery, tanks, and troops, it was easy to believe that the 32d Division was somehow deficient or they would have achieved the hoped-for objectives by the twenty-sixth.

The Australian attitude toward the plight of Harding's troops was a key in undermining Harding's standing with MacArthur. Blamey had an a priori negative opinion of the capability of American troops. He phrased this succinctly in a letter to Prime Minister Curtin: "My faith in the militia is growing, but my faith in the Americans has sunk to zero." With reference to the 32d Division and the attacks at Buna, he concluded: "It has revealed the fact that the American troops cannot be classified as attack troops. They definitely are not equal to the Australian militia, and from the moment they met opposition sat down and hardly have gone forward a yard."[3] Such a conclusion showed unwarranted ignorance of the situation at Buna and betrayed a bias that would make his recommendations to MacArthur devastating to the reputation of the 32d and its commander.

An indication of possible conflict between the 32d and General Herring's staff occurred even before the attack on the *Minnemura*. General Harding had decided to visit the forward regiments on the sixteenth and left Colonel Mott in charge of headquarters. Mott, a regular army officer of real talent, also appears to have had a temper that could be ignited quickly. Early in the morning he received a radio message from Herring that one of his staff would arrive to confer with General Harding. An unfortunate mix-up then followed. Mott wanted to inform Herring that Harding preferred to confer by phone. However, the line to Herring's headquarters went dead before Herring could be informed of Harding's whereabouts and presumably that he would soon confer by phone. Brigadier Ronald Hopkins soon arrived at the airfield, and Major Hawkins, the G-2, suggested that Mott go to the airfield to fill in Hopkins on the details. Overly irritated by what he must have considered unwarranted interference from the Australians at a critical time, Mott vetoed the suggestion, saying, "No, the hell with them." Hopkins, angry at this unnecessary slight, flew back to report to Herring on what had happened. This led Herring to conclude that Harding was refusing to cooperate with the Australian command.[4]

A similar misunderstanding occurred later as Harding was moving to his new headquarters at Dobodura. After the forward echelon of sixty men had marched all day in the heat, Harding found Lt. Col. W. T. Robertson, an emissary from Herring, waiting for him. Robertson wanted a full dress report, and Harding explained that he couldn't comply because of the ongoing movement of his headquarters. He further informed Robertson that it would be some time before the signal corps people would be able to move their heavy equipment forward. Robertson was clearly dissatisfied with Harding's explanation and informed him that Herring would soon arrive to find out the situation for himself.[5]

At Port Moresby the feeling of anxiety over the Buna stalemate matched that of late August when General Vasey had found that the attitude there was "like a bloody barometer in a cyclone."

MacArthur was not the picture of the steely, confident commander in charge of the situation. Despite the multiplicity of duties, he was surprisingly unaware of the actual situation at Buna. Rather, he had listened to the Australians who had painted a bleak picture of the 32d. This reinforced his earlier optimistic notion that the defeat of the Japanese there would be an easy matter. Major Hawkins, whom Harding had sent to Port Moresby to attempt to minimize friendly air attacks by giving more accurate positions to the air force, was called to MacArthur's headquarters and grilled extensively by Blamey, Kenney, and Sutherland. However, any further input he might have given was blocked by his hospitalization with an acute attack of malaria.

Blamey had been pressing for more reinforcements for Vasey's sector. Because of limited reserves, he tried to convince MacArthur that Harding's requests were not justified. He wanted the 21st Brigade to be flown to the Sanananda front. MacArthur hesitated on the question of reinforcements, although he suggested that the entire 41st Division could be moved forward to Buna. He decided to send a fact finder to the Buna area. This was Lt. Col. David Larr, a deputy to MacArthur's G-3, Brig. Gen. Stephen Chamberlin. In retrospect, the choice was unfortunate, because Larr was a staff officer with no combat experience.

A further unfortunate situation developed at Dobodura that colored Larr's view of the situation. Once again it was Colonel Mott at the center of a confrontation. Mott, who had just been appointed to take over Urbana Force, was still at Dobodura when Larr arrived and demanded a jeep. There were only two jeeps available, one for hauling supplies and the other that Mott needed to move to the Urbana area. Short tempered, Mott was obviously put off by Larr's demands, and a noisy squabble ensued. The immediate result was that Larr, who considered his orders more important than Mott's need, was left on foot. In all probability the confrontation with Mott colored Larr's attitude toward the 32d and predetermined his negative report.[6]

There is no way of being certain exactly what Larr reported to MacArthur. He left no written report and was later killed in a plane crash. From the accounts of others, it is known that what he said was mainly negative. He recommended that Colonels Mott and Hale be removed from command of the Urbana and Warren fronts. He believed that neither was fit for such command and they were retained only because of Harding's reluctance to relieve them. He stated that the commanders remained too far back to control the situation at the front despite the fact that Harding was moving his headquarters forward at the time of his visit. Larr's report on the men of the 32d was particularly damaging. He charged that many were skulking in rear areas, that most were deathly afraid of snipers, and that some had even abandoned their weapons. These damaging accusations convinced MacArthur and his staff of the incompetence of the 32d's leadership and the near cowardice of the troops.

General Kenney, who had never inspected the situation on the ground at Buna, would later repeat these accusations, although in a modified form, which hinted at the reality of the problems at Buna. He wrote:

The troops were shot full of dysentery and the malaria were [*sic*] starting to show up. We were flying back a lot of sick every day as well as a few wounded. The troops were green and the officers were not controlling them. They threw away their steel helmets and then wouldn't go forward because they didn't have them. They were scared to death of snipers and beginning to imagine that every coconut tree was full of them.[7]

One aspect of the report was absolutely correct. The troops were afraid of snipers who, although not in every tree, were in enough trees to cause serious damage to the infantry in exposed positions. The standard way of dealing with the sniper problem—directing rifle fire at all trees that might conceal a sniper—did not always work, because some of the Japanese defenders at night would climb the trees, cut down any of their dead comrades, then take their place. Later, Eichelberger witnessed firsthand how effective snipers could be when, inspecting the Urbana front, General Waldron was drilled through the shoulder, a wound that ended his career. A few minutes later, Eichelberger narrowly escaped when a bullet from a sniper's rifle whizzed by his head and struck his senior aide, Capt. Daniel Edwards, in the side.[8] Contrary to Larr's and Kenney's belief, fear of snipers was simply a normal reaction to the situation at Buna.

The twin accusations of incompetent leadership and cowardice deeply affected MacArthur, who decided to send his trusted chief of staff to Dobodura to confer with Harding. Sutherland was hardly an unbiased investigator. He had listened to Blamey and Larr and had read Robertson's report. Even before deciding to send Sutherland to Buna, MacArthur apparently had decided on a change of command. He had already instructed Chamberlin on the twenty-ninth to send an alerting message to Eichelberger at Rockhampton. In a phone conversation on Sunday afternoon, Chamberlin told Brig. Gen. Clovis Byers, Eichelberger's chief of staff, "If you are going into combat, you'll get the warning order about midnight tonight and you'll leave at daylight tomorrow morning."[9]

On the morning of 30 November, Sutherland flew to Dobodura to confer with Harding and Herring, who had arrived earlier. He discovered that the two generals were at loggerheads over a number of issues. Chief among them was Harding's request for additional firepower and more troops. Specifically he wanted the rest of the 126th, then operating under Vasey, returned to the Buna sector. He also wanted the 127th, then at Port Moresby, flown in as quickly as possible.

Herring had a detached but negative view of Harding's problems. It was not unreasonable for Harding to believe that Sutherland, given the facts, would support his views. He was surprised to find that, on the contrary, Sutherland supported the Australian arguments.

Sutherland informed Harding that the movement of the 127th was beyond the logistical capabilities of the theater at that time. This was surprising, because less than a week before, MacArthur had suggested bringing in the entire 41st Division. Sutherland was correct; the air force could not ferry both the 21st Brigade to Vasey's front and the 127th to reinforce the Buna offensive. It was clear that Blamey, in his downgrading of American forces and insistence on having the 21st Brigade, had won the logistical argument.

Sutherland never was closer to the front line than Harding's headquarters at Dobodura, and he flew back to Port Moresby in the afternoon. Before leaving, he informed Harding of some of the items that Larr had touched on. More specifically, he indicated that headquarters believed that Mott and Hale should be replaced. Harding defended both, but particularly Mott, who had had command of the Urbana Force for only one day when Larr arrived. Further, he pointed out that Larr detested Mott and was therefore incapable of arriving at an unbiased conclusion. This argument did not sway Sutherland, who indicated that MacArthur was going to confer with Eichelberger and would probably send him to Buna. On arrival back at Port Moresby, Sutherland advised MacArthur to relieve Harding, because he refused to get rid of incompetent subordinates.[10]

Eichelberger received the warning order just before midnight of the twenty-ninth. MacArthur had sent two C-47s, one his own plane, to pick up Eichelberger, six officers, and nine enlisted men of I Corps headquarters. It was obvious that MacArthur was in a hurry to get his corps commander involved in the Buna stalemate. This change in attitude must have surprised Eichelberger, because he later recalled that the first indication that all was not going well at Buna was the warning order.[11] After arriving at Port Moresby, Eichelberger and Byers were met by an orderly at MacArthur's bungalow who informed them that MacArthur wanted to see them at once. Byers recalled the scene on the veranda:

> There was General Sutherland sitting over at General MacArthur's desk swinging and rotating around in his swivel chair. Kenney was on my left and Bob [General Eichelberger] on my right. General MacArthur paced back and forth across the floor as he said, "Bob, I never thought I'd be told that American soldiers were throwing away arms, running, and wouldn't face their enemy."[12]

General Eichelberger remembered clearly MacArthur's concern when he left no doubt of what he wished. MacArthur said:

> Bob, I'm putting you in command at Buna. Relieve Harding. I am sending you in, Bob, and I want you to remove all officers who won't fight. Relieve regimental and battalion commanders; if necessary put sergeants in charge of battalions and corporals in charge of companies—anyone who will fight. Time is of the essence; the Japs may land reinforcements any night.

He then gave Eichelberger a further melodramatic order, "Bob, I want you to take Buna, or not come back alive." He pointed to Byers and said, "And that goes for your chief of staff too. Do you understand?"[13]

A number of conclusions can be drawn from this meeting. The first is that MacArthur was afraid of a large-scale Japanese landing. Further, he had agreed with Larr and the Australians that there was a breakdown in command and that large numbers of the men of the 32d Division were cowards. Neither conclusion was later supported by facts. However, he expected Eichelberger, who had until then been kept in the dark about events at Buna, to rescue the situation. His peremptory command left Eichelberger with little maneuvering room. He had been told to relieve Harding and any of those who wouldn't fight. It appears that Eichelberger became aware during that evening during briefings that all was not as simple as those at headquarters imagined. Nevertheless, he prepared to leave for Buna after breakfast on 1 December. Before he left, MacArthur took him into his office and promised him that if he took Buna, he would be awarded the Distinguished Service Cross and be recommended for a high British decoration. A further inducement given by MacArthur was that he would allow Eichelberger's name to be released for newspaper publication.[14]

It took just forty minutes for Eichelberger and his small staff to fly to Dobodura; they landed there at 1100 and encountered for the first time "the stink of the swamp." On arriving, Eichelberger informed his old friend Harding: "I have been ordered to relieve you but get behind me and I'll see if I can hold you here."[15] This clearly indicated Eichelberger's discomfort with MacArthur's peremptory order. Two hours later he had assumed command and so informed General Herring, who immediately sent Brigadier Hopkins to confer. Hopkins informed him that Herring was not interested in the capture of Buna village but wanted Buna Mission taken. Eichelberger, who hadn't had time to completely grasp the tactical situation, nevertheless knew that he could not afford to allow the Japanese to hold the village and thus threaten the rear and flanks of any troops occupying the mission; he so informed Hopkins. Hopkins also complained that Harding was not transmitting requests for air support through New Guinea Force headquarters. Later, Harding vociferously denied the accusation.

In his report to Sutherland on 1 December, Eichelberger appeared optimistic. He wrote: "The picture I give you tonight is not as bad as I had expected. Mott has been attacking today and is within 75 yards of Buna Village. He will attack Buna Village tonight."

That evening, Mott reported that his attack had stalled and the Japanese were counterattacking in force across the "island" seven hundred yards southwest of the mission. A heavy artillery concentration stopped the Japanese, but the promising attack by Urbana Force was blunted. Eichelberger decided to go forward the next day to see for himself the actual conditions.[16] Eichelberger discovered that the major Japanese attack reported to him had not occurred. Instead, the Japanese had simply sent out a number of probing attacks. This undermined his confidence in whatever was told him of the situation at the front.

On 1 December there was a further attempt on the Urbana front to take Buna village. Company E of the 126th, reinforced by the headquarters companies of both battalions, advanced through the open area just below the bridge over the Girua River. The attack was preceded by fire from the 25-pound artillery pieces and all available mortars. Several bunkers were destroyed by this bombardment.

The attack appeared to be going well when Company E inexplicably withdrew, perhaps because of a mix-up in communications. Mott therefore canceled the attack and planned to resume it the following day. That evening a report reached Eichelberger that Urbana Force was under heavy attack. The report proved to be false. On the second, Mott continued the attack with two companies, E and F from the 126th, plus a platoon from the 128th. In a repetition of all previous attacks, this too was halted by heavy enemy fire across all avenues of approach.

It was obvious that the men were played out. Major Roger Egeberg, a visiting medical officer, reported to Eichelberger on 1 December that the men looked like "Christ off the Cross."[17] This and other comments should have modified Eichelberger's view of the situation. They did not. Only after assuming command and discovering for himself the difficulty of the task of defeating the Japanese in their bunkers did he admit to the deplorable condition of the men. Later in his recollection of the events of early December, he noted: "Shortly after I arrived in Buna I ordered the medicos to take the temperature of an entire company of hollow-eyed men near the front. Every member, I repeat, every member of that company was running a fever." He also remarked that to evacuate all the sick would mean victory for the enemy.[18]

The situation on the Warren front was no better. General Harding had decided to shift the attack from Cape Endaiadere and to concentrate on the new strip area. On 1 December he therefore ordered a halt of all activity except demonstrations in McCoy's sector. The attack on the first was basically exploratory, with two companies trying to find weak spots in the Japanese defenses. The attack on 2 December began with an air attack, but the planned artillery barrage was late. As in previous attacks, the Japanese simply took to their bunkers to wait until the air and artillery assaults ended. Eventually the infantry went forward, but once again the Japanese stopped any meaningful gains. The weather was hot, and many troops began to drop due to heat exhaustion. The Japanese, satisfied with their defense, did not attempt any counterattack. It was after the action had been completed that Eichelberger's investigators arrived at the front.

Eichelberger decided to inspect the Urbana front on 2 December and left Dobodura at 0930. At the same time, he sent Col. Clarence Martin and Col. Gordon Rogers to the Warren front. Eichelberger was accompanied by Harding and Waldron. Both teams had to proceed most of the way on foot. Eichelberger's party stopped at an aid station, where he found unwounded men who had been sent back with fever and exhaustion and a few with combat fatigue. Eichelberger was not impressed with the reasons why they were not still at the front. Reportedly he was angry before they reached Mott's headquarters. His humor was not improved by discovering that the attack had failed. The two generals then went forward and were not fired upon by the Japanese. Eichelberger concluded from this not that there was a lull in the fighting but that there had been scant opposition. He also discovered that the troops, although hungry, had not been allowed to start fires to cook rice captured from the Japanese. He was not mollified by the explanation that such fires would draw the attention of the Japanese to specific positions.

Further inspecting the troops, he was disturbed by not seeing a continuous front. He criticized the placement of a machine gun manned by U.S. soldiers, viewing it as proof that the troops were not active enough in pressing a weak enemy. What followed would have been comical had the results not been so serious. Eichelberger questioned the men on where a nearby path led and was told that an enemy machine gun had it covered. He didn't believe them and offered to decorate any man who would run fifty yards down the trail. When they declined his offer, he concluded that the men were cowards. Both Harding and Major Smith believed that the offer was not all that alluring. Smith noted later that a hank of ribbon would "look damn artificial to a soldier who is filthy, fever ridden, practically starved, living in a tidal swamp, and frustrated by seeing his buddies killed."[19]

Returning to Mott's headquarters, Eichelberger with his a priori prejudice vented his anger on Mott and Smith, pointing out the unwounded men in the aid station and the hesitance of the machine gunners. He even intimated that the troops had not fought that day. Later he apologized, telling them that he had not realized what they were up against. In the course of the discussion, Colonel Mott, who in all probability had difficulty restraining himself, exploded and vehemently pointed to the suffering and bravery of his men. Harding made it clear that he agreed with Mott, emphasizing his point by throwing his cigarette to the ground. Eichelberger was not finished and said, "You're licked." Shortly afterward he left Mott's command post to confer with his staff and await the report of Martin and Rogers.[20]

While Eichelberger was at Urbana front, Martin and Rogers had gone to Colonel Hale's command post, reaching it about noon, then gone forward to McCoy's command post, arriving there in midafternoon. Before they arrived, there had been intense fighting with all available reserves on the line. By the time they arrived, the action was over and, as Martin reported, it was as quiet as a church.

He could not understand why the men were not pushing ahead against what appeared to be little opposition. Later, after he had some experience with the Japanese defenses, he admitted that the attacks, even if continued throughout the day, would not have been successful. However, at that time, Eichelberger's lieutenants questioned whether there had been any fighting at all. They noted the scruffy looks of the troops, describing them as deplorable, and said the men seemed primarily concerned with being relieved. Martin was also concerned about the unsanitary conditions he saw. After only a brief observation, Martin and Rogers made their way back to Dobodura, arriving there at 2200, to discover that Eichelberger had already relieved Harding.[21]

In his report to Sutherland on 3 December, Eichelberger was terse in relating the relief. He wrote: "Yesterday I received nothing but excuses. Harding was ready to fight for his men and his men had nothing to offer." He had found that the units had been "scrambled like eggs." He noted that "the rear areas were strong but the front line was weak as described by MacArthur." The inspection of the right of the line by Colonels Martin and Rogers confirmed his own quick summary.[22] Later in his book relating his experiences in World War II, Eichelberger admitted that the reason for the units being scrambled was the way they had been flown or marched in piecemeal and almost immediately thrown into battle, this urgency prompted by pressure from MacArthur's headquarters.

Eichelberger's decision to relieve Harding came as something of a surprise to Harding, who, despite the differences between them earlier that day, believed that his command was still safe. He and his staff worked that afternoon on the plans for an attack on the following day. At the same time, Eichelberger was also meeting with Byers and other members of his staff. He reported to them what he had observed and of the confrontation with Mott and Harding. It appeared that Harding was not predisposed to get rid of any of the officers that higher headquarters considered incompetent. Eichelberger asked for their advice, and all present agreed that, given MacArthur's order, he had no choice but to relieve Harding.[23]

Unaware that his old friend and classmate had already decided to relieve him, Harding went to Eichelberger's tent with plans for a further attack on Buna on the third. He found General Waldron with Eichelberger. As Harding explained the proposal for air bombardment and large-scale infantry attacks, he noted that Eichelberger was not impressed. He was more concerned in lecturing Harding about what he had observed that day that he considered wrong. Harding disagreed on a few points and finally said, "You were probably sent here to get heads, maybe mine is one of them. If so, it is on the block." Eichelberger said that it was and that he was putting Waldron in charge of the division. Harding then asked whether he was to return to Port Moresby, to which Eichelberger said yes. Harding then left the tent. Waldron followed him outside and expressed his regret, and Eichelberger came out and apologized for having to let him go.[24] Shortly afterward, Martin and Rogers arrived and made their report, which not surprisingly confirmed to Eichelberger that he had made the right decision.

The following day, Harding visited a portable hospital near his command post, then went to the airfield for the flight to Port Moresby. Later that day he met with Sutherland, who indicated only that he would be sent to Australia. Harding made it clear to Sutherland that he had no intention of pleading his case to him or anyone else. That evening Harding had a lengthy, friendly interview with MacArthur, who seemed genuinely sympathetic. MacArthur promised that nothing would go on the record about the events of the previous day and tended to dismiss the problems at Buna by a reference to new troops having to learn in their first battle. Harding queried the supreme commander as to why he was relieved, to which MacArthur replied, "I haven't the faintest idea." It was a surprising reply by the man who had set the entire process in motion. Noting that Harding did not look well, MacArthur ordered him to Australia for a month where he was to forget about the war.[25] As to Harding's future, nothing was said at that time. General Kenney, who was present at the meeting with MacArthur, later reported his pessimistic views of that future. He noted: "I was really sorry for him. He might have made good and become a 'big wheel,' but no luck, General MacArthur did a nice considerate job of letting him down."[26]

Meanwhile in Papua, Eichelberger continued to remove those senior officers whom Harding had steadfastly defended. On the evening of 2 December, he appointed Colonel Martin to replace Hale as commander of Warren Force. The following day he removed Mott as commander of Urbana Force. The earlier confrontation had obviously changed Eichelberger's mind, because he had reported previously that Mott was doing a good job. Colonel McCreary was appointed in his place. However, on 4 December, Waldron protested that he needed McCreary to command the artillery. Eichelberger then named Col. John Grose, who had been the corps inspector general, to take over Urbana Force. The responsibility for taking Buna now rested squarely on Eichelberger and these newly appointed commanders. The instrument that Eichelberger had to work with remained the tired, hungry, and maligned troops of the 32d Division. The swamps were still there, disease was epidemic, and the Japanese still held their defense lines almost completely intact. Eichelberger, facing the same problems as Harding, soon discovered that taking Buna was far more difficult than he and those at General Headquarters at Port Moresby had imagined.

Chapter XI
Sanananda Stalemate

The lack of lateral trails and the swampy jungle between the main trails channeled the Allied attacks west of the Girua River in two discrete actions. One was directed at capturing the village of Gona, which covered the main anchorage at Basabua. The other, farther to the west, involved the attempt to reach the Sanananda area via the Soputa-Sanananda trail. Here was the largest concentration of Japanese troops, numbering more than 3,000 men, organized by Colonel Yokoyama in two distinct defensive belts. The other area of conflict, Gona, was at first believed by the high command to be undefended. In actuality there were approximately 800 Japanese there commanded by Maj. Tsume Yamamoto. These troops were ensconced in a complex series of bunkers, pillboxes, trenches, and firing pits similar to those encountered by the 32d Division at Buna. Any attack on the Gona defenses was channeled by Gona Creek to the west. To the south were heavily jungled areas where the commander had placed many defensive positions. To the east were extensive hidden firing pits along the shoreline.

The early attacks had wreaked havoc on the Australians. The 25th Brigade had only 750 men left, most of whom were exhausted and sick. On the twenty-fifth, Blamey and Herring visited MacArthur, both seriously concerned about the stalemate and the possibility that the Japanese would succeed in landing substantial reinforcements. The night before, the air force had intercepted a convoy of four destroyers and forced them to turn back, although some men had been landed. It was obvious that more troops had to be sent north. MacArthur at first wanted to send in the 41st Division, but Blamey disagreed. He wanted an Australian unit; he said he knew they would fight. MacArthur swallowed this insult and agreed to the dispatch of the 21st Brigade, then recuperating at Port Moresby.[1]

The first unit of the 21st Brigade, Lieutenant Colonel Challen's 2/14, was landed at Popondetta, and by 29 November most of the brigade had been flown across the Owen Stanley Range. Despite their brief rest, the men of the 21st were not fully recovered. Previous action had taken its toll. The 2/14 had only 19 officers and 322 men, and the 2/27 had 22 officers and 301 men, whereas the 2/16, with only two companies, had 256 men. Thus the total complement was 63 officers and 879 men, approximately the normal strength of a battalion.[2]

Brigadier Vasey decided to use the brigade to move westward and take Gona instead of using it to aid in clearing the Sanananda area. He rushed the 21st into position and planned to begin the attack toward Gona on the twenty-ninth. The 21st's commander, Brigadier Dougherty, asked for a postponement until the thirtieth, citing the need to reconnoiter the ground over which the assault was to be mounted. Vasey said he agreed if higher headquarters approved.

Fearing Japanese reinforcements, Blamey refused the request and noted how imperative the quick capture of Gona was for the resolution of the campaign. What was not recognized was that the Australians at Gona, like their American counterparts at Buna, were operating blind. There were no good maps of the area, and patrolling was made difficult by the alert Japanese. The confrontation with Japanese defenses actually began the evening of the twenty-eighth when Challen's 2/14, the only force then available, attempted to gain a starting point for the main attack by securing both sides of Small Creek, then attacking westward. Patrols had reported that the area was free of Japanese. They were wrong. They had not penetrated far enough to see the Japanese defenses. At dusk, the Australians, moving at first through the jungle, then a swampy area, reached the beach, where they were caught by enfilade fire from the bunkers. They were forced into a grim retreat back through the swamp. This abortive attempt cost the Australians forty-six casualties.[3]

The plan for the thirtieth was for the 2/14, supported by all available mortar fire, to eliminate the Japanese east of Small Creek. At the same time, the 2/27 would move up from the south, then turn westward. Preceding the movement of the infantry, the air force was to bomb and strafe the Japanese positions. The bombers and fighters arrived on time but were too few to eliminate the defenses. With their positions still intact, the Japanese, in a three-hour firefight, kept the 2/27 from making any substantial gains. The battalion suffered fifty-six casualties. The 2/14, to the east, was more successful, taking the village of Banumi, but all the attempts to move west were halted.

At 0200 on 1 December, the Japanese attempted to reinforce Gona with two hundred men from Giruwa. They were driven back by men of the 2/27, who ambushed the barges six hundred yards east of Gona. Pressure on the Japanese was continued by Dougherty, who was planning to attack eastward with the 2/27 aided by a company of the 2/16. They were to be joined by the 3d Battalion on the left and thus drive through to Gona. The usual artillery and mortar barrage preceded the advance. At first all went well, but the 3d Battalion did not link up as planned. A company of the 2/27 broke into the mission area of the village, but the Japanese mounted a heavy counterattack and drove them out. The casualties were once again heavy and, except for attrition on the enemy, little was accomplished.[4]

On 2 December, Lt. Col. R. Honner's 39th Battalion, the advance unit of Brig. Selwyn Porter's 30th Brigade, arrived. The heavy casualties suffered by the 21st Brigade convinced Vasey that Porter's brigade should relieve the 25th. The stalemate on the Sananada trail forced a change in plan. Vasey decided to send the 39th and the 2/14 under Dougherty to reinforce the troops there. He also combined the depleted 2/27 and 2/16 into one composite battalion. Gona was to be simply contained by this composite unit and the played-out 25th Brigade.

All the attacks were carried out in constant rain. When the troops were not attempting to advance, they sat in their weapon pits half

filled with water. Early on the morning of the third, the shift of
forces began along a coastal trail that soon led to an impassable
swamp. As the troops bunched up on the beach, they noticed that
Australian Beaufighters were strafing a derelict Japanese transport.
As one soldier recalled: "I remember saying to someone, 'I hope
those RAAF blokes know we're on this beach.' Just then one of the
Beaufighters finished its half-circle and straightened up to sweep
along the beaches again. We were watching him and it didn't look
good at all. And the next minute, flame from the front of him—he's
opened up with his machine-guns and strafed virtually the whole
battalion."[5] The casualties fortunately were few from this example
of mistaken identify, but once again the air units had shown the
ground troops that they were not always friendly.

After Dougherty reported that the coastal track was impassable,
Vasey again altered his plans. He now would continue the attempt
to take Gona. He relieved the remnants of the 25th Brigade and
had them flown back to Port Moresby. He then assigned the task of
taking Gona to the composite 2/27-2/16, the 2/14, and the fresh
39th Battalions. Only aggressive patrolling was undertaken between
the third and fifth as Dougherty prepared the assault on Gona.
Early on the morning of the sixth, the attack began, with Lt. Col. Albert Caro's composite battalion moving west along the beach. At
the same time, Honner's 39th advanced from the south, attacking
northwest.

The heavy preliminary mortar attack again proved ineffectual.
The 39th was caught in heavy enfilading fire and gained only a few
yards through the kunai grass. Caro's attack through the Coconut
Grove was almost equally fruitless, although a few men broke into
the Japanese defenses, destroying one post and killing a number of
Japanese. The projected attack the following day was called off at
Honner's request, because his air support was dropping bombs be-
hind his troops. He wryly commented, "Give me a squadron of
Stukas."[6] He asked that, in the future, aircraft not be used in preparation for the infantry attack.

The second attempt by Gen. Hatazo Adachi at Rabaul to reinforce his beleaguered forces was on 2 December. The 3d Battalion
of the 170th Infantry and attached troops were loaded onto four de-

stroyers. Accompanying them was Maj. Gen. Tsuyuo Yamagata, who was scheduled to assume command of the defense. Rabaul sent a strong fighter plane escort for the destroyers, and at first these blunted the attacks by B-17s and B-25s of the Fifth Air Force. The ships managed to reach Basabua but were forced by continuing air attacks to leave before the infantry units could go ashore. They moved north and began unloading the troops near the mouth of the Kumusi River, despite the night attacks by Allied planes. An estimated five hundred Japanese and their supplies were landed before the destroyers fled for safety. The men were soon joined by the 41st Infantry troops of Colonel Yazawa. Yamagata, now with a considerable force ashore, found that the Australians were between him and Gona. He quickly moved toward the beleaguered village and crossed to the east side of the Amboga River, a small stream two miles from Gona, on the fourth.[7]

Yamagata's force confronted the Chaforce Company of the 2/16, led by Lt. Alan Haddy, which had been posted to the west bank of Gona Creek. After being strafed by Allied and Japanese planes and taking part in aggressive patrolling, the Australian company, hardly larger than a platoon, was located at a small village later called Haddy's village. On 6 December the village was surrounded by the Japanese. Haddy had sent back to Chaforce base for help. Only fifteen men were immediately available, but Brigadier Dougherty, on learning of the situation and recognizing the need to check the Japanese advance on Gona, sent an additional fifty men of the 2/14. Led by Lt. Robert Dougherty, they surprised the Japanese and drove them back, killing an estimated ninety. That evening Colonel Challen arrived with the rest of the 2/14, which forestalled any further Japanese advance. Haddy's village was not retaken until 18 December, but the continuing advance by the Australians after the sixth forced Yamagata ultimately to set up a perimeter on the Napapo-Danawatu area, a few miles northwest of Gona. With his left flank now secure, Dougherty planned to launch on 8 December what he believed would be the final assault on Gona.[8]

Brigadier Dougherty considered that the attack on the eighth would be the last because his depleted force could hardly make any further attacks without substantial reinforcements. His brigade had less than eight hundred men, fewer than a normal battalion. Vasey agreed with Dougherty's desire to take Gona but warned that if the attack on the eighth were unsuccessful, further attacks would be ruled out. The Japanese there would simply be contained, while the 39th would be shifted to aid in the capture of Sanananda.[9] The plan was for the 39th Battalion to make the major effort, attacking the Japanese compressed into a narrow position approximately two hundred yards in width. The 39th would attack the southern defenses while the composite 2/16-2/27 would attack along the coast. The assault was preceded by a fifteen-minute mortar and artillery barrage, which began at 1230. The artillery used delayed fuses set to go off eighteen inches below ground instead of the high-explosive fuses that detonated on impact. Company C of the 39th would attack the southern defenses while A Company struck from the southeast.

When the attack began, the composite battalion, charging over open ground, took many casualties and was halted with no gain. However, the two companies of the 39th were more successful. Honner ordered both of the assault companies to advance before the bombardment had ceased. On the left, C Company could not advance, but the men of A Company who had crawled up to the enemy lines charged ahead while shells were still dropping on the Japanese positions. They broke through, at first destroying a machine gun and killing thirty-eight enemy before moving on to destroy four more posts. Honner now committed C and D Companies to the breech. The Japanese gave no ground, but the Australians, now inside the defenses, systematically cleared one strong point after another.[10]

Major Yamamoto, in charge of the defense of Gona, had received permission from Colonel Yokoyama to attempt to break out with as much of his force as possible and attempt to reach Giruwa. His troops tried two routes, one between the scrub and ocean and the other by wading out to try to go around the Australians along the beach. Brigadier Dougherty later recalled:

And at the end of the day I had to report that the attack was unsuccessful whereas in fact it had been successful, because the Japanese at midnight on the night of 8–9 December staged a breakout. Frank Sublet [C.O. Composite Battalion] rang me and told me that they were being infiltrated, and I said, "Frank, just order your men to stay in their holes and just shoot anything that moves on top of the ground. It doesn't matter what it is, shoot it." These men were the Japanese remnants of Gona; they were finished.[11]

The Australians killed an estimated one hundred of those attempting to escape, but it is probable that a large number did manage to make their way to the Sanananda area.

The following day, A Company of the 39th moved toward the beach, clearing out the Japanese in a few remaining gun pits. Men of the composite battalion moved up the beach line, taking care of the few remaining Japanese. Early on the ninth, Honner transmitted to Dougherty the laconic message, "Gona gone." Approximately eight hundred Japanese of the impoverished Japanese garrison had fought with such ferocity, determined to hold their positions to the end, that they had not even attempted to bury their dead. They had used the corpses along with rice bags to buttress the rifle pits and also as firing steps. They could not move from their position for fear of being shot, so they used them as latrines, adding to the stench of rotting corpses. The overriding remembrance of Australian veterans was the horror of viewing the many dead and the smell. Colonel Honner recalled:

We reverently buried our gallant dead and moved out as burial parties went in to dispose of the Japanese—they had buried 638 of them by the end of the next day, but many days later we still stumbled over the ones they didn't find, or momentarily stopped brushing our teeth in the lagoons as decayed bodies nudged past us. We did not envy the burial parties in their task. We had seen the Japanese put on their respirators when our bombardments churned up the stench of their comrades' corpses. And many of our battle-hardened veterans, fighting their way forward over polluted ground, were unable to face their food. It was sickening to breathe let alone eat.[12]

The cost to the Australians in taking Gona was heavy, resulting in a total of 734 battle casualties, and the effort to clear the Japanese westward to Haddy's village claimed even more lives.

East of Gona the Australian advance toward Sanananda Point was being contested by an even larger Japanese force, commanded by Lt. Col. Hatsuo Tsukamoto, whose main defenses lay just south of the Killerton and Soputa-Sanananda trail junction. The 2/1 Battalion of the 16th Brigade had encountered the southern outpost of the Japanese defenses near Soputa on the morning of 20 November. Attacks against the center of the defenses were contained, but a company under Capt. B. W. T. Catterns, on the left, flanked the Japanese and set up a defensive position two miles in the rear of the Japanese forward positions. On the right, two companies of the 2/2 moved ahead one and a half miles and took an enemy rice dump in an abandoned plantation one-third mile east of the trail. On the twenty-first, Catterns's men beat off a succession of attacks, inflicting heavy casualties on the Japanese. However, by the time of the Japanese withdrawal, the Australians had suffered sixty-seven casualties from a force of ninety men.[13] The Australian advance, coupled with severe losses, forced the remaining Japanese in the forward positions to fall back to the main defense line. The 16th Brigade now had an east-west line that on the right was only forty yards from the main Japanese defenses, but in the center it was several hundred yards away.

Despite the success of 21 November, it had been obvious to Vasey that the 16th Brigade was played out. In two months of action it had lost a third of its strength, having suffered 561 casualties. Most of the 1,037 men available for duty were hungry and exhausted, and a large number of these were sick.[14] General Herring, upon Vasey's report, appealed to higher headquarters for fresh troops. General Headquarters believed that the Sanananda front was more important than Buna and should be the arena of greatest effort. Therefore it was decided to divert the U.S. 126th Regiment to the Sanananda offensive instead of using it as the left wing of Harding's attack on Buna. Colonel Clarence Tomlinson, commanding the 126th, had already begun the movement of his regiment to the Buna area when he received the surprising order. Despite Harding's vehement protests, the order stood, and the 126th began the march through rain and mud to the new sector. The leading elements reached Soputa on the evening of the twenty-first. Vasey placed Tomlinson under Brigadier Lloyd's command and planned to have the first elements of the 126th committed on the twenty-second to hold the positions won the previous day. The 16th Brigade was placed in reserve. The Americans assumed the responsibility of driving the Japanese from their main positions at the juncture of the trails.

The American command had little idea of the conditions forward of the junction. The maps that the Australians were using were inadequate, and there was little time for good reconnaissance before Vasey planned to use the regiment. Colonel Tomlinson and Capt. William Boice (the S-2) made a hasty trip forward. Based on this and discussions with Vasey and Lloyd, Tomlinson concluded that the Japanese main position was an inverted V. He therefore planned to attack it in an expanded V. Major Richard Boerem's two companies of the 1st Battalion would spread out and attempt to envelop the enemy position. Tomlinson would hold the 2d Battalion in reserve.

Before the plan could begin, Tomlinson received orders to detach the 2d Battalion and send it to the Buna sector, where it would be a part of Harding's left flank attack. After a difficult river crossing and an exhausting march, the battalion arrived to become part of Colonel Smith's operation.[15]

This shuttling back and forth of units of the 126th was another example of poor tactical planning at General Headquarters. The initial order sending the 126th to aid the Australians had removed almost half of the forces available to Harding when he began the assault on Buna. The later order detaching the 2d Battalion from Tomlinson's command shifted approximately 1,500 men back to the Buna sector, leaving Tomlinson with fewer men than that to carry out the proposed advance up the trail. Many of the Australians welcomed the Americans but were put off by the attitude of some who, not having tasted combat against the Japanese, arrogantly informed the veteran Australians that they could go home, because the 126th was there to clean things up.[16] They would soon find that cleaning things up would be more difficult than any of them could imagine.

Despite the departure of the 2d Battalion, the assault on the Japanese positions began early on the morning of the twenty-second. The flanking companies on the left encountered small Japanese patrols, which they managed without difficulty to drive back. However, they became disoriented after the firefights trying to maneuver in the deep bush and discovered by evening that they had not advanced far enough to suit Tomlinson's plan. Meanwhile, the companies on the right encountered heavy fire almost immediately after they attempted to advance. They were forced to halt and dig in only two hundred yards from their start. Colonel Tsukamoto chose to commit a large number of relatively fresh troops who had only recently landed at Basabua in order to try to dislodge the American units. Supported by two Australian companies, the Japanese counterattack was thwarted and the Japanese again sustained heavy casualties.

Work on grading for the airfield at Popondetta began on 19 November, and four days later the first C-47 transport plane landed. That day, considerable needed supplies were flown in. Most welcome were the four 25-pound artillery pieces and ammunition for them, giving the Australians the first artillery support since they began the trek across the mountains. By evening the guns had been set up and were registered.[17]

Despite the artillery, the attacks on the Japanese on the twenty-third and twenty-fourth were abortive. On the left, the two companies, I and K, had moved ahead approximately 1,200 yards and were by the evening of the twenty-fourth located a thousand yards west of the Killerton trail. Japanese attacks during the night forced the men back into the swamp, scattering the units. On the right, L Company had been able to advance only a few yards and was substantially in the same location as it had been on the twenty-second.

The attack on the twenty-sixth opened with heavy mortar and artillery preparation and did no better than previous assaults, being contained by heavy Japanese fire. The increased artillery and mortar support was a mixed blessing. On the twenty-fifth an erratic mortar shell fell on the command post of Capt. J. M. Blamey, commander of the Australian 2/2, mortally wounding him, killing one of his men, and wounding five others. The next day another mortar round landed on a group of Australian soldiers, killing five and wounding eight.[18] Despite such tragedies from friendly fire, the attack on the twenty-sixth continued all day but gained little ground. When the troops dug in that evening, Tomlinson had lost more than a hundred men killed or wounded. The situation deteriorated further on the twenty-seventh as Tsukamoto launched a series of very heavy attacks on the Allied right wing. These assaults were broken up with the aid of the 25-pound artillery pieces, whose fire was directed by Lt. A. N. Daniels, the forward observer who switched their fire from one sector to another. Nevertheless, both Maj. Bert Zeeff's L Company and the Australians in the plantation area sustained heavy casualties. Tomlinson ordered Zeeff to prepare in the next offensive to move his unit northwest to try to make contact with the companies on his left.[19]

General Vasey had hoped to move Australian troops westward over the Killerton trail to the Soputa-Sanananda trail, considerably north of where the Americans were attacking. He sent Lt. K. M. Boyer, of the 22/3 Battalion, on the twenty-third with a large patrol to investigate the feasibility of such a plan. Boyer moved into the swamps, and his men waded for two days before reaching the Killerton trail on the twenty-sixth. The size of the swamp between the patrol and the Soputa-Sanananda trail prevented any direct linkage. After a brief skirmish with a Japanese patrol, Boyer's patrol returned to Vasey's headquarters with the bad news that the farthest north that it was practical to go in such a maneuver was where the Americans were already attacking.

Tomlinson planned for the next major attempt on the Japanese positions to begin on 30 November. Before this he sent his executive officer, Maj. Bernd Baetcke, to the left flank to take command of the planned main effort from Maj. George Bond. He had available I and K Companies, parts of M Company, the 3d Battalion headquarters, and the Cannon and Antitank Company. The plan was to have simultaneous attacks in all areas, but he hoped for a breakthrough on the left.

The assault began early in the morning with L Company on the right advancing only a few yards before the Japanese from prepared positions pinned them down. The two companies, C and D, in the center were also halted. However, on the left, as Tomlinson hoped, there was a substantial gain. Company I led the way and pushed ahead four hundred yards before being met with withering fire as they crossed a grassy patch. Bond was wounded and the attack was momentarily halted. Baetcke came forward, took charge, and got the companies moving again. They moved past the kunai grass patch until being stopped by a large swampy area. However, led by Capt. John Shirley, I Company slowly advanced and discovered a well-used trail that led to a Japanese bivouac area. Driving the Japanese from this, Shirley's men established a large perimeter astride the main trail almost a mile behind the track junction. Tomlinson now had a trail block that, if held, would cut off the Japanese defenders of the junction area from the troops manning the second defense line three hundred yards to the north.[20]

Tomlinson now ordered Major Zeeff, whose center force had been held up on the thirtieth, to attack northward the next day and link up with Shirley's troops at the roadblock. At first the units met little opposition as they crossed the trail and dispersed some of the Japanese defenders. Tomlinson, gratified by the early success, ordered Zeeff to have his men dig in and as soon as possible move them eastward to the roadblock. Before settling in for the night, Zeeff sent a patrol forward and discovered a large concentration of Japanese in very well-prepared defenses. He concluded that his force was inadequate to the task. Tomlinson agreed and decided to pull back Zeeff's men. Early that evening the retreat began as the men, proceeding in single file and carrying their sick and wounded, moved south, then east to the banana plantation near where they had started.

The roadblock, approximately 250 yards long and 150 yards wide, was located in a generally open space in the midst of swampland. There was little natural cover, and the tall trees around the block gave Japanese snipers good vantage points. Shirley had I Company, the Antitank Company, a machine-gun section of M Company, and a communications detachment. He placed the machine guns at the northern and southern ends of the block, emplaced his two 60mm mortars with I Company west of the trail, put the Antitank Company east of the trail, and waited for the Japanese counterattacks. They were not long in coming. The Japanese attacked from the north almost immediately, but they were halted. During 1 December the defenders beat off five heavy attacks.[21]

Major Baetcke, the task force commander, with two companies, was west of the roadblock. He had planned to commit one of the companies in conjunction with Maj. Richard Boerem's frontal attack to relieve Shirley's men. When the central attack failed on the thirtieth, Baetcke called off the advance. Instead, the next day he sent a small party ahead with ammunition and rations, led by Capt. Meredith Huggins. They fought their way through to the block by midday. Soon afterward, Shirley was killed, and Huggins took command. The roadblock henceforth would be called Huggins block. Huggins recalled:

> I ordered the establishment of a double perimeter two men to a foxhole. . . . The Japanese came up behind and established another one behind us. And so it went. I was shot in the head by a sniper. Luckily, I didn't have any brains so I wasn't badly hurt. We were surrounded at the time. Aussies were a few hundred yards away but so were the Japs.
>
> You measured things in inches. I laid wounded in a hole for five days, I think, until a relief party came through and moved me out.[22]

For the next few days the Japanese continued to attack the block; their efforts were fruitless. However, they checked any advance of the U.S. troops from the west and south. They also established their own block farther north up the trail. The ordeal of the men within the Huggins block continued until 22 December, when the Australians finally pushed through the Japanese defenses. Because the major concern in early December was the maintenance of the roadblock, General Eichelberger argued that Tomlinson and his headquarters staff were not needed west of the Girua, and he requested their return. Herring agreed. With Tomlinson's departure, Major Baetcke took over command of U.S. forces in the Sanananda area. By this time they had sustained numerous casualties, and most were ill.

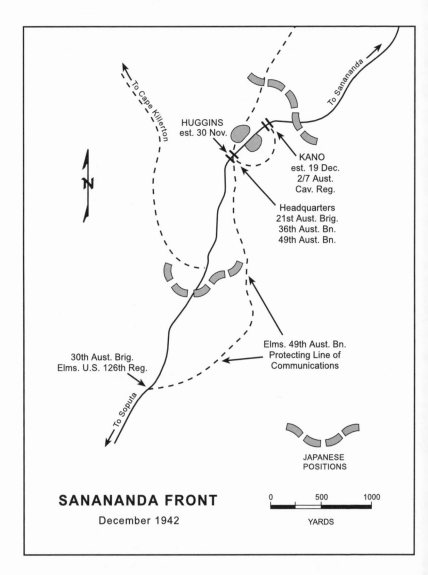

To Cape Killerton

To Sanananda

HUGGINS
est. 30 Nov.

KANO
est. 19 Dec.
2/7 Aust.
Cav. Reg.

Headquarters
21st Aust. Brig.
36th Aust. Bn.
49th Aust. Bn.

Elms. 49th Aust. Bn.
Protecting Line of
Communications

30th Aust. Brig.
Elms. U.S. 126th Reg.

To Soputa

JAPANESE
POSITIONS

SANANANDA FRONT
December 1942

0   500   1000

YARDS

The next major attempt to advance was planned by Vasey and
Brigadier Lloyd to begin on the fifth. Before then there was active
patrolling west and south of the block probing for weak parts in the
Japanese defenses. One such probe was led by a young lieutenant,
Dan DeYoung, who recalled a typical patrol firefight with the
Japanese:

I led a patrol out forward from where we were. There had been a machine gun firing at us. We couldn't see anything, couldn't see 20 yards away, just complete jungle. Couldn't see where the machine gun fire was coming from. I took a part of my platoon and tried to get behind this gun.

All of a sudden we were under heavy fire. Of six men I had, three were hit right away. One sergeant was seriously wounded in front of me. The pain was so much that before we could reach him he shot himself. I wasn't wounded then but was shot by a sniper at dusk as we were trying to get away.[23]

The plan of attack for the fifth was that Baetcke, from the position west of the trail, would attack the Japanese defenses north of Huggins with K Company while Boerem, with more than two hundred men of C and L Companies, attempted to move north. Early in the morning K Company began the attack after a fifteen-minute mortar and artillery preparation. Moving blindly through the kunai grass, they had gone three hundred yards before Japanese machine guns and mortars opened up and stopped any further advance. Boerem's frontal attack also was halted after advancing less than a hundred yards. For all the preparation, there was no substantial gain; the attackers suffered ninety casualties. The plight of the men at Huggins was becoming more desperate. They were down to one day's ration and almost out of ammunition after repulsing Japanese attacks on the fifth and sixth. Captain Huggins was wounded but could not be evacuated immediately. Lieutenant Peter Dal Ponte, with sixty men carrying forty-pound packs, attempted to break through to Huggins, but after fighting all day he was turned back.[24]

Malaria and exhaustion were taking a toll on the men inside and outside the block. On 7 December both Boetcke and Zeeff were so incapacitated by malaria that they had to be evacuated, leaving Boerem in command of the American contingent. By this time a new frontline commander, Brig. Selwyn Porter, had arrived with 30th Brigade militia troops, fresh but generally inexperienced, to replace the played-out 16th. The first units of the brigade arrived at Soputa on the fourth. Porter sent the Australians forward quickly to relieve C, D, and L Companies of the 126th and placed the Americans in supporting positions. There were only three battalions in the brigade, as the 39th was then deeply involved in the assault on Gona. Each of the three battalions of the 30th Brigade was facing its first action. The 49th was the original battalion stationed at Port Moresby at the beginning of the Kokoda defense. The men had been employed in construction projects and unloading cargo, as were the troops of another battalion, a composite organization of the 55th and 53d Battalions. Neither had much actual combat training. Perhaps the best prepared was the 36th Battalion. Lieutenant Colonel O. C. Isaachsen, its commander, recalled:

> When we got over to Sanananda, when Brigadier Porter found that quite a few of the fellows had never fired a Bren-gun or Tommy-gun—never thrown a grenade—he ordered that these fellows come back not far from his Brigade Headquarters and be given actual experience in firing a Bren, a Tommy-gun and throwing a few grenades. This was within a few days of us arriving at Soputa.[25]

These were the men whom Porter planned to use to crack the Japanese defenses on the seventh. As with a number of senior officers in the Papuan campaign, he had no detailed knowledge of the situation. Nevertheless, he directed these men to make direct frontal attacks on the main Japanese positions at the trail intersection. After an artillery barrage, Lt. Col. O. A. Kessels's 49th Battalion began the attack at midmorning. Soon, the advance companies were met with withering fire, and by early afternoon all forward momentum had been stopped. Despite the heavy casualties sustained by the 49th, Porter then committed the composite 55/53 Battalion, passing it through the line of the 49th. After advancing a few yards, the men were caught in a murderous cross fire. By evening it was apparent that Porter's attack was a complete failure. The 30th Brigade had suffered 229 casualties, roughly 48 percent of the total strength of the troops engaged.[26]

After the seventh, in contrast to his earlier false optimism, Porter defined his new strategy: "To position minimum troops on present front for purposes of security and holding frontally. To maintain maximum troops in hand for mobile offense and conservation of health and energy."[27] What this meant was that Porter no longer had the troops to gain a decision in the Sanananda sector, and the Australians were forced to accept a stalemate. Except for the beleaguered Huggins block, the Japanese defenses were as strong as they had been before the weeklong Allied attacks.

Chapter XII
Clearing the Buna Approaches

The change of commanders in the Buna area did not noticeably affect the weary, frustrated, and maligned troops that Eichelberger would need to carry out MacArthur's dictum. However, there were changes that became apparent during the two weeks after Harding's removal. Eichelberger began to receive the support that had been denied his predecessor. A fleet of small boats, sent to replace those lost in November, began to operate on a regular schedule from Milne Bay. The navy even agreed to provide four corvettes for the protection of this vital supply route. On 3 December they brought five thin-skinned, under-armed Bren gun carriers to be used in the planned attack on the Warren front. Ammunition, particularly for the one 105mm howitzer, began to arrive after 10 December in considerable quantities, much to the relief of the artillery commanders. Most important was the arrival of reinforcements, something that Harding had pleaded for. It was as if General Headquarters realized that they had to trust Eichelberger's judgment and provide him with the men and materiel he believed necessary to take Buna.

The improvement in the fortunes of the Allied forces in Papua was tied directly to the actions of the Fifth Air Force and the RAAF. They were charged with a number of separate but complementary missions. Bombers of the Fifth Air Force attacked Rabaul and outlying Japanese island bases regularly. There was also a constant patrol of the sea routes between New Britain and Papua in order to detect any attempt by the Japanese to resupply their garrisons there. General Hatazo Adachi, the new commander of the Eighteenth

Army, in his second attempt had sent a battalion of infantry with a new overall commander, Maj. Gen. Tsuyuo Yamagata, which managed to land near the mouth of the Kumusi River.

Another attempt to reinforce the New Guinea garrison left Rabaul on 7 December. In this convoy was Maj. Gen. Kensaku Oda, who was to take General Horii's position in command of the South Seas Detachment. On 9 December the convoy was detected and driven back to Rabaul. On 15 December a larger convoy of two cruisers and three destroyers was observed heading for the Vitiaz Strait. Under cover of bad weather and darkness, it managed to reach an anchorage off the mouth of the Mambare River and land the eight-hundred-man battalion and General Oda. The supplies were hastily unloaded, and the ships quickly moved out to sea. The next morning, with the weather clearing, medium bombers of the Fifth Air Force, guided by an Australian coast watcher, Lyon Noakes, attacked the supply dumps, destroying most of what had been landed the night before, while heavy bombers struck at the withdrawing ships. This was the last attempt on the part of the Japanese to reinforce the Papua garrisons. Despite the air attacks, Oda and his troops were ashore and, by using barges and hugging the coast at night, managed to get to Yamagata's headquarters. Oda later moved to take command in the Sanananda area, a separate command from Yamagata's.[1]

Direct air support of the many Allied infantry attacks was hampered by the difficulty of good observation and the closeness of the lines between the attackers and defenders. Thus there were a number of cases of misdirected bombs, which caused casualties and convinced many infantrymen that air support was as dangerous as the Japanese. Nevertheless, the A-20s, P-39s, and P-40s did yeoman service in support of each major offensive.

The results of this close support can be judged in part by what some of the Japanese in the enclave wrote in their diaries. On 18 November one wrote: "Enemy bombers and fighters raided rear positions and afterward strafed. Because of that our forces could not move." Another diarist noted four days later: "Enemy planes again flew over and because of this we could not step outside." On the twenty-eighth another soldier made the plaintive entry: "From morning we are heavily bombed. It is more terrifying than that of the 25th. The daily air raids and assaults kill off my comrades and there is nothing I can do but await death."[2]

The Allies ruled the air over Papua. Japanese raids became fewer as the Guadalcanal losses reduced the available planes at Rabaul. Kenney's strikes against the airfields there reduced even further the Japanese ability to interfere with the action over Papua. This dominance became even more noticeable after the Fifth Air Force received a number of high-performance Lockheed P-38s, which could challenge the Zero at high altitudes.

However vital the bombing campaign was, the most important contribution of the air forces was the delivery of men and supplies to the front. With the navy relatively inactive, it was left to the air transports to be the main support of the infantry. However, air action of the Fifth Air Force was costly. Between July 1942 and January 1943, a total of 380 airmen were killed and 200 were missing.[3] Flying through bad weather over the high Owen Stanley Range, the transports from the beginning of the offensive at Buna and Gona kept the infantry supplied with everything needed to sustain them. The task was made easier with the opening of new airstrips at Popondetta and Dobodura. As many as thirty transports a day landed at these forward fields. Between 13 November and 23 January, crews of the 374th Troop Carrier Group either dropped or landed almost 5 million pounds of rations and supplies.

Another major service provided was evacuation of the wounded or sick. By mid-December, 1,500 patients a week were being shuttled back to the hospital at Port Moresby. By the end of the campaign, ten specially equipped DC-3s and ten C-60s were available for air evacuation. Continuing demands of the Fifth Air Force caused Kenney to ask the Australians for any help they could provide. In response, the government assigned its Special Transport Flight of fifteen Hudson bombers, a DC-2, and eleven other planes taken from the civilian sector. The unit arrived on 14 December and immediately began dropping supplies to Soputa.[4]

MacArthur, who had at first been antagonistic to the air force, came to understand how important the Fifth Air Force was to all phases of his planned operations in New Guinea. By November, any suspicions he had earlier about the effectiveness of the air force command had been laid to rest by the actions of Kenney, Whitehead, and lower-echelon officers. It became obvious to General Headquarters that the Papuan campaign could not be successfully fought without major participation by the airmen. The bulk of the 32d Division had been flown across the mountains prior to the beginning of the Buna offensive, as was the 30th Brigade and other troops delivered to the Sanananda area. Eichelberger's spent troops were reinforced by the 127th Regiment, the advance elements of which arrived on 4 December. With this fresh regiment and a steadily improving supply system, Eichelberger was convinced that he could accomplish quickly what had eluded Harding.[5]

Eichelberger, who had been disturbed by the mixing of units, set about immediately to regularize the command structure. He was not able to accomplish this completely, because the 1st Battalion of the 126th was on the left flank of the two battalions of the 128th on the Warren front. The other battalion of the 128th was operating on the Urbana front. The lack of connecting east-west trails between the fronts meant that it would take days to shift these battalions to bring them under the correct commander. Eichelberger had appointed regimental commanders whom he believed he could trust to be aggressive. On 3 December, Colonel Martin went forward and took command of the Warren front. In contrast to his negative report, given when he made the quick inspection that contributed to Harding's removal, he now reported that his forces had few weapons with which to dislodge the Japanese in their fortified positions. Colonel John Grose, a veteran of World War I and Eichelberger's choice to command the Urbana front, had been the I Corps' inspector general, and he hadn't arrived in Papua until the third and did not take command until the next day. Despite all the problems facing the 32d, Eichelberger had planned a general offensive on both fronts to begin on the fourth. Grose, noting that he had no time to familiarize himself with his command, the terrain, and Japanese dispositions, asked Eichelberger to postpone the attack for a day. Eichelberger agreed.

The Japanese and the terrain dictated the type of attack that could be made on their positions, so there was nothing particularly new about Eichelberger's plan. It called for heavy air attacks on the new strip and Duropa Plantation, facing the 128th Regiment in the Warren Force area, and against Buna village and the Triangle in the Urbana front area. This would be followed by concentrated mortar and artillery fire in the hope that the inadequate 25-pound artillery pieces somehow would destroy the Japanese positions. The only new factor was the five Bren gun carriers, which were to lead the advance up the coast.

Many who observed the light armored, open-top vehicles and the small-caliber gun were convinced that they would be useless. Another negative factor was that the route of advance was over ground dotted with tree stumps, on which the carriers could hang up.[6]

The attack on the Warren front began on schedule, with L Company of Lieutenant Colonel Miller's 3d Battalion of the 128th attacking on a wide front supported by the Bren gun carriers. I Company followed. In the center, Lieutenant Colonel McCoy's 1st Battalion of the 128th, with A Company leading, attacked the Japanese positions at the eastern end of the new strip. The 1st Battalion of the 126th, on the extreme left, moved out against the bridge between the airstrips. The Australian Independent Company, placed between the center and left, was basically in a holding position.

As many predicted, the Bren gun carriers had a difficult time traversing the stump-filled ground, and L Company encountered a barricade near the coast. The Japanese, using machine guns, grenades, and sticky bombs, soon destroyed all the Bren gun carriers. After two hours, L Company had advanced only 400 yards. Meanwhile, after initial forward momentum, the attack in the center was also stopped by Japanese fire and the extreme heat. B Company managed to reach the eastern end of the strip before being forced to dig in. On the extreme left, Lieutenant Colonel Carrier's battalion had done little better. After some success with an antitank gun knocking out a number of emplacements, the forward advance was stopped 150 yards from the bridge. Thus, at the end of the day, it was obvious that Eichelberger's first offensive on the Warren front had failed as badly as any of those undertaken while Harding was in command.[7]

This action convinced Eichelberger of two things. One was that the men he had previously maligned would fight. He also concluded that continued direct frontal attacks on the defenses in the Warren zone would fail unless he received reinforcements. He decided to concentrate the offensives in the immediate future against the Japanese in front of the Urbana Force. He accepted General Herring's suggestion that the objectives for Warren Force should be to systematically reduce the defenders' strength by destroying individual pillboxes and machine guns while keeping up the pressure by aggressive patrolling. For the next thirteen days, action along this part of the front amounted to a type of siege warfare, with the line advancing very little but with small-scale infantry operations and mortar and artillery attacks taking a toll on the defenders.[8]

Meanwhile on the Urbana front, Eichelberger, de Graff, Rogers, McCreary, and Tomlinson were at the forward observation post to watch the action. The 2d Battalion of the 126th attacked toward Buna village at 1030, just after the B-25s had finished the bombing. The Cannon Company of the 128th, without its guns, moved to clear the east bank of the Girua River. On the right, E and G Companies engaged the Japanese defenses directly in front of the village. The Cannon Company, as it entered an open space, was met with a hail of gunfire. However, by the next morning it had advanced to the outskirts of the village. To the right of Cannon Company, E Company was able to advance to the main Japanese defense line, fifty yards from the village, before being halted. G Company, led by Lt. Cladie Bailey, was also stopped short of the village.

There then occurred one of the more bizarre episodes of the entire New Guinea campaign. Eichelberger had gone forward with Grose to Bailey's command post. The arrival of a three-star general that far forward surprised Bailey. Even more surprising was Eichelberger taking personal charge, in essence becoming a company commander, a position normally filled by a captain. He believed that he could take the village by sending F Company through the depleted G Company to continue the attack. Colonel Grose protested that he had intended to use F Company on the left and that there was no hurry. However, Eichelberger felt he needed to take Buna village that day. Lieutenant Robert Odell, the nominal company commander, was summoned to the observation post and given ten minutes to get his men ready to take the village. Odell had the impression that Eichelberger believed that the village could be taken by a bayonet charge. The reality proved to be tragically different. The company attack was halted, with four men killed and eighteen wounded of the forty men who had begun the attack.[9]

There is no question of the bravery of the senior officers at this juncture of the campaign, although one might have reservations about corps and division commanders exposing themselves to sniper fire. The danger was clearly shown as Eichelberger and several members of his party decided to follow Odell up the trail. General Waldron had earlier been hit in the shoulder, a wound that, although not life threatening, eventually ended his military career. Even worse for Eichelberger was the wounding of his senior aide, Capt. Daniel Edwards, who was struck in the face by a sniper's bullet. Luck had been with Eichelberger; the sniper had chosen to zero in on Edwards rather than on him. He immediately helped evacuate the wounded from his party to the field hospital in the rear, where he learned of the only genuine success of his first offensive.[10]

A platoon of eighteen men from H Company, led by SSgt. Herman Bottcher, an experienced soldier who had fought in the Spanish Civil War, moved north on the far right. They knocked out several pillboxes, crossed a creek, and finally reached the beach by late afternoon. Bottcher had the men dig in; then he emplaced his light machine gun and waited for the Japanese counterattack. This came quickly from both the village and mission areas. Bottcher, manning the machine gun, and his riflemen beat off a succession of attacks. His breakthrough to what became known as Bottcher's Corner, combined with the earlier advances along the entire west bank of Entrance Creek, effectively cut off the village from the mission area. As soon as Bottcher's action was known to Colonel Smith, a fresh platoon from H Company was sent as reinforcements. For his action, Eichelberger gave Bottcher a battlefield promotion to captain and was later instrumental in him receiving the Distinguished Service Cross.[11]

General Waldron was evacuated to Port Moresby and General Byers succeeded to command of the 32d Division. Tomlinson became commander of Urbana front on 7 December; Grose, as had been promised, took command of the 127th. Tomlinson planned to follow up on Bottcher's success by launching an all-out attack on the seventh. At 0600 the Japanese upset the time schedule for this by attempting to infiltrate Bottcher's position. However, they were discovered by Cpl. Harold Mitchell, who alone charged them. This so surprised the Japanese that they hesitated. The noise of Mitchell's yelling alerted Bottcher's men. When the Japanese resumed their attack, they were cut to pieces by Bottcher's machine gun. Surprisingly, Mitchell was not wounded, and for his quick action he later received the Distinguished Service Cross.

The attack by E and G Companies of the 2d Battalion of the 126th finally began in the early afternoon but generally made no progress. Attacking from Bottcher's Corner, Lieutenant Odell's platoon advanced a few yards before fire from the village halted even this slight advance. During the afternoon the Japanese air force made one of its few large-scale attacks on the Buna area. Bad weather over the mountains grounded Fifth Air Force planes; thus the twenty-one Japanese bombers were not interfered with. The worst results of the raid were the bombs that struck the hospital, causing forty casualties.[12] During the evening, Captain Yasuda attempted to send reinforcements from the mission area to the village by barge. The movement was detected by Bottcher, who sprayed the barge, setting it on fire.

The attack on the village was resumed the afternoon of the following day, with the same dismal results. The effect of artillery and mortars on the Japanese was again minimal. One of the main obstacles was a large bunker located on the southern edge of the village. It was decided to use one of the flamethrowers, which had arrived only the previous day. The action was later described in an official report:

Under covering and diverting fire from the men on the left flank of the box the operator advanced from his position at the end of the shallow trench some seven to eight yards without being fired upon. At that point the initial burst of the flame thrower was released. With that, those who were to rush the box advanced from behind the breastworks. One rifleman was hit immediately and returned to cover. Instead of a 25 yard burst of flame a mere 10 to 15 foot dribble of flame came out of the flame thrower. The operator, bending low, continued to advance, trying time and again to get the machine to function properly, but without success. He was finally hit less than 15 yards from the box and fell to the ground. Lt. Davidson [the chemical officer] was killed outright.[13]

The defenders in the bunker continued to hold up all serious forward movement until the bunker was finally taken late in the afternoon of the following day.

Captain Yasuda made his last attempt to link up with the village defenders when he launched an attack from the mission coordinated with an attack from the village during the evening of the eighth. The heavy weapons of the 2d Battalion cut the attackers to pieces. The following day the attempt to broach the Japanese defenses continued, with only minimal gains, until the bunker was taken. By then the assault companies of the 126th had been reduced to less than 50 percent effectiveness and after numerous direct assaults were able only to maintain their position. There was a pause in the attacks on the village while the 3d Battalion of the recently arrived 127th Regiment replaced the worn-down 126th. This was completed by the eleventh; the following day, probing attacks were begun, which registered a few small gains. The village was hit by a large quantity of artillery and mortar fire in preparation for what was believed to be the final assault on the fourteenth. The Japanese defenders estimated at fewer than a hundred men, sensing the inevitable, slipped away during the night of the thirteenth, filtered through the U.S. positions, and reached Giruwa. Thus, when the assault on the morning of the fourteenth began, there was no opposition. The village fell without a shot. But the defenders had blunted fifteen attacks and cost the 126th heavy casualties.[14]

The Coconut Grove, with its maze of trenches and bunkers, was now all the Japanese held on the left bank of Entrance Creek. Byers informed Colonel Smith just after noon on the fifteenth to prepare for his 2d Battalion of the 128th to attack these positions at once. Smith and his executive officer, Maj. Roy Zinser, had already worked out a plan of attack but were hampered by a lack of men in the direct locality, because his unit was stretched out to defend more than a mile of front. Denied reinforcements, he had only about a hundred men to carry out the attack. The approach was split by a large open space, so he divided his meager force, sending Zinser to the left while he moved to the right with E Company.

The mortar preparation as usual had little effect on the Japanese defenders as they slowed the advance with heavy fire and forced men in both prongs to dig in for the night, where their lives were made more miserable by the heavy rain, which filled their positions with water. The next morning any advance was halted by enemy fire from bunkers. Zinser called upon a flamethrower team to reduce one of them, but the results were the same as the earlier use before the village: It fizzled out.[15] The bunker was finally reduced by rifle fire and grenades, but as the troops moved forward, they encountered an even larger bunker, which dominated the approaches to the grove. Two men from E Company, Corporal Rini and Pvt. Bernardino Estrada, protected in part only by covering fire, crept close to the bunker, and Rini jumped on top of it and fed grenades through the gun slits, killing all the defenders. Ordering an all-out attack, Smith led the way. All the bunkers and trenches were cleared, and the fighting was over by noon. Smith did not halt in the grove but moved his men immediately to attack the Japanese positions in the Triangle. They captured the skeleton of a bridge by which the village trail crossed Entrance Creek, then they moved to establish themselves firmly on the eastern side before being halted. Realizing that they did not have enough force to advance farther, Smith's men dug in and prepared to hold their position.[16] Now only the Triangle remained to be cleared before an attack could be mounted to isolate Buna Mission by advancing to the sea east of Giropa Point.

During this period, Eichelberger was keeping General Headquarters informed of what was occurring. By the sixth he had apparently reversed his opinion of the 32d when he reported that morale was high and the men had performed bravely and had much to be proud of during the action of the previous day. He assured Sutherland that MacArthur could stop worrying about the conduct of the division in battle.

Perhaps sensing that this was not enough to convince a head-quarters still obsessed with the fear of massive Japanese reinforcements, Eichelberger wrote: "Tell the General to be patient, I shall do my best and I trust that that will be no mean effort."[17]

That MacArthur was not convinced by the success of the Australians and Eichelberger's comments that all was going well can be seen in a letter to Eichelberger on 13 December, addressed "Dear Bob":

Time is fleeting and our dangers increase with its passage. However admirable individual acts of courage may be; however important administrative functions may seem; however splendid and electrical your presence has proven, remember that your mission is to take Buna. All other things are merely subsidiary to this. No alchemy is going to produce this for you; it can only be done in battle and sooner or later this battle must be engaged.

Hasten your preparations and when you are ready—strike, for as I have said, time is working desperately against us.[18]

His impatience to take Buna, and the underlying fear of a greater Japanese commitment, intensified during the month despite all indications that the campaign was progressing favorably.

The major limitation to Eichelberger's strategy on the Warren front was the lack of firepower needed to reduce the pillboxes. Commenting on the effectiveness of the 25-pounder and 3.7-inch guns, General Waldron had said earlier that they simply annoyed the Japanese. Even grouping the mortars and moving the 25-pounders closer to the front did little to improve their effectiveness. The artillery weapon that had proved more effective was the 105mm howitzer. However, the gunners had quickly run out of the initial small supply of ammunition. The gun stood idle while more than eight hundred rounds of ammunition rested in a supply dump at Brisbane. Despite the urgent requests of the supply officers at Port Moresby, until mid-December there was not a sufficient number of rounds available to allow the gunners to begin plunging fire against the Japanese defenses.

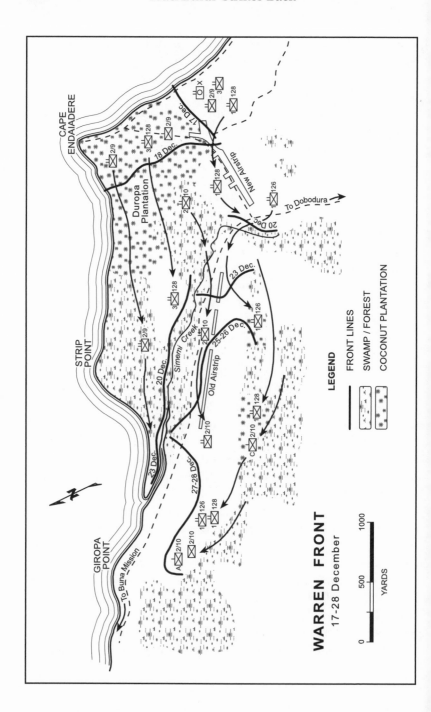

CAPE ENDAIADERE

STRIP POINT

GIROPA POINT

To Buna Mission

Duropa Plantation

New Airstrip

To Dobodura

Simemi Creek

Old Airstrip

17 Dec.

18 Dec.

20 Dec.

23 Dec.

25-26 Dec.

27-28 Dec.

20 Dec.

23 Dec.

2/9

3/128

1/128

2/9

3/128

2/10

1/128

1/126

3/128

1/126

2/9

2/10

2/10

C 2/10

1/128

1/126

1/128

A 2/10

2/10

WARREN FRONT
17-28 December

LEGEND

FRONT LINES

SWAMP / FOREST

COCONUT PLANTATION

0   500   1000
YARDS

More firepower became available with the arrival of the 3,300-ton Dutch ship *Karsik* on 11 December, bringing, in addition to infantry reinforcements, a troop (four) of Stuart M-3 light tanks of the Australian 2/6 Armored Regiment. On the fifteenth, another troop was landed. In addition, despite being attacked by RAAF bombers, the ships unloaded the 2/9 Battalion of the 18th Brigade from Milne Bay on the eleventh and six days later brought in the 2/16. The Australian commander, Brigadier Wootten, who had arrived earlier, was given command of the Warren front; Colonel Martin became his second in command. Thus Eichelberger had a much stronger force by mid-December with which to assail Cape Endai-adere and the government station. He assumed direct command of the 32d Division on the seventeenth, when Byers was wounded and had to be evacuated. If there ever had been a doubt as to who controlled the offensive, that was laid to rest after Eichelberger took over the division in addition to his responsibilities as corps commander.[19]

Eichelberger planned for Warren Force on the eighteenth, now with tanks, to move toward the Duropa Plantation and Cape Endai-adere as well as the new strip. At the same time, Urbana Force was to clear the Triangle and move to the coast, isolating the Japanese at Giropa Point and Buna Mission from one another. On the Warren front, most of the tanks would advance into the plantation area, closely followed by three companies of the 2/9, followed by the 3d Battalion of the 128th. After securing the cape, the troops were to turn toward Simemi Creek and thus be in the rear of the Japanese defenses along the airstrip. Supported by the remainder of the tank force, a company of the 2/9 would then attack the east end of the strip. Except for the tanks, there was nothing new in this plan. It was overly optimistic, considering that the major elements in the plan had already been attempted.

Early on the morning of the eighteenth, the artillery opened up, including the 105mm, which now had ammunition enough to support the attack. Then planes began a ten-minute bombing and strafing attack, the noise of which masked that of the tanks moving up. A and D Companies, following five tanks, advanced north while C Company and two tanks moved northwest toward the eastern end of the strip. Pressure was maintained against the Japanese at the bridge and the western end of the strip.

The Japanese of the 144th and 229th Infantry were taken by surprise by the tank attack. The Stuart tanks, with their 37mm guns firing at close range, systematically destroyed the bunkers, driving the Japanese into the open, where they were finished off by the infantry. Within an hour the Australians had reached the cape, although they had suffered 171 casualties, one-third of their strength, and had lost two tanks.

Changing the axis of the attack on the right, they moved westward toward Strip Point and beyond to Simemi Creek. There they encountered a defense line of bunkers and trenches not previously known, and they were forced to halt. Meanwhile, the 3d Battalion of the 128th had also moved to the west, mopping up a considerable force of Japanese still in the coastal area. The assault by C Company of 2/9 had not gone as well. Although reinforced by the 1st Battalion of the 128th, they could not drive the Japanese from their positions.[20]

Eichelberger ordered a regrouping of his forces on the nineteenth preparatory to resuming the attack the following day. He reported to General Headquarters his satisfaction with the results of the day's operation. Partially to justify what MacArthur believed to be an unnecessary delay in taking Buna, he wrote: "I know General MacArthur will be glad to know that we found concrete pillboxes with steel doors interlocked in such a way that it would have been impossible for infantry unassisted to get across." He concluded that, without the tanks, the attack would not have succeeded.[21]

Before the attack resumed, ships brought in more supplies, larger-caliber mortars, and the rest of the 2/10, which would be sorely needed due to the casualties to and illness of the engaged forces. On the morning of the twentieth, Wootten ordered the 2/9, supported by four tanks, to move west toward Strip Point. Aided by units from the 3d Battalion of the 128th on its left, the Australians were able to move up to Simemi Creek after a full day's action. Continued attacks during the following three days cleared out all Japanese east of the creek with the exception of a few located near the creek's mouth. The 1st Battalion of the 126th, attacking from the west, closed up with units of the 128th and destroyed the bunkers in front of the bridge and cleared out the new strip area. Yamamoto, however, was able to extricate some of his troops, pulling them back across the creek. He also reinforced the small unit holding the little island at the mouth of the creek.

The next problem facing Wootten was how to get across the creek. The most obvious was by means of the 125-foot-long bridge over the creek and adjacent swamp. However, there was a large gap in the bridge caused by an artillery shell, and the Japanese had the approaches well covered. An attempt was made on the twentieth by men of the 1st Battalion of the 128th, but they were driven off by the intense fire. It was imperative to find an alternate crossing. A patrol of the 128th tried to ford the stream north of the bridge but was driven back by the Japanese. A similar attempt south of the bridge also failed. The next day, a patrol of A Company of the newly arrived 2/10, after a difficult patrol where the men had to wade in neck-deep water, discovered a place where the creek could be forded a quarter mile north of the bridge. The rest of the battalion began to cross immediately, and by the end of the afternoon of the twenty-second, most were safely across and in position to attack the east end of the old airstrip. The following day they attacked southward, driving the Japanese from their bunkers. Meanwhile, the engineers, despite heavy enemy fire, had repaired the bridge, enabling the tanks to cross over by the twenty-fourth.

When the Australians resumed the attack on the twenty-fourth, they faced a series of formidable obstacles. Yamamoto had excellent defenses along the old airstrip. His men had dug several trench lines perpendicular to the runway, and these were covered by bunkers with machine guns located to the north and south. In addition to mortars, he had two 75mm and two 37mm guns and several 25mm pom-pom guns to bolster the defenses. North of the strip he had emplaced two 3-inch dual-purpose naval guns.

The Australian attack began early on the morning of the twenty-fourth with two companies of the 2/10 on the right led by two tanks while one company with another tank moved down the runway. At first all went well; then the 3-inch guns pinpointed the tanks, destroying two of them. Counterbattery fire knocked out one naval

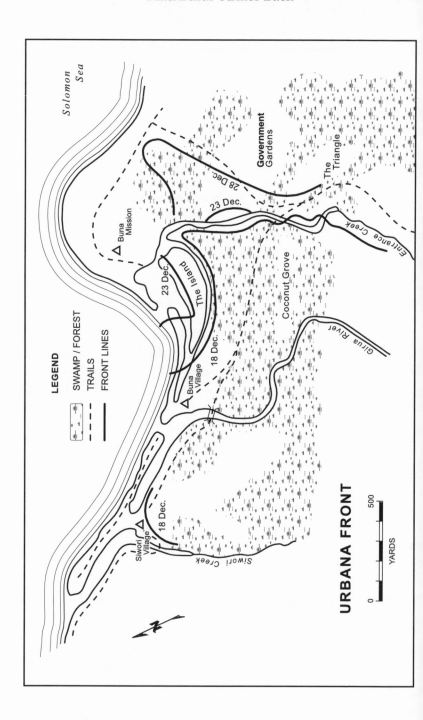

LEGEND

SWAMP / FOREST

TRAILS

FRONT LINES

URBANA FRONT

YARDS

0   500

gun, but the other could not be located. The third tank overturned in a shell hole. Without the tanks, the infantry, subjected to intense artillery and rifle fire, was halted after advancing less than a quarter mile. A series of night attacks gained nothing.[22]

Brigadier Wootten decided against committing any more of his tanks until the enemy guns could be located. Instead he would concentrate on trying to flank the Japanese bunker system while also continuing to attack frontally. On Christmas Day he sent a company of the 2/10 to the far left to try to find a way through the swamp. The men made little progress. Colonel Martin also decided to attempt to find a way through the swamp. He sent fifteen men of A Company, led by Lt. George Hess, to the right. After sloshing through waist-deep mud, by early afternoon they emerged on dry ground in the rear of the Japanese right flank. By evening, C Company had arrived at the position. The next morning, in conjunction with frontal attacks, C Company overran the Japanese defenses, capturing two of the multipurpose guns, whose crews, without regular ammunition, desperately fired blank rounds, then attempted to set them on fire.[23] The Japanese air force sent fifty-four bombers from Rabaul staging through Lae to attack the Allied positions, but they did little damage. In all probability the planes caused more damage to the Japanese defenses. The infrequent Japanese raids almost stopped after this, because they lost fourteen planes to the Fifth Air Force interceptors.

The success on the left flank prompted Wootten to move A Company of 2/10 from the right to support his further attacks. Some of the 25-pounders below the bridge had run out of ammunition, but one by its accurate fire was responsible for cracking the Japanese defenses along the old strip on the twenty-seventh. The battery commander, Maj. W. H. Hall, manning a seventy-foot-high observation post in a banyan tree, had a clear view of the entire area. Using armor-piercing shells at a thousand-yard range, the gunners knocked out one of the 75mm guns in a bunker and later one of the pom-poms. In conjunction with the heavy mortars, the accurate artillery fire forced the Japanese out of many bunkers and into a general retreat. The next day, despite heavy fire from the dispersal bays and from positions at the west end of the strip and the Government Plantation area, the Australians pressed forward. There was scant opposition from the Japanese adjacent to the strip, and mopping up began before noon. As the Japanese tried to escape into the swamp, they were picked off by troops earlier ordered into the swamp by Maj. Gordon Clarkson.

That evening the Japanese began a series of counterattacks, at first on the center of the re-formed Allied line and later on the far right. Early the next morning, one group managed to reach the command post of C Company of the 128th without being detected. Before being driven off, they killed fifteen men and wounded an additional twelve.[24] The major Japanese counterattacks had gained no ground. The old strip was firmly in Allied hands. Warren Force was within striking distance of Giropa Point, the last Japanese stronghold on its front.

While Warren Force was slowly destroying the Japanese defenses east of Giropa Point, Urbana Force was involved in a desperate attempt to secure the mission. With the loss of Buna village, the Japanese were constrained into a small area around the mission, defined by Entrance Creek to the west, the Triangle in the south, and the swampy area north of Government Gardens. The overly optimistic plans of Advance New Guinea Force was for Urbana Force to seize the island located immediately southwest of the mission by 18 December, the same day that the attack was begun on the Warren front, then drive the Japanese from the Triangle the following day. A platoon was sent past Siwori village, three-fourths of a mile to the west, to block any reinforcements from the Giruwa area. The attack on Musita Island would be made by the fresh 127th. The depleted 126th was given the task of taking the Triangle.

Possession of Musita Island was important because it would enable enfilading fire to be directed at the main Japanese positions near the mission, less than five hundred yards away. There was also a footbridge over the creek connected to the mainland. The task of taking the island wasn't easy, because the once accessible bridge from the 127th's area had been destroyed and the creek was too deep to be forded. On the eighteenth, swimmers from L Company pulled a cable across the stream, which allowed two platoons to cross to the island. They met little opposition until they approached the bridge to the mission area and came under heavy fire. Believing that they were outnumbered, they retreated across the creek. The first attack on the island had failed.

The attack on the Triangle, a natural fortress dominating the main trail to the mission, which had been greatly improved by the Japanese, had also been checked. After heavy bombing of the mission area and mortar fire on the Triangle, two companies, E and G of the 126th, started the attack from just below the trail junction at midmorning. Japanese machine-gun and rifle fire halted the advance almost immediately. Shortly after noon a concentration of white phosphorus smoke was fired into the Triangle followed by a second infantry attack. This, too, was stopped. A heavy mortar barrage preceded the third attempt later that afternoon; it did little to blunt the Japanese response. By evening, nothing had been gained, with a cost of forty men killed and wounded.[25]

The 126th, reduced to less than three hundred men, was in no condition to continue the attack on the Triangle and went into reserve. The 127th took over the assault on the twentieth, with the plan for E Company to attack from the Coconut Grove across the two bridges. The men were to advance close up to the white phosphorus rounds, which, along with the heavy mortars, were to soften up the enemy defenses.

Despite this artillery preparation, the Japanese resistance was such that the attack was called off just before noon. A further attack by a reinforced platoon, which attempted to infiltrate the defenses, was caught by enfilading fire and almost wiped out. The attacks were halted early in the afternoon. E Company had sustained 40 percent casualties and retreated back to the Coconut Grove. After a month of continuous action, Colonel Tomlinson was exhausted and asked Eichelberger to replace him as commander of Urbana Force with Colonel Grose, the 127th commander. Eichelberger concurred and Grose took over Urbana Force for the second time.

Eichelberger decided to shift the main focus of the attacks farther to the north. He ordered two companies to contain the Japanese within the Triangle while, on the twenty-second, Companies I and K moved across the creek into the northwest part of Government Gardens. In I Company's area a footbridge had been constructed; in K Company's area the creek was much wider and there was no bridge. Grose attempted to explain to Eichelberger that it would be more profitable to move K Company to the bridge, then move north after crossing. Eichelberger vetoed the suggestion that the attack be postponed and ordered it to proceed as planned. Numerous evening attempts to get a rope across the creek by K Company swimmers were met with concerted Japanese fire. Finally one man got across and secured the rope. By early morning, seventy-five men had crossed. The frontal attack had cost eight killed and forty wounded. Meanwhile, I Company had moved over the bridge without losing a man. Eichelberger now had a strong bridgehead in Government Gardens on the east side of the creek.[26]

Farther north on 22 December two companies crossed the bridge to Musita Island and encountered only slight resistance from the Japanese. The island was fully occupied by midday. A 37mm gun was brought across and, in conjunction with another located on a spit of land east of the village, began a continuous harassing fire on the mission area. Eichelberger, however, instead of attempting a crossing directly from the island to the heavily defended mission area, decided to eliminate the Japanese in the Gardens area. This abandoned area was overgrown with kunai grass, which led to a swamp, on either side of which was a coconut plantation. The attackers had only a half mile to go before reaching the sea, but Yasuda had every foot of ground covered. Along the coastal trail, which connected the mission to Giropa Point, were many bunkers, and there were others along the coast. The Japanese were well hidden in the kunai grass and in trees in the swampy area.

Colonel Grose had five companies, with two in the direct attack from the bridgehead eastward into the kunai grass. After an artillery preparation, the troops moved forward on a four-hundred-yard front early on the morning of the twenty-fourth. Soon, I Company was halted after clearing out a few bunkers. Every attempt to move forward was thwarted. Three hours later, Grose replaced I Company with G Company. It had some initial success in clearing out three bunkers and establishing a position astride the trail before it, too, was halted. L Company on the left, although provided with heavy machine-gun and mortar support, had even less success at first. Grose ordered a platoon of A Company to attack the mainland from the island across the north bridge. This diversion was a tactical success, although eight of the platoon were killed as Yasuda weakened his position in order to counter the attack. A platoon from L Company charged ahead and broke through the Japanese front as far as the Coconut Grove; there it encountered two bunkers, which blocked further advance. Sergeant Kenneth Gruennert, covered by fire from the platoon, crawled forward and destroyed the first bunker. Although wounded, he pressed on. Throwing his grenades, he forced the Japanese from the second bunker before being killed by a sniper. For his actions he was posthumously awarded the Medal of Honor.

However, the platoon was isolated. Colonel Grose did not learn of the breakthrough until noon, when he ordered K Company to advance to the platoon's position. Yasuda had meanwhile plugged the hole in his defenses and halted all forward movement. The remnants of the audacious platoon made their way back to their own lines two days later. Eichelberger related to MacArthur, in a letter written on Christmas Day, that the failure of the offensive was "the all time low of my life."[27]

On the twenty-fifth, MacArthur's headquarters released a brief communiqué to the press relative to the fighting in Papua. It read: "On Christmas Day our activities were limited to routine safety precautions. Divine services were held." Eichelberger much later remarked on how off the mark this was. There was desperate fighting and "the outcome of the whole miserable tortured campaign was in doubt."[28] In retrospect Eichelberger's statement was an exaggeration. The campaign was not in doubt at that time, but Eichelberger believed that unless the mission was soon taken, he would be replaced. It appeared that the end of the "miserable" campaign could not be predicted in spite of all that could be hurled at the Japanese in their bunkers and trenches. The attack on Christmas Day seemed to confirm his pessimism. A ruse was tried, with the troops making a great show that the major attack would be from the island across the north bridge. Instead, A and F Companies attacked directly

across the Gardens. F Company did break through, and after suffering heavy casualties, A Company joined them later. However, the
defensive perimeter they established at the edge of the Coconut
Grove was still two hundred yards from the sea and six hundred
yards from the mission. An attack on the Triangle later that afternoon also was halted with no appreciable gain. The bunkers there
were too well defended.

Colonel Grose decided to make the attack on the twenty-sixth in
the direction of the two companies tied down near the coast.
Frontal attacks by two companies in the central area destroyed a
number of bunkers, but C Company, the one charged with breaking through to the coast, was generally contained by the Japanese.
However, a platoon did manage to reach the beleaguered troops.
The position was reorganized, the dead were buried, the wounded
were given medical attention, and communications were established to the main area to the rear. On the twenty-seventh Grose
put Col. J. S. Bradley, chief of staff of the division, in command of
the continued attempt, with two companies to open a corridor to
the coast. By evening small numbers of reinforcements had
reached the perimeter. Eichelberger was informed of the situation
that evening and called a conference of senior officers. The report
had stated that the companies had suffered heavy casualties and
the troops, suffering from battle shock, could not advance. His advisers believed the situation to be desperate. However, when he
went forward to the Urbana command post, he found that the situation, although bad, was far from desperate.[29] That morning,
Companies C and G moved through to relieve the battered F and
B Companies and thus opened up a broad corridor from Entrance
Creek to the Coconut Grove.

Establishment of the corridor presented Yasuda with a major
problem. The defensive positions in the Triangle were still intact.
However, with the loss of control of the Gardens, those positions
had been flanked and his men in the Triangle were likely to be cut
off and annihilated. Yasuda ordered the immediate evacuation of
that heretofore nearly impregnable position. A patrol from E Company moved cautiously into the Triangle that evening and discovered that the fourteen bunkers and trench lines had been hurriedly

abandoned. Colonel Grose's forces were well established in the Coconut Grove and controlled the trail junction near the coast; in addition, the Japanese in the mission area were separated from those at Giropa Point. It was now only a matter of time before Buna Mission would also fall.

Chapter XIII

Final Offensives

The concluding phase of the Allied offensive was divided into three separate campaigns. The first was along the Warren front, where Brigadier Wootten, with a preponderance of Australian troops, confronted the Japanese defenses between Giropa Point and Simemi Creek. Farther to the west, three U.S. regiments making up Urbana Force were bogged down south of Buna Mission. Finally there was the stalemated Sanananda front, where the Australians, augmented by a few Americans, had established roadblocks along the main trail, the most important of which was the Huggins block. For weeks, activity in this area was generally confined to patrolling and defending the roadblocks as Generals Herring and Eichelberger gave primacy in their planning to capturing Buna Mission.

The supply situation, which had earlier been a nightmare, was largely solved. Six small freighters were now making regular trips to Oro Bay. In the two weeks after 12 December, they had brought in 4,000 tons of cargo, almost twice the amount that the Fifth Air Force was able to deliver to the 32d Division during the entire period of its involvement.[1] They also brought welcomed reinforcements for Brigadier Wootten. On the twenty-eighth, Lt. Col. A. S. Arnold arrived with his 600-man 2/12 from Goodenough Island. With the arrival of the 2/12, Eichelberger had more than 4,000 men available on the Warren front. By 31 December, the 2/12 had relieved the exhausted 2/10 on line and would take over much of the burden of offense against Giropa Point. The most important additions to the troops in that area were the Stuart light tanks. Seven more of these tanks had arrived with the 2/12, giving Wootten ten serviceable tanks. He now had his mobile artillery. The 37mm guns firing at point-blank range could reduce the bunkers, something that the inadequate artillery and mortars could not accomplish.[2]

Wootten used the morning of the twenty-ninth for regrouping his forces for an attack northeast toward the coast in the afternoon. It was planned for a company of the 2/10 to be preceded by six tanks. These were late in arriving; when they eventually came up, they charged ahead, outrunning the infantry. This mix-up allowed the Japanese to hold their positions and eventually throw the Australians back to the edge of the Coconut Grove. After this failure, Wootten realigned his units. The 2/12 replaced the 2/10, and the 3d Battalion of the 128th replaced the 126th troops on the line.

The movement of the new units was not complete until the evening of the thirty-first, in time for a new attack on New Year's Day. The plan was for an artillery and mortar preparation prior to a two-phase assault. The 2/12, accompanied by six tanks, would strike northeast toward the coast, then turn southeast, completing the encirclement of the Japanese strong points west of Simemi Creek. Then, in conjunction with the 2/10 and the 3d Battalion of the 128th, they would destroy those positions.

The attack began early in the morning, with the 2/12 moving northward as planned while three companies of the 128th attacked the fortifications in the dispersal bay area. The 2/10 was in a blocking position at the end of the old strip. Within half an hour the tanks and infantry of the 2/12 had overrun the Japanese defenses in Giropa Point, then reached the coast and turned eastward along it. By evening, despite desperate Japanese opposition, they had cleared the beach as far as Simemi Creek.

The intense fighting can be measured by the casualty figures. The 2/12 had suffered 62 killed and 128 wounded. Meanwhile, troops of the 128th had slow going against the entrenched Japanese in the dispersal bay area. The end for the Japanese on the Warren front came the next morning as the 3d Battalion of the 128th with six tanks cleared the dispersal bays and the Australians destroyed the last pockets of resistance in the areas overrun the previous day.

Later that day Wootten ordered the 2/12 and the 128th's 3d Battalion to begin to move westward toward Buna Mission on 3 January. These orders were canceled when contact was made with Urbana Force and it was learned that the attack on the mission was already unfolding.[3]

Eichelberger's attitude after the events of the twenty-fifth convinced MacArthur, ever pessimistic, that the Allied situation in Papua was in a bad way. His feelings can be seen in his meeting with Herring, who visited him at Port Moresby on Christmas Day. MacArthur greeted him by saying, "Well we're not getting on very fast are we? . . . If we do not clear this position quickly I will be finished and so will your General Blamey, and what will happen to you, young man, I just don't like to think."[4]

There is no way of ascertaining the seriousness of MacArthur's fears of being relieved, but he was concerned enough to send Sutherland to visit Eichelberger's command post. Earlier, Eichelberger had sent MacArthur a captured ceremonial sword, and Sutherland brought with him a message of thanks and a letter from the commander in chief containing gratuitous advice that also showed how far removed MacArthur was from the reality of the fighting at Buna. He wrote:

> Where you have a company on your firing line, you should have a battalion; and where you have a battalion, you should have a regiment. And your attacks, instead of being made by two or three hundred rifles, should be made by two or three thousand . . . I beg of you to throw every ounce of energy you have into carrying out this word of advice from me, as I feel convinced that our time is strictly limited and that if results are not achieved shortly, the whole picture may radically change.[5]

On the twenty-eighth, Eichelberger took Sutherland and Colonels Bowen, Rogers, and Harding from Buna Force headquarters forward to Grose's command post. The units of Urbana Force were then cleaning up isolated Japanese resistance in the newly won corridor. Grose had just pulled the 3d Battalion of the 127th out of the line for a much needed rest. However, Eichelberger, perhaps to impress Sutherland by taking the mission, ordered Grose to attack with the 3d Battalion immediately. Startled by the order, Grose nevertheless hurriedly moved to organize a plan. What he decided on was a two-phase attack from the island. The first phase involved using five Australian assault boats, which had just arrived, to cross to the mainland. The other was for some men to attack directly across the damaged north bridge.

After artillery preparation, six volunteers carried heavy planks across to the far side of the bridge to repair the damage done earlier by an artillery shell. Despite Japanese fire, the men managed to lay down the planks. Meanwhile, the boats pushed off and tried to land on the spit opposite the island. They were fired on not only by the Japanese but also by troops of E Company who mistook them for Japanese. The boats were sunk. Fortunately there were no casualties, but this part of the plan had failed.

The proposed attack across the bridge also was a failure. As soon as the planks had been put in position, men of K Company, despite heavy fire from the mainland, began to cross. As the first two men reached the repaired section, the planks fell into the creek. The two men fell in also, then spent the next twenty-four hours hiding in neck-deep water until they could be rescued. Eichelberger's hasty order had resulted in a fiasco and certainly would not impress Sutherland.[6]

Despite this setback, the noose was tightened further on the 29th as B Company of the 127th moved two hundred yards up the coast, and just before midnight a patrol of H Company found a shallow area in the creek. They waded across from the village sand spit to the one projecting from the mission area. Based on this, a new plan was drawn up for the thirty-first. This called for E Company to cross over, taking the route discovered by the patrol. Once across they were to turn inland. Meanwhile, Major Shroeder's I Company along the coast would attack westward while the men in the Triangle would continue to root out the remaining Japanese and complete the conquest of the Gardens area. The Japanese discovered the move across the creek, and their heavy fire panicked the men of E Company, who began to withdraw in disorder. However, F Company moved up and, with the aid of a reassured E Company, after a day-long fight established a bridgehead and began attacking northward against a line of bunkers close to the mission. The action in the Gardens area was a success, and patrols from Urbana Force made contact with those of Warren Force, moving west along the coast.[7]

On the basis of the continued fanatical resistance of the Japanese, there was no reason to suspect that the Japanese High Command had decided to give up Buna. However, they had. A number of reasons dictated the Japanese decision. From a tactical viewpoint, the Japanese garrison had done all that could be expected. It was impossible for General Imamura, the army commander at Rabaul, to reinforce or supply the defenders unless he was prepared to divert support from Guadalcanal. This he refused to do. The Eighteenth Army there was in an increasingly desperate condition, and General Hyakutake on Guadalcanal daily bombarded Rabaul with pleas for more aid. Imamura believed he had a divine order to do everything possible for the troops on Guadalcanal. Before leaving Tokyo to take up his command in New Britain, he had met with the emperor at the Imperial Palace. As he was leaving, Hirohito had said, "Imamura, I understand that my soldiers are suffering terribly on Guadalcanal. Go as soon as you can to save them. Even one day is important."[8]

With the primacy of Guadalcanal and the worsening situation at Buna, Imamura and Adachi on 26 December decided to reverse the situation on a bold last attempt. Yamagata was ordered to move all available troops to Giruwa by sea preparatory to reinforcing Buna. If the garrison could not be relieved, the troops should be prepared to hold Giruwa. On the twenty-eighth the orders were modified, and Colonel Yazawa was ordered to build up a special force to move along the beach, break through to the mission, reorganize those who were there, and withdraw to Giruwa. Yamagata had already ordered 430 men to proceed by barge to Giruwa; he arrived two days later. Yazawa was to begin his rescue mission as soon as enough men could be concentrated there to make the attack feasible. This desperate plan was never put into effect, however, because of the imminent fall of the mission.[9]

On New Year's Day, Grose planned what he believed would be the final attack on the mission enclave. Early in the morning following a heavy mortar barrage, B Company moved eastward while E Company attacked from the bridgehead at the spit. Major Shroeder's men struck from the southeast. The Japanese defenses held on all fronts, denying the capture of Buna that day.

However, there were signs that Japanese morale was cracking. That afternoon, troops to the east spotted several Japanese attempting to swim away from the mission. On the morning of 2 January, a large party of well-armed Japanese attempted to reach landing barges on the spit but were machine-gunned by troops of E Company. Later that morning, many more Japanese were detected in the water either swimming or clinging to rafts or logs, and mortar and machine-gun fire was directed at them. Then at 1000, the air force arrived and began systematically strafing those trying to escape. At the same time, the troops from the spit attacked southeast while the two companies in the swamp moved north and two others advanced through the Coconut Grove. The artillery firing white phosphorus shells set fire to the huts within the mission, driving the Japanese into the open. The envelopment was completed after engineers repaired the north bridge, allowing H Company to cross. By 1630, the mission had been overrun. The few remaining Japanese were searched out and destroyed later that day or the next morning. Japanese resistance eastward toward Giropa Point was ended by a two-company attack. By noon on the third, 150 Japanese dead were counted in the mission area; eventually 190 would be buried there and an additional 300 at Giropa Point. It was learned later that both Yamamoto and Yasuda had committed suicide.[10]

Eichelberger had given MacArthur his victory at Buna a month after he had removed Harding and optimistically assumed direct control of the operation. The cost had been high, with 620 men killed, 2,065 wounded, 132 missing, and a high percentage of the troops suffering from one or more tropical diseases. At the conclusion of the Buna campaign, 2,900 men from the 32d Division were still hospitalized.[11]

Congratulations on the capture of Buna were tendered by Blamey. Herring and even George Marshall sent a note of appreciation to MacArthur. However, Eichelberger had to wait six days before receiving a message from MacArthur, on the eve of his return to General Headquarters at Brisbane. The note mainly discussed plans for the 32d Division and what MacArthur wanted Eichelberger to do once he returned to Australia. It closed with the short, personal comment: "I am so glad that you were not injured in the fighting. I always feared that your incessant exposure might result fatally. With a hearty slap on the back."[12]

In accordance with his instructions, Colonel Yazawa had left Giruwa on his rescue attempt on 2 January. Shortly afterward he learned that the mission had been captured. He then decided to try to rescue as many survivors as possible. This meant that he had to regain control of the spit off Tarakena village on which a patrol of twenty-two men of the 127th, commanded by Lt. Louis Chagnon, had established a perimeter. Late in the evening, Yazawa attacked and, after a brief flurry of fighting, forced Chagnon's men out of their positions into the water, where they had to swim to safety. Ultimately, Yazawa rescued 190 survivors of Buna. Nevertheless, his position was not secure, because Grose on the fifth sent G and F Companies of the 1st Battalion across the swollen Siwori Creek to begin an advance westward to Tarakena. The Japanese made a number of brief stands before retreating toward the village. By the evening of the seventh, G Company had reached the outskirts of Tarakena. C and A Companies, having relieved the assault companies, stormed into the village the next morning. By evening, the village had been secured, with minimal losses.

Continuing westward, the 127th was to cross Konombi Creek, a wide tidal stream. All attempts on the ninth to cross using a damaged bridge were driven back by Yazawa's troops. Early the next day, Grose sent a few men in his two available boats across the creek. Despite continual Japanese fire, volunteers managed to swim back across to secure a cable to guide the boats. By evening, both assault companies were across and had secured a firm bridgehead. However, no trail leading from the coast to the interior was found. The next few days were given over to patrolling in an attempt to find a way through the swamp. Eichelberger replaced Grose, who returned to headquarters, with Col. Merle Howe, previously the 32d Division G-3. Eichelberger ordered Howe to resume the attack westward in conjunction with the proposed attack at Sanananda.

After surveying the situation, Howe reported to Eichelberger:

> This damn swamp up here consists of big mangrove trees, not
> small ones like they have in Australia, but great big ones. Their
> knees stick up in the air . . . as much as six or eight feet above
> the ground, and where a big tree grows it is right on top of a
> clay knoll. A man or possibly two men can . . . dig in a little bit,
> but in no place do they have an adequate dug-in position. The
> rest of this area is swamp that stinks like hell. You step into it
> and go up to your knees. That's the whole damn area, except
> for the narrow strip on the beach. I waded over the whole
> thing myself to make sure I saw it all. . . . There is no place
> along that beach that would not be under water when the tide
> comes in. . . .[13]

In order to carry out the attack, Eichelberger released the entire
regiment to Howe.

Public relations officers on MacArthur's staff on 8 January released a communiqué calling the last phase of the Papuan campaign a mopping-up operation. This was but another example of
overoptimism on the part of the rear echelon, who still seemed to
have no real knowledge of the situation at the front. Eichelberger
was named commander of Advance New Guinea Force on 13 January, when Herring moved to Port Moresby after MacArthur and
Blamey returned to Brisbane.

Neither Eichelberger nor Vasey was under any such illusions concerning Sanananda. The campaign to drive the Japanese from their
strongly held positions along the trail, and at Sanananda and
Giruwa, would be long, frustrating, and bloody. The main effort on
that front had been north along the trail before the worn Australian
and American units had been halted. The major success before the
stalemate had been the establishment of roadblock Huggins. Later,
on 20 December, the 2/7 Australian Cavalry had seized another
block three hundred yards northeast of Huggins. The 49th Battalion then fought its way into Huggins and established a firm supply
route to the southeast.

On 22 December, Brigadier Dougherty, with 21st Brigade Head-quarters, took over command of the 49th Battalion, the 2/7, and the U.S. troops at Huggins. He moved his command post to Huggins. Brigadier Porter was left to command two battalions of the 20th Brigade whose task was to mop up the remaining pockets in the trail junction area. The 126th Infantry troops, after twenty-two days at Huggins, were finally relieved by the 39th Battalion. Porter's forces, attacking west of the trail, found clearing the Japanese a difficult and costly venture, because the defenses were at least three-quarters of a mile in depth. Their counterattacks continued to thwart any definite breakthrough. The same situation prevailed farther north in Dougherty's area. The front there was also stale-mated. Exhaustion and disease cut down the effectiveness of any planned operation. The American presence, which had been 635 men when Major Boerem took command from Baetcke, had by New Year's Day dwindled to only 244 men. American casualties west of the Giruwa during that period were 73 killed, 234 wounded, 84 missing, and 588 sick and evacuated. Yet they could not be relieved, because many of the Australian units were also in bad shape and Porter did not have any replacements. By late December the battalions of both the 30th and 21st Brigades were down to only company strength. It was obvious that reinforcements and relief were necessary if Sanananda was to be captured.[14]

General Herring had requested that the 163d Regiment of the 41st Division, which had arrived at Port Moresby on 27 December, be sent immediately to Sanananda. Blamey agreed. Herring, after meeting with MacArthur, was assured that he had no objection to this arrangement. Eichelberger, whose forces were closing in on the mission, had also requested Col. Jens Doe's regiment. On the day that the regiment arrived in New Guinea, MacArthur changed his mind and decided to send it to Eichelberger's front, and he so informed Blamey. This vacillation brought a vigorous reaction from Blamey. After pointing out that sufficient men were available for the final offensive at Buna, he made it clear that the 21st Brigade had to be relieved. Its active strength was such that it could no longer function adequately. He reminded MacArthur that Herring had been promised the 162d and had made plans accordingly. He then lectured MacArthur:

> I do not for one moment question the right of the Commander-in-Chief to give such orders as he may think fit, but I believe that nothing is more contrary to sound principles of command that the Commander-in-Chief or the Commander, Allied Land Forces, should take over the personal direction of a portion of the battle. This can only result in disturbing the confidence of the inferior commanders.[15]

The following day, MacArthur replied and stated the reasons for his change of mind. He considered the Buna-Giropa site as the most important and believed that, once it was cleared, "the Sanananda sector would present no difficulties and can rapidly be rolled up." He noted that it would take time to transport the regiment, and if the Buna area were cleared, the 163d would be employed at Sanananda. In reply to Blamey's testy comments about interference, MacArthur disclaimed any attempt to interfere with the tactical arrangements, claiming that his action dealt only with strategy and was only advice.[16] His verbal advice was, however, taken for what it was—a decision on how to insert a new unit into the campaign. This exchange between the two senior commanders once again showed how confused the nature of command in Papua was. Only much later would it be clarified. The exchanges would be illustrative only of this tension, because the capture of Buna Mission on 2 January, rendered the arguments moot. The 163d was actually to be moved to Sanananda.

On 4 January, Herring conferred with Eichelberger, Vasey, Berryman, and Wootten at his headquarters to work out the general details for the reduction of Sanananda. Despite a lack of specific information as to the numbers of Japanese in the various locations, they devised a three-phase plan. Urbana Force, now primarily the 127th Regiment, would move westward toward Giruwa and if possible delude the Japanese into believing that this was the main effort. That, however, would fall to the newly arrived Australian 18th Brigade and the U.S. 163d Regiment. They would clear the area between the Huggins (renamed Musket) and Kano (renamed Fisk) blocks and establish control over a portion of the Killerton trail. The 18th Brigade would continue the efforts to clear the Japanese from south of Musket.

On 5 January, advance elements of the 18th Brigade with four tanks reached Soputa. Further reinforcements of artillery and tanks were held up on the east side of the river, because the rains had caused heavy flooding. The rains also briefly disrupted air supply; the airfields at Popondetta and Dobodura were unusable.

Despite the problem caused by the rains, all infantry units to be used in the campaign were present by the seventh, and in the following days there was a general realignment. The 39th and 49th Battalions were placed in reserve, and the 126th, now with fewer than two hundred men, was finally relieved. The 1st Battalion took over responsibility for the roadblocks, with two companies at Musket and two at Fisk.[17] By then, Musket, located on dry jungle-covered ground four feet above the swamps, had been well developed. Foxholes had been dug for an entire squad and were arranged in a square or circular pattern. Positions were about fifteen yards apart. There were two sections within the perimeter. The outer wing consisted of rifles and automatic weapons; the inner ring contained higher headquarters, the switchboard, 81mm mortars, ammunition dumps, and the aid station. Between the rings were small supply dumps, the kitchen, and lower headquarters. Slit trenches were everywhere, and the area was densely crowded, especially when troops were in transit to other points. It had become basically a command area. Trouble with Japanese snipers had been taken care of by establishing antisniper units in forward trenches or in the trees.[18] Fisk, although not as elaborate, had also been improved defensibly, as had another defense position located four hundred yards to the east of Musket to cover the supply route.

The Japanese between Musket and Fisk had two very strong positions. One, the largest and best defended, was located two hundred yards north of Musket on either side of the trail; another was just south of Fisk on dry ground. These defenses were groups of bunkers about five yards apart in circular or oval patterns. Automatic weapons were arranged to fire from six to eight inches above the ground and along fire lines so carefully constructed that little disturbance of the jungle was apparent. The position could be approached directly only by road or through the swamp.

On 8 January, B Company, moving west and north from Musket, attacked the strongest position while C Company attacked the smaller one closer to Fisk. Each of the attacks failed as the Japanese laid down a heavy volume of fire, forcing a retreat back to the safety of the roadblocks. The probing attacks continued north of Musket, and on the tenth a patrol discovered that the Japanese, for inexplicable reasons, had abandoned the smaller roadblock near Fisk, leaving behind considerable equipment. There was also evidence that the Japanese there, desperate with hunger, had resorted to cannibalism. The day before, the 2d Battalion had moved southwest of Musket against slight Japanese resistance and set up a new block, code named Rankin, on the Killerton trail. The Japanese at their main defenses at the junction were thus cut off from easy escape.[19]

The next phase of the attack, as planned by Vasey, was to clear the trail junction. This began on 12 January, with the 2/9 Battalion attacking on the right and the 2/12 on the left. The 2/9 would attempt to circle the Japanese left flank and attack its rear. The main effort would be that of the 2/12 and a portion of 2/10 accompanied by three tanks. Troops from Musket would support the Australian attack to the south.

However well conceived, the plan failed because the Japanese commander, Colonel Tsukamoto, had been hoarding some 3-inch antitank shells, enabling his artillery firing at point-blank range to knock out the tanks. The infantry, without the tanks, continued on, destroying a large number of Japanese and wrecking a few fixed positions before being halted. The 2/9 on the left had made only a few gains. The attack on both flanks had not seriously dented the Japanese defenses.

Eichelberger visited Vasey's headquarters the following day to discuss the impasse. He suggested that the Japanese be totally surrounded and their position be subjected to attrition. Such a siege would not be necessary. Without supplies and almost completely surrounded, Colonel Tsukamoto decided to abandon his strong trail junction defenses. The Australians, keeping pressure on the Japanese, discovered on the fourteenth that there were few Japanese left behind. Vasey then ordered an all-out attack by troops of the 18th Brigade from the south and those of the 163d moving down from Musket in order to block the Japanese escape routes. By the end of the day, the area had been swept clean of Japanese after killing more than 150. However, many of Tsukamoto's troops escaped to the north and west. With the trail junction defenses captured, the way was cleared for the final assault on Sanananda.[20]

The worsening condition of the Japanese can be seen in the many diaries kept by common soldiers and recovered after the fighting. One particular diary, kept by Pvt. Kiyoshi Wadu, who perished at Giruwa, is especially important in tracing the growing pessimism and despair. On 28 December he wrote: "Received about 8 Shaku [five ounces] of rice. Due to lack of rain the well dried up so I went to get water from the stream. On the way the jungle was full of the dead. The planes that fly overhead are enemy planes and the guns that roar continuously by day and night are enemy guns." On 7 January he noted: "We live on borrowed time, but it is a wonder that I can go on living without eating. Our planes do not come over."

By the fourteenth he believed that the patients in the hospital would be evacuated and he hoped he would also. His last entry was made four days later: "Heavy rain is falling tonight. Reinforcements have not come. There are no provisions. Things are happening just as the enemy says. It is a difficult situation. . . ."[21]

The diary of another soldier recorded the same observations but also echoed the determination to resist: "We can't eat today. Mess gear is gone because of the terrific mortar fire. . . . Everyone is depressed. Nothing we can do. . . . It is only fate that I am alive today. This may be the place I shall find my death. I will fight to the last. . . ."[22]

General Oda, commanding the troops at Giruwa, was more pessimistic than the common soldier. Communicating to his superior at Rabaul on the twelfth, he urged that reinforcements be sent to the Gona area at once or the Japanese would lose their foothold in eastern New Guinea. He reported on the condition of his troops:

Most of the men are stricken with dysentery. Those not . . . in bed with illness are without food and too weak for hand-to-hand fighting. . . . Starvation is taking many lives, and it is weakening our already extended lines. We are doomed. In several days, we are bound to meet the same fate that overtook Basabua and Buna.[23]

Japanese Imperial Headquarters had already made two bitter decisions. They recognized that the situations on Guadalcanal and in Papua were desperate and it did not appear that they could be reversed. Therefore, on 4 January, orders were issued for the evacuation of what was left of Hyakutake's army on Guadalcanal. General Imamura at Rabaul was also ordered to begin the evacuation of the troops at Sanananda and Giruwa after reinforcements were sent to bolster the defense of Lae.

Imamura left the details of implementing the imperial order to General Adachi. He dispatched a regiment for Lae and Salamaua on the seventh, and the ships managed to get through despite Allied air attacks. Adachi's plan for the evacuation was to load the sick and wounded and as many able-bodied soldiers as possible on board barges or motor launches. The rest would be forced to try to break through the Allied forces in the Gona region to areas in the west still held by the Japanese.

On the thirteenth he gave the order to begin evacuating the sick and wounded. However, he did not understand how desperate Yamagata's and Oda's forces really were, because he set the date for the breakout toward Gona for the twenty-fifth. The situation a week before this scheduled attempt was so bad that Yamagata ultimately would order the attempt to begin on the twentieth.[24]

In planning for a general attack on the sixteenth, General Vasey moved the 39th, 49th, and 18th Brigade troops one and a half miles north of Rankin while positioning the 2/12 at a trail junction one and a half miles east of the plantation. The 2/10 secured Killerton village, located three-quarters of a mile south of the cape. Vasey planned for the 3d Battalion of the 163d to continue to attack the large enclave in the south while the 1st Battalion attacked northward. Farther to the east, the 127th had been mired in the swamp

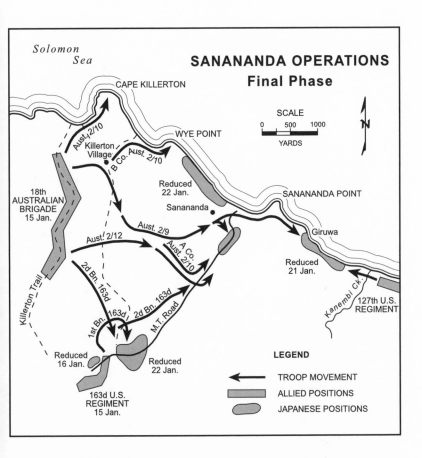

east of Giruwa. However, the new commander, Colonel Howe, who had been given the entire regiment, sent one company to the south to find a way around the swamp while two companies attacked westward along the coastal strip.

On the sixteenth, C and D Companies of the 2/10, moving north, reached the coast without being opposed and turned eastward toward Wye Point. They encountered heavy fire from the Japanese defending a bridge over a creek. Wootten then ordered B Company, which had taken Killerton village, to proceed northeast toward the point. Moving through a swamp, they were met by heavy fire from many bunkers and could not advance farther. A

Company, on the right, had reached the Soputa-Sanananda road one and a half miles north of the main Japanese defense line before being halted. Although temporarily blocked on the sixteenth, they were more successful the following day as the 2/10 captured Cape Killerton and Wye Point. The 2/9 marched eastward toward a big kunai grass strip only a few hundred yards from Sanananda Point. The strip was undefended, and from this vantage point the next morning the battalion moved through a swamp and by afternoon had captured Sanananda village. The 2/12 had also advanced eastward and by the evening of the seventeenth had reached the Soputa-Sanananda road. Turning north, its units met those of the 2/9. By evening the beach, except for a 1,500-yard strip between Wye Point and Sanananda, was controlled by the Australians.

Three companies of the 163d attacked directly the western side of the road beyond Fisk. That was halted by the Japanese, but another company moved around the Japanese right flank and established a new position west of the road. Early in the afternoon the last enemy resistance between Musket and Fisk was overcome. Meanwhile, the 2d Battalion had moved southward along the trail, then northeast, where it made contact with the 2/12. By the end of the day, both the 1st and 2d Battalions of the 163d were north of the main Japanese defense line. Lieutenant Colonel Doe and his battalion were now in a position to wipe out the enemy enclave straddling the road.[25]

In another example of Allied rivalry, Vasey believed that the progress of the 163d was too slow and visited Doe at Musket to urge him on. The attacks on the enclave by three companies on the seventeenth were halted, which brought forth a complaint from Vasey to Herring about what he considered lack of aggressiveness by the Americans. Eichelberger, at his new command post at Somboga, received the complaint forwarded to him by Herring. He decided to see the situation firsthand and, accompanied by Vasey and some staff officers, went forward to Fisk. He and Vasey crawled down to Doe's command post. Eichelberger recalled:

It had a roof of sorts and revetments to protect it. I said, "Where are the Japs?" Doe answered, "Right over there, see that bunker?" I saw it and Vasey saw it, and it was only 50 yards away. Doe was in the front line and so were we. He gave us some hot tea and went on with the attack. Vasey was satisfied with Doe's determination, and so was I.[26]

Although blocked temporarily on the seventeenth, the 163d had destroyed an estimated 250 Japanese and had the survivors surrounded. Farther to the east, where the 127th was operating, the swamps made it difficult for any major breakthrough. Nevertheless, on the eighteenth, Howe's men advanced three hundred yards against weakening opposition.

A factor in the campaign against Sanananda not usually encountered was the presence of so many unburied dead. The swampy area and high water table made it impossible for the Japanese, even if they could have spared the time and manpower, to bury their dead. Lieutenant Colonel A. S. Arnold, commanding the 2/12, wrote of the conditions in the area south of Sanananda:

> The whole area, swamps and rivers included, are covered with enemy dead . . . the stench from which is overpowering. It is definitely the filthiest area I have ever set eyes upon. In a great many cases the Japanese bodies are fly-blown, and others reduced almost to skeletons.[27]

Although it was apparent that the campaign was in its last stages, the fanatical Japanese defense of the strong points continued. Elements of the 2/9 and 2/10 west of Giruwa were briefly halted on the nineteenth. However, men of A Company of the 2/10, moving through shoulder-deep water, charged one of the salient points. Colonel Arnold wrote of these events:

> The enemy resistance collapsed and the company advanced 500 yards killing 150 Japs many of whom were hiding in huts and captured three large dumps of medical and other stores. As in many other cases enemy wounded engaged our troops and had to be shot. This may give rise in the future to Jap propaganda but they are doing it so consistently that our troops cannot take chances.[28]

The 2/12, attacking northward also through a swamp in conjunction with 2/9 units moving south, reduced a well-defended roadblock south of Sanananda before moving to the coast. All that was left in this area south of Sanananda was mopping up scattered Japanese units.

By the twenty-first, except for the strong roadblock in the area of operations of the 163d, the entire Soputa-Sanananda road was controlled by the Allies. The reduction of what had been the main Japanese line of defense took time. Pounded by mortar and artillery fire, the Japanese nevertheless used their bunkers, trenches, and natural features to thwart attacks from every direction on the nineteenth and twentieth.

However, the final attack, on the morning of the twenty-first, found the Japanese defenses faltering. Heavy mortar and artillery fire on the last defense line pinned down the Japanese. A and K Companies' attack caught most of the Japanese in their shelters and killed them in droves. Dazed and exhausted, many of the Japanese wandered into the open, only to be shot down. Some of the men who had previously held out so stubbornly panicked and tried to escape up the road, making easy targets for the American riflemen. B and C Companies in the western area surged forward and cleaned out the bunker lines. Moving southward, they enveloped the last Japanese in the perimeter. At day's end, at a cost of one man killed and six wounded, the 163d had destroyed more than five hundred Japanese, their largest single day's loss of men since Gorari.[29]

Elsewhere, the 2/9 and 2/10, in a triple envelopment on the twenty-second, attacked an enemy pocket west of Sanananda. The Australians met surprisingly little resistance from the Japanese, who, after such sustained fighting, seemingly had lost the will to resist. After the position was taken, the Australians counted two hundred bodies. Another factor in the weakening of the Japanese defenses was the knowledge that evacuation of the sick and wounded first, followed by the able bodied, was to begin at Giruwa. In the early evening on the nineteenth, after giving orders to Oda and Yazawa, General Yamagata, accompanied by his staff and 140 sick and wounded, left in two large motor launches. Although bombed, they arrived safely near the mouth of the Kumusi River. After supervising the loading of the wounded and movement of troops seeking to escape westward, Oda said to a soldier, "That's the end of that. I am going to smoke one cigarette at leisure." He did not take much time to enjoy his cigarette, but shot himself almost immediately. His supply officer, Lt. Col. Yoshinobu Tomita, had also committed suicide. Colonel Yazawa, attempting to slip through the Allied lines, ran into an Australian outpost and was killed.[30]

With the Japanese giving up any concerted defense, Giruwa was quickly taken on the twenty-first by units of the 127th who had earlier found some solid ground and pushed on to a junction with the Australians on the east bank of the Giruwa lagoon. A patrol of Company E, exploring the area east of Giruwa after its capture, chanced upon what remained of the Japanese 67th Line of Communications hospital. They took fire from a Japanese patrol before penetrating through the perimeter to the huts. Sick and wounded were scattered throughout the area, and there were many unburied dead. Some of the ambulatory patients were like walking skeletons. Despite their condition, many of the patients fought back; others blew themselves apart with grenades. Taking no chances, the riflemen of E Company soon had ended all resistance in the hospital huts. Twenty Japanese in the hospital were killed and sixty-nine others, perhaps too weak to resist, were taken prisoner.[31]

The last major action along the Sanananda front was in the 163d area, where two companies, I and L, at midmorning of the twenty-second, attacked and eliminated all serious resistance there. Thus the bitter and desperate first phase of the New Guinea campaign came to an end six months to the day after it had begun with the Japanese landings at Buna. The Japanese had first been thwarted in their offensive operations against Port Moresby and Milne Bay, and later their enclaves at Buna, Gona, and Sanananda had been destroyed. Only the broken remnants remained near the mouths of the Kumusi and Mambare Rivers. The victory had been costly, a total of 8,335 major battle casualties. The Australians had lost 2,037 killed and 3,533 wounded; U.S. casualties amounted to 847 killed and 1,918 wounded. These figures reflect only part of the effects of the campaign, because entire battalions were reduced to only company size as a result of disease. It is difficult to know how many

Japanese troops were involved and what their casualties were. Estimates based on Japanese sources place the total number committed at approximately 18,000. Of these, 12,000 were killed, an estimated 3,400 escaped, and 2,000 were evacuated by barge before the main fighting for the enclaves began. In addition, 1,900 men were landed at Milne Bay and 300 were stranded on Goodenough Island.[32]

For all his fears and at times ill-conceived decisions, MacArthur had his victory. For the first time in World War II, the Japanese defending well-fortified, in-depth positions had been totally defeated by Allied forces operating at a distance from their sources of supply and without adequate equipment. Taken with the final evacuation of the Japanese from Guadalcanal on 7 February, the Papuan victory totally reversed the initiative that had been theirs since Pearl Harbor.

Epilogue

The criticism of the handling of the Papuan campaign began soon after the last Japanese outpost had been taken and most of the exhausted Australian and U.S. units were relocated. These mainly concerned the way that higher headquarters had behaved during the long, trying ordeal. Although subdued in their criticism, Australian officers faulted General Blamey for his actions in removing competent commanders without just cause and his ignorance of the conditions along the Kokoda Trail and later at Gona and Sanananda. This latter accusation was also leveled at General Headquarters by many of the U.S. commanders, including Generals Harding, Eichelberger, and Doe, who lamented that those in control at Port Moresby and Brisbane did not understand the nature of the fighting in Papua. MacArthur and most of the senior U.S. staff never visited the front, and those who did, such as Sutherland, did not venture beyond Dobodura. It was a considered opinion of many Australian commanders that the Japanese enclaves after 20 December could simply have been sealed up and the defenders left to perish or surrender, thus saving thousands of Allied casualties. Their conclusion was that General Headquarters needed to celebrate a total victory, the first over a major Japanese force since the beginning of the war. This was certainly MacArthur's attitude.

At the conclusion of the campaign, MacArthur, after reviewing the cost, resolved never again to force a head-on, grinding type of action against Japanese defenses. He stated, "No more Bunas." In large part during the rest of the New Guinea campaign he would make good on this vow, not because he had completely altered his attitude, but because the strategic situation had changed radically. The construction of airfields at Dobodura and Popondetta extended the range of Kenney's bombers, which could more easily attack the Japanese positions at Lae, Salamaua, and Rabaul. Allied control of the air, which had been a major factor in the Buna-Sanananda campaign, became even more evident with the steady flow of planes to the Fifth Air Force. The Japanese never recovered from their grievous air and naval losses in the Solomons; therefore, MacArthur could plan his subsequent offensives without fear of devastating air attacks.

By early 1943, MacArthur also could devise future operations knowing that he had naval support. Allied naval officers had charted safe routes through and around the coral reefs, so that any future attacks could be supported by naval gunfire. The authorities in Washington also finally took notice of MacArthur's requests for landing craft. While never in great supply, these gave him the flexibility to bypass Japanese strongholds and attack his selected targets along the thousand-mile New Guinea coast from the sea. He would never get all the ships and landing craft that he believed he needed, and his private differences with Admirals King and Nimitz would continue throughout the war; but eventually he would have a naval force, the Seventh Fleet, which would be strong enough to meet his immediate tactical needs.

During the months following the Buna campaign, MacArthur moved to simplify the command structure. He was never satisfied with having General Blamey in command of all Allied ground forces, but at first, for political reasons, he could do nothing about the situation that rankled U.S. commanders. Eventually he resorted to subterfuge, by creating the special Alamo Force, which comprised most U.S. ground troops. This was placed directly under his command. Ultimately the Alamo Force became the U.S. Sixth Army. Blamey, although not ignored, would gradually be shunted aside and for practical purposes command only Australian troops, which were generally confined to operations in the interior, while U.S. Army units assumed the responsibility of amphibious operations.

MacArthur made few changes of higher-echelon personnel. The Bataan Gang continued to be dominant at General Headquarters. However, MacArthur did manage to rid himself of some officers in whom he had little confidence. Thus Admiral Carpender was replaced by Vice Adm. Thomas Kinkaid, who, although not totally submissive to MacArthur, served him with a minimal amount of friction. The arrival of Rear Adm. Daniel Barbey, an amphibious expert, gave MacArthur the naval commander most needed to carry out the bulk of his offensives against the Japanese. Finally, with the assignment of Lt. Gen. Walter Krueger to command Alamo Force, MacArthur had completed his team, which would allow him in the next eighteen months to secure the entire north coast of New Guinea, bypassing thousands of Japanese in his leapfrogging offensives.

The later victories that would bolster MacArthur's reputation as a brilliant strategist rested upon the all-but-forgotten earlier Papua campaign. In this he had shown little of the brilliance he would later display. Beset by political difficulties and provided with few of the supplies he needed, he compounded the problem by underestimating his enemy and not realizing the actual combat conditions facing his forces. The mistakes of both MacArthur and Blamey, operating with little knowledge but nevertheless deciding a priori on the tactical situation, did not show either commander at his best. The ultimate victory depended not on brilliant generalship but on the courage and dogged determination of thousands of tired and sick troops who gave the Allies their first victory and paved the way for all subsequent successful actions in New Guinea.

Notes

Chapter I

1. This phase of the war is covered by many general works. For example, see Harry A. Gailey, *The War in the Pacific: From Pearl Harbor to Tokyo Bay* (Novato, Calif.: Presidio Press, 1995), pp. 104–32, and Roland Spector, *Eagle Against the Sun* (New York: The Free Press, 1985), pp. 72–141.

2. Gailey, pp. 133–40.

3. Samuel Milner, *The War in the Pacific: Victory in Papua* (Washington, D.C.: Office of the Chief of Military History, 1957), p. 8.

4. George C. Kenney, *General Kenney Reports* (New York: Duell, Sloan and Pearce, 1949), p. 21.

5. Milner, p. 7.

6. Hugh Buggy, *Pacific Victory* (Canberra: Ministry of Information, n.d.), pp. 46–50.

7. Paul Hasluck, *Australia in the War of 1939–1945,* Series Four, Vol. II, *The Government and the People, 1942–1945* (Canberra: Australian War Memorial, 1970), p. 137.

8. Ibid., pp. 140–41.

9. Pat Robinson, *The Fight for New Guinea* (New York: Random House, 1943), pp. 32–33.

10. Samuel Eliot Morison, *History of United States Naval Operations in World War II,* Vol. IV, *Coral Sea, Midway and Submarine Actions* (Boston: Little, Brown & Co., 1949), pp. 65–68.

11. Milner, p. 3.

12. Hasluck, p. 15.

13. Ibid., pp. 16, 21.

14. John Robertson and John McCarthy, *Australian War Strategy, 1939–1945* (St. Lucia, Australia: University of Queensland Press, 1985), pp. 230–39.

15. Winston Churchill, *The Second World War,* Vol. IV, *The Hinge of Fate* (New York: Houghton Mifflin Co., 1950), pp. 157–65.

16. Hasluck, p. 80.

17. Ibid., p. 95.

18. Robertson, pp. 263–65.

19. Ibid., p. 297.

20. Douglas MacArthur, *Reminiscences* (New York: Crest Books, 1964), p. 157.

21. Ibid., pp. 152–58.

22. Gavin Long, *MacArthur as Military Commander* (London: B. T. Batsford, 1969), p. 81.

23. Buggy, p. 13.

24. MacArthur, p. 161.

25. William Manchester, *American Caesar* (New York: Dell, 1978), pp. 325–26.

26. Milner, p. 20.

27. Ibid.

Chapter II

1. Milner, pp. 22–23.

2. Long, p. 89.

3. Ibid., p. 90.

4. Ibid., p. 89.

5. Milner, p. 27.

6. Ibid., pp. 27–32.

7. "Seek and Strike: The Story of 75 Squadron Royal Australian Air Force in the Air Battle for Port Moresby, 1942." Stencil copy in Library RAAF Museum, Point Cook, Australia.

8. Wesley F. Craven and James L. Cate, *The Army Air Forces in World War II,* Vol. IV, *The Pacific: Guadalcanal to Saipan* (Chicago: University of Chicago Press, 1964), pp. 7–8.

9. Ibid., pp. 102–3; "Seek and Strike."

10. *The Marauder: A Book of the 22d Bomb Group* (Sydney: Halstead Press, 1944), p. 24.

11. D. Clayton James, *The Years of MacArthur*, Vol. II, *1941–1945* (Boston: Houghton Mifflin Co., 1975), p. 197.

12. Kenney, p. 52.

13. James, pp. 198–99.

14. Samuel Eliot Morison, *History of United States Naval Operations in World War II*, Vol. VI, *Breaking the Bismarcks Barrier* (Boston: Little, Brown & Co., 1950), p. 32.

15. MacArthur, p. 162.

16. Milner, pp. 24–25.

17. Hasluck, p. 193.

18. Milner, pp. 41–42.

19. Samuel Eliot Morison, *History of United States Naval Operations in World War II*, Vol. III, *The Rising Sun in the Pacific* (Boston: Little, Brown & Co., 1961), pp. 266–67.

20. Ibid., pp. 387–88.

21. Morison, Vol. IV, pp. 10–12.

22. Ibid., pp. 21–28.

23. Ibid., pp. 33–64.

24. Ibid., pp. 69–159; Gordon W. Prange, *Miracle at Midway* (New York: Penguin Books, 1982).

25. Robertson, p. 321.

26. Ibid., p. 322.

Chapter III

1. Long, p. 100.

2. Milner, pp. 47–48.

3. Lida Mayo, *Bloody Buna* (Garden City, N.Y.: Doubleday & Co., 1974), pp. 13–16.

4. Peter Brune, *Those Ragged Bloody Heroes* (Sydney: Allen & Unwin, 1991), pp. 24–31; Milner, pp. 58–60.

5. Interview with Col. William Pitt, Philip Island, Australia, 8 December 1998.

6. Victor Austin, *To Kokoda and Beyond* (Melbourne: Melbourne University Press, 1988), pp. 68–69.

7. Chester Wilmot, Dispatches from the New Guinea Area for the Australian Broadcasting Commission, Disc. No. 314, Australian War Memorial (AWM) 422/7/8.

8. Brune, pp. 25–31.

9. Col. William Pitt, "Dobodura," p. 3. Stencil copy in author's files.

10. Milner, pp. 51–52.

11. Ibid., p. 53.

12. Saburo Hayashi and Alvin Cook, *Kogun: The Japanese Army in the Pacific War* (Quantico, Va.: The Marine Corps Association, 1959), p. 51.

13. Seizo Okada, "Lost Troops." Manuscript translated by Seiichi Shiagiri, from book published by *Ashahi Shimbuiin,* p. 9, AWM 492/7/22.

14. Milner, pp. 54–55.

15. Okada, p. 10.

16. Milner, pp. 70–71.

17. General details of the Australian retreat are taken from Raymond Paull, *Retreat from Kokoda* (Melbourne: Mandarin Books, 1989); Milner, pp. 56–65, 72–100; Brune, Chapters 7–12; Austin, Chapters 4–7; Mayo, Chapters 2–4.

18. Paull, p. 55.

19. Ibid., p. 57.

20. Milne Bay and Goodenough Island Areas, Messages Related to Operations, AWM 422/7/8.

21. New Guinea Force Reports, Maroubra Operations, Kokoda, 21 July–4 August, Appendix A, AWM 54, 577/7/29, part 21.

22. Austin, pp. 54–55.

23. Paull, pp. 74–85; Brune, pp. 59–71.

24. Brune, pp. 87–91.

25. Wilmot Dispatches, dated 9/23/43, AWM 422/7/8.

26. Brune, pp. 106–21.

27. Austin, pp. 162–63.

28. Capt. G. H. Vernon, M.C., Manuscript Diary of Services on the Owen Stanley–Buna Campaign, 1942, AWM PR 00787; Allan S. Walker, *Australia in the War of 1939–1945*, Series Five, *The Island Campaigns* (Canberra: Australian War Memorial, 1962), p. 20.

29. Walker, p. 25.

30. Ibid., p. 21.

31. Ibid., pp. 21–44.

32. Conversation between Major General Morris and Major General Vasey as quoted in Paull, p. 88.

33. Okada, p. 10.

34. James, pp. 203–4.

35. Mayo, pp. 46–47.

36. Paull, p. 191.

37. Brune, p. 183.

38. Long, p. 108.

39. Paull, p. 222.

40. Okada, p. 14.

Chapter IV

1. Dudley McCarthy, *Australia in the War of 1939–1945*, Vol. V, *South-West Pacific Area* (Canberra: Australian War Memorial, 1959), pp. 155–58; Morison, Vol. VI, pp. 34–35.

2. Morison, Vol. VI, pp. 36–37.

3. Milner, pp. 77–78; Buggy, pp. 162–63.

4. McCarthy, pp. 157–59.

5. Milner, p. 79.

6. Buggy, p. 154.

7. Morison, Vol. VI, p. 35.

8. Kenney, pp. 83–84.

9. McCarthy, pp. 164–65.

10. Milner, p. 82.

11. McCarthy, pp. 168–71.

12. Craven, p. 97.

13. Secret Cipher Clowes to General Headquarters, 29 August, AWM 54 422/7/8.

14. Morison, Vol. VI, p. 38.

15. Capt. A. S. Palmer, Report on Operations, Milne Bay Area, 1942, AWM 54/417/20/47.

16. Buggy, 166–67.

17. McCarthy, pp. 177–80.

18. Walker, pp. 52–57.

19. Buggy, p. 71.

20. Morison, Vol. VI, p. 36.

21. McCarthy, pp. 183.

22. Ibid., p. 185; Walker, p. 57.

23. Buggy, pp. 172–73.

24. Commonwealth Department of Veterans Affairs, *War Cemeteries and Memorials in the Papua New Guinea & Indonesia Region* (Canberra: Office of Australian War Graves), p. 12.

Chapter V

1. James, p. 220.

2. Ibid., p. 218.

3. Ibid., p. 211.

4. D. M. Horner, *High Command: Australia and Allied Strategy, 1939–1945* (Canberra: Australian War Memorial, 1982), Appendix II.

5. Kenney, p. 124.

6. James, p. 212.

7. Jay Luvaas (ed.), *Dear Miss Em, General Eichelberger's War in the Pacific, 1942–1945* (Westport, Conn.: Greenwood Press, 1972), p. 30.

8. James, p. 209.

9. Ibid, p. 208.

10. Secret message, Sutherland to Blamey, AWM 54, 422/7/8.

11. James, p. 209.

12. Kenney, pp. 93–94.

13. Horner, p. 214.

14. John Hetherington, *Blamey* (Melbourne: F. W. Cheshire, 1954), pp. 151–57; Brune, pp. 191–92.

15. Brune, p. 192.

16. Hetherington, p. 158.

17. Brune, p. 193.

18. Hetherington, p. 163.

19. Ibid., pp. 164–65.

20. Ibid., p. 165.

21. Ibid., p. 170.

22. Brune, pp. 195–96.

23. Telegram from MacArthur to Blamey, 17 October 1942, MacArthur's USAFPAC Correspondence, Allied Land Forces, Box 6, Folder 2, MacArthur Archives, Norfolk, Va.

24. Brune, pp. 212–13.

25. Hetherington, p. 178.

26. Paull, p. 254.

27. Ibid., pp. 257–58; Brune, pp. 198–202.

28. Robertson, Appendix II; Brune, pp. 204–5.

Chapter VI

1. Thomas B. Buell, *Masters of Sea Power: A Biography of Admiral Ernest J. King* (Boston: Little Brown & Co., 1980), pp. 219–20.

2. Samuel Eliot Morison, *History of United States Naval Operations in World War II,* Vol. V, *The Struggle for Guadalcanal* (Boston: Little Brown & Co., 1949), pp. 15–16.

3. Samuel B. Griffith II, *The Battle for Guadalcanal* (Baltimore: The Nautical & Aviation Publishing Co., 1963) is a good, concise account of the extended battle for the island.

4. Doris Hart, translator of the Japanese book *Southern Cross* by Kane Yoshihara, Tsutomi Yoshihara, and Nomi Yoshihara, Transcript File AWM MSS 0725, p. 4.

5. Gailey, Chapter 7.

6. James, p. 220.

7. Kenney, pp. 120, 126.

8. Okada, p. 14.

9. Paull, p. 267.

10. Okada, pp. 16–17.

11. Ibid.

12. F. C. Jorgensen, translator of *Nankai Shitai, War Book of the 144th Regiment* (Japanese), AWM File PR 00297, p. 14.

13. Ibid., p. 15; Paull, p. 269.

14. W. B. Russell, *The History of the Second Fourteenth Battalion* (Sydney: Angus & Robertson, 1948), p. 178.

15. Brief memoir in papers of Irvine F. Lloyd, AWM File PR 00322, p. 2; Milner, p. 104.

16. Paull, p. 272.

17. Mayo, p. 61.

18. McCarthy, pp. 285–306.

19. Buggy, p. 188.

20. Brune, p. 211.

21. Paull, p. 285.

22. Brune, p. 213.

23. Mayo, p. 65.

24. Paull, pp. 280–81.

25. Jorgensen, p. 16.

26. Ibid., p. 15; McCarthy, pp. 300–303.

27. Paull, pp. 286–87; McCarthy, p. 314.

Chapter VII

1. Robert L. Eichelberger, *Our Jungle Road to Tokyo* (New York: Viking Press, 1950), p. 14.

2. Milner, p. 92.

3. Leslie Anders, *Gentle Knight: The Life and Times of Major General Edwin Forrest Harding* (Kent, Ohio: Kent State University Press, 1985), pp. 205–10.

4. Interview with William de Mers, Palo Alto, Calif., 22 July 1997.

5. Thirty-second Infantry History Commission, *The 32d Infantry Division in World War II* (Madison, Wis.: History Commission, 1955), pp. 22–25.

6. Ibid., p. 25.

7. Eichelberger, pp. 12–13.

8. Anders, p. 225.

9. E. J. Kahn, Jr., "The Terrible Days of Company E, Part I," *The Saturday Evening Post,* 8 January 1944, p. 11.

10. Kenney, p. 99.

11. James, p. 234.

12. Milner, p. 102.

13. Kahn, "The Terrible Days," p. 12.

14. Mayo, p. 67.

15. Kahn, "The Terrible Days," p. 43.

16. Interview with Dan DeYoung, Palo Alto, Calif., 13 July 1999.

17. Ibid.

18. McCarthy, pp. 346–49.

19. Craven, pp. 113–14.

20. Kenney, pp. 75, 109–10.

21. McCarthy, p. 346.

22. Milner, p. 116.

23. Craven, pp. 106–12.

24. Anders, p. 233.

25. Milner, p. 107.

26. 32d Infantry Division, Report of Action, Papuan Campaign, September 1942–March 1943, National Archives, College Park, Md., File 332-0.3.

27. MacArthur to Blamey, 20 October 1942, MacArthur Archives, Norfolk, Va., USAFPAC Correspondence, Box 6, Folder 2.

28. Anders, p. 237.

29. Milner, pp. 121–23, 236.

Chapter VIII

1. Walker, pp. 63–66.

2. Yoshimara, p. 11.

3. McCarthy, p. 322.

4. Ibid., pp. 327–29; *Nankai Shitai*, pp. 21–23.

5. *Nankai Shitai*, pp. 24–25.

6. Okada, p. 24.

7. Ibid., p. 25.

8. McCarthy, p. 333.

9. James, p. 239.

10. Milner, pp. 144–46.

11. Lt. Col. B. A. Kessler, Report on Operations in New Guinea, Sanananda Area, 2 December–January 1943, Serial 18, AWM 54, File 577/7/29.

12. Craven, p. 122.

13. Milner, p. 147.

14. Brune, pp. 218–19.

15. McCarthy, Chapter 16; Milner, pp. 147–49.

16. Milner, p. 150.

17. McCarthy, pp. 384–94.

18. Mayo, p. 97.

Chapter IX

1. Anders, p. 237.

2. Milner, p. 138.

3. Report of Action (G-2 Section) to Commanding General 32d Infantry Division, 3 April 1943, pp. 2–3, National Archives, File 332-3.

4. 32d Infantry Division, Report of Action Papuan Campaign, September 1942–28 March 1943, National Archives, File 332-0.3.

5. De Mers interview.

6. Blamey to MacArthur, 19 November 1942, USAFPAC Correspondence, Allied Land Forces, MacArthur Archives, Box 6, Folder 1.

7. Ibid, 27 November 1942.

8. Kenney to Arnold, 24 October 1942, cited in Craven and Cates, p. 119.

9. Anders, pp. 241–44.

10. 32d Infantry Division Report of Action Papuan Campaign, National Archives, File 332-0.3 and Milner, pp. 168–70.

11. Robert White, "Report of the Commanding General Buna Force on the Buna Campaign, December 1, 1942–January 25, 1943," MacArthur Archives.

12. Milner, p. 141.

13. Ibid., p. 135.

14. White, p. 15.

15. Ibid., p. 15ff.

16. Mayo, p. 97.

17. Milner, pp. 177–78.

18. De Mers interview.

19. World War II Operations Report, 32d Infantry Division, National Archives, File 332-3.

20. Ibid.

21. Anders, p. 251.

22. Milner, p. 185.

23. Ibid., pp. 182–93.

24. Ibid., pp. 180–82.

25. Ibid., pp. 191–95.

26. Interview with Robert Curtis, 28 August 1997, Sumner, Washington.

27. Eichelberger, p. 29.

28. De Mers interview.

Chapter X

1. James, pp. 257–59.

2. Luvaas, p. 28.

3. Hetherington, p. 182.

4. Anders, p. 244.

5. Ibid., p. 259.

6. Ibid., p. 260.

7. Kenney, p. 150.

8. Eichelberger, p. 29.

9. Transcript of Oral Reminiscences of Lt. Gen. Clovis Byers by D. Clayton James, 24 June 1971, p. 12, MacArthur Archives.

10. Milner, pp. 201Ff.

11. Eichelberger, p. 20.

12. Clovis Byers's Diary, 1942, Hoover Institution Archives, Stanford, Calif.; Byers's Oral Reminiscences, p. 12.

13. Ibid.; Paul P. Rogers, *The Good Years: MacArthur & Sutherland* (New York: Praeger, 1990), p. 336.

14. Eichelberger, p. 22.

15. Anders, p. 262.

16. Letter from Eichelberger to Sutherland, 1 December 1942, Sutherland Microfilm Records, MacArthur Archives.

17. Milner, p. 207.

18. Eichelberger, p. 23.

19. Anders, p. 264.

20. Ibid., p. 265.

21. Milner, p. 211.

22. Letter from Eichelberger to Sutherland, 3 December 1942, Sutherland Microfilm Records, MacArthur Archives.

23. Ibid.

24. Harding's Diary, 2 December 1942, quoted in Milner, p. 212.

25. Anders, pp. 267–68.

26. Kenney, p. 159.

Chapter XI

1. Kenney, pp. 150–51.

2. Brune, pp. 224–26.

3. Russell, pp. 188–203.

4. Ibid.; McCarthy, pp. 430–33.

5. Austin, p. 195.

6. Brune, p. 252.

7. Milner, p. 214.

8. Ibid. p. 217; Brune, pp. 253–55.

9. McCarthy, p. 440.

10. 7th Division Report, Kokoda Trail to Gona, 13 August to 2 December 1942, AWM 54, File 577/7/34, pp. 25Ff.

11. Cited in Brune, p. 259.

12. Ralph Honner, "This is the 39th," *The Bulletin,* 3 August 1955.

13. McCarthy, p. 394.

14. Ibid.

15. 32d Division, Report of Action Papuan Campaign, September 1942–28 March 1943, National Archives, File 332-0.3.

16. McCarthy, p. 394.

17. Ibid., p. 397.

18. Ibid., p. 398.

19. Milner, pp. 162–63.

20. Ibid., pp. 163–64.

21. Ibid., p. 219.

22. Eric Bergerud, *Touched with Fire: The Land War in the South Pacific* (New York: Penguin Books, 1996), p. 369.

23. Interview, Dan DeYoung.

24. McCarthy, p. 404.

25. Brune, p. 276.

26. Report on Operations in New Guinea, 30 Australian Brigade, Sanananda Area, 2 December 1942–January 1943, AWM 54, File 577/7/29; Milner, p. 223.

27. McCarthy, p. 412.

Chapter XII

1. Craven, p. 122; Milner, p. 218.

2. World War II Operations Report 32d Infantry Division, G-3 Journal, National Archives, File 332-3.2.

3. Craven, p. 127.

4. Ibid., p. 121; Douglas Gillison, *Australia in the War of 1939–1945,* Series Three, *Royal Australian Air Force, 1939–1942* (Canberra: Australian War Memorial, 1962), pp. 661–62.

5. Letter from Eichelberger to Sutherland, 5 December 1942, Sutherland Microfilm Records, MacArthur Archives.

6. White, p. 10.

7. Milner, pp. 236–41.

8. 32d Division, Report of Action Papuan Campaign, September 1942–28 March 1943, National Archives, File 332-0.3.

9. Mayo, p. 119.

10. Eichelberger, p. 30.

11. Milner, pp. 243–44.

12. Eichelberger, pp. 38–39.

13. Report on the Activities of the 32d Infantry Division Chemical Section during Papuan Campaign, 18 February 1942, National Archives, File 332-3, p. 7.

14. Milner, p. 252.

15. Chemical Section Report, National Archives, File 332-3, p. 9.

16. McCarthy, p. 382; 32d Division Report of Action, National Archives, File 332-0.3.

17. Letters from Eichelberger to Sutherland, 6 and 7 December 1942, Sutherland Microfilm Records, MacArthur Archives.

18. MacArthur to Eichelberger, 13 December 1942, USAFPAC Correspondence, Allied Land Forces, MacArthur Archives, Folder 1, Box 6.

19. McCarthy, pp. 451–52; Milner, pp. 256–57.

20. McCarthy, pp. 455–62.

21. Letter from Eichelberger to Sutherland, 18 December 1942, Sutherland Microfilm Records, MacArthur Archives.

22. McCarthy, pp. 467–69.

23. Ibid., p. 272.

24. Ibid., p. 274; Milner, pp. 280–81.

25. Milner, pp. 284–85.

26. Ibid., pp. 288–89.

27. Ibid., pp. 295–98.

28. Eichelberger, p. 47.

29. Ibid., p. 48; Milner, p. 300.

Chapter XIII

1. Milner, p. 307.

2. Byers, World War II Operations Report, 32d Infantry Division, G-3 Journal, National Archives, File 332-3.2.

3. Milner, pp. 306–9; McCarthy, pp. 482–84.

4. James, pp. 269–70.

5. Mayo, p. 147.

6. Ibid., pp. 151–52.

7. Milner, pp. 312–14.

8. John Toland, *The Rising Sun,* Vol. 1 (New York: Random House, 1970), p. 521.

9. Milner, p. 315.

10. Ibid., pp. 317–19.

11. McCarthy, p. 495.

12. Eichelberger, p. 49.

13. Milner, pp. 353–54.

14. Ibid., pp. 228–30.

15. Letter from Blamey to MacArthur, 27 December 1942, US-AFPAC Correspondence, Allied Land Forces, MacArthur Archives, Folder l, Box 6.

16. Letter from MacArthur to Blamey, 28 December 1942, US-AFPAC Correspondence, Allied Land Forces, MacArthur Archives, Folder l, Box 6.

17. McCarthy, p. 511; Milner, pp. 332–35.

18. William F. McCartney, *The Jungleers: A History of the 41st Infantry Division* (Washington: Infantry Journal Press, 1948), p. 36.

19. Ibid., pp. 37–38.

20. McCarthy, pp. 513–16.

21. Paull, pp. 298–305.

22. Eichelberger, p. 20.

23. Milner, p. 347.

24. McCarthy, pp. 527–28.

25. Milner, pp. 356–58.

26. Eichelberger, p. 67.

27. McCarthy, p. 525.

28. Ibid., p. 521.

29. Milner, pp. 363–64.

30. Mayo, p. 169.

31. Milner, p. 363.

32. McCarthy, p. 531; Milner, p. 370.

Bibliography

PRIMARY SOURCES

Australian War Memorial, Canberra, Australia

Battle Casualties Buna-Gona Coastal Campaign, Australian Military Forces, November 1942–22 January 1943, AWM 54, File 171/2/25.

Broadcast BBC. Copy of talk by British officer from Buna-Gona front. AWM 54, File 132/2/10.

Honner, Ralph. "The 39th at Isurava," *Stand To,* July–August 1956. PR 87/008.

Lessons from Milne Bay Operations, August–September 1942, AWM 54, File 417/1/1.

Messages Milne Bay, AWM 54, File 422/7/8.

Milne Bay and Goodenough Island Areas, Messages related to operations, AWM 54, File 422/7/8.

Nankai Shitai, War Book of the 144th Regiment, Japanese translated by F. C. Jorgensen, PR00297.

New Guinea Force Reports, Maroubra Operations, Kokoda, 21 July–4 August 1942, AWM 54, File 577//7/29.

Okada, Seizo, "Lost Troops" manuscript, translated by Seiichi Shiagiri, AWM File 492/7/22.

Palmer, A. S., Report on Operations, Milne Bay Area, 1942, AWM 54, File 417/20/47.

Papers of Irvine F. (Jack) Lloyd, PR00322.

Papers of Lt. Alf Salmon (39th Battalion), PR00297.

Report on Operations in New Guinea, 30 Australian Infantry

Brigade Sanananda Area, 2 December–January 1943, AWM 54, File 577/7/29, Serial 18.

Report on Operations, 39th Australian Infantry Battalion, Kokoda Area, July–August 1942, AWM 54, File 577/7/29.

7th Division Report on Operations, Kokoda Trail to Gona, 13 August–2 December 1942, AWM 54/File 577/7/34.

Summary of Operations carried out by No. 4 Army Co-operation Squadron in Papua, Soputa, Gona-Buna, November 1942–January 1943, AWM 54, File 85/3/50.

Transcript File AWM MSS 0725.

25 Australian Infantry Brigade, Notes on the New Guinea campaign, AWM 54, File 577/7/31.

Vernon, Capt. G. H. Manuscript Diary of Service on the Owen Stanley–Buna campaign 1942, PR00787.

Wilkerson, John. Typescript, Owen Stanley campaign, July–November 1942, PR00267.

Wilmot, Charles. Dispatches from New Guinea Area for Australian Broadcasting Commission, AWM 422/7/8.

Yoshihara, Kane, Tsutomu Yoshihara, and Nomi Yoshihara. *Southern Cross*, Doris Hart, transl.

Hoover Institution Archives
Byers, Lt. Gen. Clovis. Diary, 1942.

MacArthur Archives, Norfolk, Va.
MacArthur's USAFPAC Correspondence, Allied Land Forces, Box 6, Folder 1.

MacArthur's USAFPAC Correspondence, Allied Land Forces, Box 6, Folder 2.

Microfilm Records of Lt. Gen. Richard Sutherland.

Transcript of Oral Reminiscences of Lt. Gen. Clovis Byers by D. Clayton James, 24 June 1971.

White, Robert. "Report of the Commanding General Buna Force on the Buna Campaign, December 1, 1942–January 25, 1943."

National Archives, College Park, Md. Record Group 407.
Birkeness, Lt. Col. Ralph. Report of Air Action Against the Enemy, 20 April 1943, File 332-3.

Byers, Brig. Gen. Clovis. World War II Operations Report, 32d Infantry Division, File 332-3.

———. World War II Operations Report, 32d Infantry Division, G-3 Journal, Buna (Papua), File 332-3.2.

Kindig, Maj. Earl. World War II Operations Report, 32d Infantry Division (Artillery), File 332-ART - 0.l to 0.3.

107th Quartermaster Detachment Report, 27 March 1943, File 332-3.

Report of Action (G-2 Section) to Commanding General, 32d Infantry Division, 3 April 1943, File 332-3.

Report on the Activities of the 32d Infantry Division Chemical Section during Papuan Campaign, 18 February 1942, File 332-3.

32d Infantry Division, Report of Action Papuan Campaign, September 1942–28 March 1943, File 332-0.3.

Units in Contact Papuan Campaign, 23 July 1943, File 332-0.3.

Interviews by Author
John Curtis, Palo Alto, Calif., 15 August 1997.
Robert Curtis, Sumner, Wash., 28 August 1997.
William de Mers, Palo Alto, Calif., 22 July 1997.
Dan DeYoung, Palo Alto, Calif., 13 July 1999.
Col. William Pitt, Philip Island, Australia, 8 December 1998.

SECONDARY WORKS
Anders, Leslie. *Gentle Knight: The Life and Times of Major General Edwin Forrest Harding*. Kent, Ohio: The Kent State University Press, 1985.

Austin, Victor. *To Kokoda and Beyond: The Story of the 39th Battalion 1941–1943*.

Bartholomew, Frank H. *Bart*. Sonoma, Calif.: Vine Book Press, 1983.

Bergerud, Eric. *Touched with Fire: The Land War in the South Pacific*. New York: Penguin Books, 1996.

Blakeley, H. W. (Maj. Gen.). *32d Infantry Division in World War II*. Madison: State of Wisconsin, n.d.

Brune, Peter. *Those Ragged Bloody Heroes: From the Kokoda Trail to Gona Beach 1942*. Sydney, Allen & Unwin, 1991.

Buell, Thomas B. *Master of Sea Power: A Biography of Fleet Admiral Ernest J. King*. Boston: Little, Brown & Co., 1980.

Buggy, Hugh. *Pacific Victory: A Short History of Australia's Part in the War Against Japan*. Canberra: Ministry of Information, n.d.

Carlton, Victoria: Melbourne University Press, 1988.

Churchill, Winston. *The Second World War,* Vol. IV, *The Hinge of Fate.* New York: Houghton Mifflin Co., 1950.

Commonwealth Department of Veterans Affairs. *War Cemeteries.* Canberra: Office of Australian War Graves, n.d.

Connaughton, Richard. *Shrouded Secrets: Japan's War on Mainland Australia 1942–1944.* London: Brassey's, 1994.

Craven, Wesley F., and James L. Cate. *The Army Air Forces in World War II,* Vol. IV, *The Pacific: Guadalcanal to Saipan.* Chicago: University of Chicago Press, 1964.

Drea, Edward J. *MacArthur's Ultra: Codebreaking and the War Against Japan.* Lawrence, Kansas: University Press of Kansas, 1992.

Dull, Paul S. *A Battle History of the Imperial Japanese Navy (1941–1945).* Annapolis: Naval Institute Press, 1978.

Eichelberger, Robert L. *Our Jungle Road to Tokyo.* New York: Viking Press, 1950.

Gailey, Harry A. *The War in the Pacific: From Pearl Harbor to Tokyo Bay.* Novato, Calif.: Presidio Press, 1995.

Gillison, Douglas. *Australia in the War of 1939–1945.* Series Three. *Royal Australian Air Force, 1939–1942.* Canberra: Australian War Memorial, 1962.

Griffith, Samuel B. II. *The Battle for Guadalcanal.* Baltimore: The Nautical & Aviation Publishing Co., 1963.

Hasluck, Paul. *Australia in the War of 1939–1945.* Series Four. *The Government and the People.* Canberra: Australian War Memorial, 1970.

Hayashi, Saburo, and Alvin Cookz. *Kogun: The Japanese Army in the Pacific War.* Quantico, Va.: The Marine Corps Association, 1959.

Hetherington, John. *Blamey: The Biography of Field-Marshal Sir Thomas Blamey.* Melbourne: F. W. Cheshire, 1954.

Honner, Ralph. "This is the 39th," *The Bulletin,* 3 August 1955.

Horner, D. M. *Australia in the War of 1939–1945: High Command, Australia and Allied Strategy, 1939–1945.* Sydney: George Allen & Unwin, 1982.

James, D. Clayton. *The Years of MacArthur, Vol. II, 1941–1945.* Boston: Houghton Mifflin Co., 1975.

Kahn, E. J. Jr. *G. I. Jungle.* New York: Simon & Schuster, 1943.

————. "The Terrible Days of Company E, Part I," *The Saturday Evening Post*, 8 January 1944.

Kenney, George C. *General Kenney Reports*. New York: Duell, Sloan and Pearce, 1949.

Leary, William M. (ed.): *We Shall Return: MacArthur's Commanders and the Defeat of Japan*. Lexington, Ky.: The University Press of Kentucky, 1988.

Long, Gavin. *MacArthur as Military Commander*. London: B. T. Batsford Ltd., 1969.

Luvaas, Jay (ed.). *Dear Miss Em: General Eichelberger's War in the Pacific, 1942–1945*. Westport, Conn.: Greenwood Press, 1972.

MacArthur, Douglas. *Reminiscences*. Greenwich, Conn.: Crest Books, 1965.

McCarthy, Dudley. *Australia in the War of 1939–1945*, Series One, *South-West Pacific Area—First Year. Kokoda to Wau*. Canberra: Australian War Memorial, 1959.

McCartney, William F. *The Jungleers: A History of the 41st Infantry Division*. Washington, D.C.: The Infantry Journal Press, 1948.

Manchester, William. *American Caesar: Douglas MacArthur 1880–1964*. New York: Dell, 1979.

Mayo, Lida. *Bloody Buna*. Garden City, N.Y.: Doubleday & Co., 1974.

Milner, Samuel. *The United States Army in World War II: The War in the Pacific: Victory in Papua*. Washington, D.C.: Office of Chief of Military History, 1957.

Morison, Samuel Eliot. *History of United States Naval Operations in World War II*, Vol. VI, *Breaking the Bismarcks Barrier 22 July 1942–1 May 1944*. Boston: Little, Brown & Co., 1950.

————. *History of United States Naval Operations in World War II*, Vol. V, *The Struggle for Guadalcanal August 1942–February 1943*. Boston: Little, Brown & Co., 1949.

————. *History of United States Naval Operations in World War II*, Vol. IV, *Coral Sea, Midway and Submarine Actions, May 1942–August 1942*. Boston: Little, Brown & Co., 1949.

————. *History of United States Naval Operations in World War II*, Vol. III, *The Rising Sun in the Pacific 1931–April 1942*. Boston: Little, Brown & Co., 1961.

Paull, Raymond. *Retreat from Kokoda*. Melbourne: William Heinemann, 1985.

Robertson, John, and John McCarthy. *Australian War Strategy 1939–1945: A Documentary History.* St. Lucia, Queensland: University of Queensland Press, 1985.

Robinson, Pat. *The Fight for New Guinea: General Douglas MacArthur's First Offensive.* New York: Random House, 1943.

Rogers, Paul P. *The Good Years: MacArthur and Sutherland.* New York: Praeger, 1990.

Russell, W. B. *The Second Fourteenth Battalion.* Sydney: Angus & Robertson, 1948.

Spector, Ronald H. *Eagle Against the Sun: The American War with Japan.* New York: Free Press, 1985.

Thirty-second Infantry History Commission. *The 32d Infantry Division in World War II.* Madison, Wis.: History Commission, 1955.

Toland, John. *The Rising Sun,* Vol. I. New York: Random House, 1970.

Walker, Allan. *Australia in the War of 1939–1945.* Series V, *The Island Campaign.* Canberra: Australian War Memorial, 1962.

War Department Historical Division. *Papuan Campaign: The Buna Sanananda Operation 16 November 1942–23 January 1943.* Washington, D.C.: Center of Military History, 1990.

———. *The Marauder: A Book of the 22d Bomb Group.* Sydney: Halstead Press, 1944.

Index

Abau, 107, 111
Abau-Jaure Trail, 106
ABDA Command, 2, 3, 6, 10, 12
Abel, Cecil, 111
Adachi, Lt. Gen. Hatazo, 127, 174, 189–190, 226
Advance New Guinea Force, 220
Agatu Maru, 45
Ahioma, 60, 65, 70
air attacks (allied), 91–92, 112, 114, 120, 127, 165, 175, 190–191
Air Transport, 46, 100, 105–106, 110–111, 112, 116, 117, 137, 139, 146–147, 149, 150, 161, 191
Airstrip No. 1, 65, 71
Airstrip No. 2, 68
Airstrip No. 3, 70, 71
Akagi, 5, 32, 33
Alacrity, 140
Allen, Maj. Gen. S.F., 55, 57, 81, 82–83, 84, 86, 94, 96, 97, 98, 145
Allied air forces, 4–5
Allied aircraft, 3, 5, 8, 10, 13, 23, 24, 25, 146, 147, 148, 151, 162, 180, 190, 191, 194
Allied intelligence, 45–46, 56, 76–77, 80, 82–83, 85, 99,

101–02, 115, 136, 156–57, 159–60, 172
Allied strategy, 1–3, 9, 100–12, 13, 21–22, 26, 27, 32–33, 35–36, 40, 42–43, 49, 57, 88, 99, 101, 106, 114–16, 124–25, 127–29, 133, 135–39, 144, 151–52, 234–35
Allied tactics, 46–47, 48, 49, 50, 54–56, 69, 88–90, 94–95, 96, 100, 123–24, 130–32, 143–45, 149–50, 164, 172–73, 174, 175–77, 180–83, 189–99, 213–15, 223–24
Alola, 39, 50, 53
Amboga R., 127, 175
Amboina, 11
Anshun, 70
ANZAC area, 3, 12, 28
Arafura Sea, 6, 44
Arnold, Lt. Col. A.S., 213, 229
Arnold, Gen. Henry H. (Hap), 74–75, 139
Aru, 44
Auchinleck, Field Marshal Sir Claude, 81
Australia; army units: Australian Imperial Force (AIF), 4, 9–10, 19; Australian Military Force (AMF), 10; Volunteer Defense

Corps (VDC), 10; corps: II, 85, 104; brigades: 7th, 28, 55, 61, 65, 66, 67; 14th, 28; 16th, 57, 99, 119, 121, 123, 124, 129, 131, 132, 179; 18th, 61, 65, 66, 67, 79, 110, 201, 222, 223, 225, 226; 20th, 221; 21st, 56, 57, 81, 84, 96, 99, 131, 159, 161, 172, 173, 221; 23d, 86; 25th, 49, 54, 57, 94, 99, 100, 120, 129, 131, 173; 30th, 12, 173, 186, 192, 221; divisions: 6th, 11, 57, 86; 7th, 11, 86, 94, 127; 8th, 10; 9th, 155; battalions: 2/1,120, 121, 131, 132; 2/2, 113, 131; 2/3, 100, 113, 131; 2/4 Field Ambulance, 117; 2/6 Armored, 201; 2/7 Armored, 220; 2/9, 69, 201, 202, 224, 228, 229, 230; 2/10, 65, 111, 202, 203, 205, 213, 214, 224, 227, 228, 229; 2/12, 65, 68, 110, 213, 214, 224, 228, 229, 230; 2/14, 49, 50, 56, 173, 174; 2/16, 50, 51, 56, 173,174, 175, 176, 201; 2/23, 131; 2/25, 61, 94, 120, 123, 130; 2/27, 50, 54, 55, 56,173, 174, 176; 2/31, 94–95,120,121, 128, 130; 2/32, 129, 130; 2/33, 57, 95, 120; 3d, 130; 11th Field Ambulance, 68–69; 14th Field Ambulance, 94; 25th, 65, 66; 22/3, 181; 39th, 39, 40–41,45, 46, 49, 50, 51, 78, 173, 174, 186, 221, 223, 226; 49th, 186, 220, 223, 226; 53d, 50, 186; 52d, 51; 55th, 186; 61st, 63, 65, 66; special units: Chaforce, 99, 175; 5th Independent co., 28, 193;

Kanga Force, 28; Papuan Infantry Bn. (PIB), 45, 47; medical problems, 51–53, 68–69, 117; supply system, 41–42, 52–53, 68, 97–98, 117
Australian Northern Territories, 9, 67
Australian–U.S. rivalry, 135–136, 155–156, 157, 158
Australian War Cabinet, 12, 14, 34

Baetcke, Maj. Bernd, 181, 183, 221
Bailey, Lt. Cladie, 194
Barkey, RAdm. Daniel, 235
Barnes, Maj. Gen. Julian, 18, 36
Barton, James, 37
Basabua, 125, 127
Bataan, 1, 17
Bataan Gang, 13, 18, 235
Biak, 36
Bismarck Sea, 2, 29
Blamey, Capt. J.M., 180
Blamey, Gen. Sir Thomas, 19, 39, 40, 43, 75–76, 78–79, 81–83, 84–85, 96, 97, 98, 110, 111, 115, 132, 135–36, 138, 143, 155, 156, 157, 161, 171, 215, 221–22, 233
Boerem, Maj. Richard, 183, 221
Bofu, 115, 116, 129
Boice, Capt. William, 107, 179
Bolero Plan, 21
Bond, Maj. George, 181
Bonwin, 140
Boreo Creek, 143
Borneo, 2
Bottcher, SSgt. Herman, 195, 196

Bougainville, 25, 87, 112

Boyer, Lt. K.M., 181

Bradley, Col. J.S., 210

Bren Gun Carriers, 152

Brett, Lt. Gen. George, 3, 13, 17, 19, 45

Brigade Hill, 84

Brisbane, 12, 36, 73

Brisbane Line, 12, 27

Brooke, Field Marshal Sir Alan, 81

Broome, 7–8

Brown, VAdm. Wilson, 28–29

Buckler, Capt. S.H., 108

Bulolo Valley, 6, 28

Buna, 9, 36, 37, 42, 43, 45, 46, 62, 71, 79, 88, 100, 115, 116, 124, 125, 129, 132–53, 163, 168, 189–218, 221

Bunda, 44

Burma, 11, 12

Burns, Col. Frank, 60

Burston, Maj. Gen. Sir Samuel, 79

Byers, Brig. Gen. Clovis, 161, 162, 195

Cameron, Maj. Allan, 47–48, 49

Canberra, 3, 14, 91

Canton I., 3

Cape Endaiadere, 126, 141, 146, 148, 165

Cape Nelson, 106, 110, 113, 114, 138

Cape York, 24, 46, 62

Caro, Lt. Col. Albert, 174

Carpender, VAdm. Arthur, 27, 124, 125

Carrier, Lt. Col. Edmund J., 145, 146, 152, 193

casualties: allied, 218; Australian, 7–8, 68–69, 70, 96, 120, 121, 130, 132, 214, 231; Japanese, 57, 67, 70, 90, 92, 95, 96, 121, 132, 176, 177, 218, 229, 230, 232; U.S., 70, 147, 153, 191, 195, 197, 207, 221, 231

Catterns, Capt. B.W.T., 132, 178

Chagnon, Lt. Louis, 219

Challen, Lt. Col. Hugh, 99

Chamberlin, Brig. Gen. Stephen, 43, 159

Chicago, 3, 8

Churchill, Winston, 11, 20–21, 74

Clarkson, Maj. Gordon, 206

Clowes, Brig. (later Maj. Gen.) Cyril, 19, 61, 63–65, 67, 68, 79, 80, 148

Combined Chiefs of Staff, 74

Coconut Grove, 150, 207, 209, 214, 218

Coln, 24

Cooktown, 24

Coral Sea, 28, 29–32, 34, 40, 87

Corregidor, 17

Crace, RAdm. J.C., 31

Crutchley, RAdm. V.A.C., 26, 91

Curtin, John, 3, 10–11, 12–14, 20, 21, 27, 34, 74, 76, 78, 79, 155, 157

Dal Pointe, Lt. Peter, 185

Daniels, Lt. A.N., 181

Darwin, 6–7, 12, 13

Deniki, 39, 41, 46, 47, 48

DeYoung, Lt. Dan, 184–85

Dobodura, 42, 129, 137, 141, 143, 158, 161, 163, 165, 191, 223, 231, 234

Doe, Col. Jens, 221, 228
Dougherty, Brig. Ivan, 82, 86, 172, 174, 176–77, 221
Dougherty, Lt. Robert, 175
Duropa Plantation, 144, 148
Dutch East Indies, 2, 8, 9, 15

Eather, Brig. Kenneth, 57, 78, 95, 96, 130
Edwards, Capt. Daniel, 160, 195
Efogi, 39, 52, 55
Egberg, Maj. Roger, 164
Eichelberger, Maj. Gen. Robert, 36, 73, 101, 102, 104, 135, 149, 153, 156, 161, 162, 163–64, 165–69, 183, 189, 192–95, 198–99, 201–02, 208, 213, 215, 218, 220, 222, 224
Embesi, 111
Embogo, 116, 141, 143
Enterprise, 33, 34
Entrance Creek, 37, 141, 198
Eora Creek, 41, 49, 84, 96, 99, 100, 119
Estrada, Pvt. Bernardino, 198
Evatt, Herbert, 21

Fasari, 111
Field, Brig. John, 6l, 67
Fiji, 3, 4, 43, 87
Fisk (Kano) Block, 223, 224, 228
Fitch, RAdm. Aubrey, 30
Fletcher, RAdm. Frank Jack, 29, 31, 32, 89
Free French Army, 3
French, Corp. John, 69
friendly fire, 146–47, 148, 174, 180–81, 201
Fuller, Maj. Gen. Horace, 36

Gama R., 65
Gap, 39, 55, 76, 94
Garbutt Field, 24
Geerds, Lt. Col. Henry, 109
General Headquarters, 47, 73, 75, 76, 77, 79, 98, 106, 137, 139, 157, 165, 169, 179, 189, 209, 219, 233
Ghormley, VAdm. Robert, 35–36, 74, 88, 90, 110
Ghost Mountain, 108
Gili Gili, 59, 60, 62, 63
Giropa Point, 198, 206, 210, 213, 218
Girua R., 37, 141, 149, 164, 171, 183
Giruwa, 94, 126, 176, 206, 217, 225, 227, 229, 230, 231
Gobe, 113
Golden Stairs, 41
Gona, 9, 36, 45, 65, 116, 121–27, 129, 133, 141, 143, 171, 172–77, 191, 226, 231
Goodenough I., 62, 65, 106, 110, 152
Gorari, 45, 46, 96, 119, 120, 121, 227
Goroni, 69
Government Gardens, 206, 210
Great Britain, 10–11
Grose, Col. John, 169, 192, 195, 207, 208, 210, 211, 215–16, 217, 219
Gruennart, Sgt. Kenneth, 209
Guadalcanal, 4, 26, 36, 73–74, 87–90, 92, 93, 107, 112, 139, 155, 217, 226, 232
Guam, 2
Guri Guri, 113

Haddy, Lt. Alan, 175
Haddy's Village, 175, 176
Hale, Col. Tracy, 114, 159, 161, 166, 169, 205
Halsey, VAdm. William F., 28, 90
Harding, Maj. Gen. Edwin, 36, 102–03, 111, 112–13, 115, 135, 136, 139, 140, 142, 144, 145, 147–48, 150, 153, 156, 157, 158, 159, 162, 163, 166, 167–69, 178–79, 189, 192, 218
Hariko Point, 116, 140, 143
Hawkins, Maj. William, 151–52, 158, 159
Hayashi, Commander, 63, 67
Herring, Lt. Gen. Sir Edmund, 19, 81, 85, 132, 135, 143, 148, 157, 158, 161, 163, 171, 178, 194, 213, 215, 220, 221, 222, 228
Hirohito, 217
Hiryu, 32, 33, 34
Hobart, 3
Hong Kong, 2
Honner, Lt. Col. Ralph, 49, 173, 174, 176
Hopkins, Brig. Ronald, 158, 163–64
Horanda, 129
Hornet, 33
Horie, Maj. Tadashi, 94
Horii, Maj. Gen. Tomitaro, 44, 46, 49, 50, 51, 53, 55, 57, 58, 59, 76, 92, 93, 98, 99, 119, 121, 122, 190
Houston, 1, 2
Howe, Col. Merle, 219–20, 227, 229
Huggins, Capt. Meredith, 183, 185

Huggins' Block, 182–83, 185, 213, 220, 221
Hyakutake, Lt. Gen. Haruyoshi, 43–33, 89, 90, 92, 126, 217, 226

Ilolo, 41
Imamura, Gen. Hitoshi, 93, 127, 217, 226
Imita Ridge, 57, 78, 79, 92
Imperial General Staff, 93, 94
Inoue, VAdm. Shigyoshi, 31–32
Ioribiawa, 39, 41, 52, 56, 94, 95
Irua R., 101
Issacksen, Col. O.C., 86
Isurava, 39, 41, 49, 50, 51

Japanese air action, 1, 5, 6, 7, 50, 140, 205
Japanese air units: 25th Air Flotilla, 29, 43
Japanese aircraft, 5, 6, 8, 10, 22, 23
Japanese atrocities, 95–96
Japanese army units: armies: 8th Area Army, 93, 126; 17th, 89, 126, 127; 18th, 6, 126, 127, 190; divisions: 41st, 100, 125; regiments: 15th engineers, 44, 122, 125; 41st, 94, 129; 144th, 44, 94, 96, 99, 119, 121, 125, 202; 229th, 202; landing forces: Kure 5th Special Force, 62, 67, 110; 3d Force, 30; Sasebo Force, 62, 125; Yokosuka Special Force, 125; Yokoyama Force, 44, 45, 46; detachments: Aoba, 62, 69; Kawaguchi, 93; South Seas, 2, 5, 30, 44, 46; Yazawa

Detachment, 44; battalions: 3d/144 Reg., 119; 3d/170, 174–75; miscellaneous units: 47th Anti Aircraft Artillery, 125; 67th Line of Communications Hospital, 231; Stanley *Shitai*, 94, 96
Japanese defense plans: Buna, 135, 141–42, 147–48, 152–53, 164–65; 202–03, 205, 208, 210–11; Gona, 129–31, 171, 174–77; Sanananda, 131–33, 178–87, 223–25, 230
Japanese Imperial Headquarters, 3, 6, 43, 126, 226
Japanese intelligence service, 59, 61–62
Japanese medical problems, 53, 95, 123, 226, 230
Japanese Navy, 1, 2–3, 5, 6, 8–9, 30–32, 43, 89, 90, 127, 190
Japanese strategy, 1–2, 4, 6, 8, 26, 30, 32–33, 43–44, 59, 61–62, 69–70, 87, 89–90, 93–94, 127, 217
Japanese supply system, 57, 92, 225
Japanese tactics, 45, 49, 50–51, 55–56, 62, 65–67, 89–90, 92–93, 100, 119–21, 125–27, 142, 148, 150, 152–53, 183, 195–99, 202–03, 205–06, 208–09
Jaure, 107, 108
Java Sea engagement, 2–3
Joint Chiefs, 35–36, 42, 74, 88
Jomard Passage, 31, 32
Jumbora, 129, 141
Kaga, 5, 32, 33

Jai, 44
Kalikodobu (Kalamazoo), 105, 107
Kanga, 47
Kanjaki Barige, 111, 115
Kapa Kapa–Jaure Trail, 106, 107
Karsik, 201
Kavieng, 5, 62, 65
Keltou, 141
Kenney, Maj. Gen. George, 3, 19, 25–27, 45, 73, 74, 75, 77–78, 91, 98, 105, 111, 112, 115, 127, 139, 157, 160, 168, 192, 234
Kessels, Lt. Col. O.A., 186
Kienzle, Capt. Herbert, 41, 52
Kilabo, 60
Killerton Trail, 131, 178, 181, 224
King, Adm. Ernest J., 15, 26, 36, 73, 88, 110, 155
King John, 110, 113, 114
Kogi, 51, 94
Kongo Maru, 29
Koitaki, 84
Kokoda, 37, 39, 40, 41, 42, 44, 45, 46, 47, 48, 49, 52, 83, 92, 98, 100, 117, 119, 157
Kokoda Trail, 37–38, 40, 43, 82, 88, 106, 108, 110, 112, 115, 124, 126, 135
Konombi Creek, 219
Korean laborers, 125
Kristian Bruder (K.B.) Mission, 60, 63, 65, 66, 67, 68, 69
Krueger, Lt. Gen. Walter, 235
Kumusi R., 37, 45, 99, 101, 106, 119, 121, 122, 230, 231
Kutabul, 8
Lae, 4, 9, 21, 29, 36, 42, 73, 88, 226, 234

Larr, Col. David, 43, 159–60, 161, 163
Larum, 108
Latjens, 1st Sgt. Paul, 108–09
Leary, VAdm. Herbert, 3, 19, 27, 28
Lexington, 28, 29, 31
Lloyd, Brig. J.E., 82, 98, 119, 129, 184
Louisiade Archipelago, 31
Lunga Plantation, 87
Luzon, 1

MacArthur, Gen. Douglas: and the Philippines, 1–2, 12–14, 18–19; escape, 13, 14; assumes command in Australia, 15, 17–19; and air power, 1–2, 17, 19, 20, 25; and the Navy, 14–15, 20, 26–27; and Guadalcanal, 114–115; relations with:Arnold, 74–75; Blamey, 39, 75, 82–83, 97, 172, 221–22, 234–35; Brett, 17, 19, 25; Carpender, 137–38; Clowes, 63, 67, 77; Curtin, 20–21, 34, 78; Eichelberger, 101, 198–99, 162–63, 215, 218–19; Ghormley, 35–36, 88, 90; Harding, 137, 146, 158–63, 168; Joint Chiefs, 74; Kenney, 26–27, 157; King, 14–15, 19, 26, 35, 73, 110, 155; Marshall, 17, 18, 19, 20–22, 35; Roosevelt, 13, 200–21; Rowell, 77
MacArthur's Navy, 30–31, 91, 110, 124–25, 140–41, 138–39, 201
McCoy, Lt. Col. Robert C. , 143, 146, 147, 152, 165, 193

McCreary, Lt. Col. Melvin, 169, 194
McKenny, Lt. Col. Lawrence, 110, 113, 140
McNab, Lt. Col. Alexander, 151
MacNider, Brig. Gen. Hanford, 101, 107, 111, 113–14, 116, 129, 140, 143, 144, 149, 151
Magarey, Maj. Rupert, 52, 53
Malaya, 2, 10–11
Manunda, 70
Mareeba, 24
Maroubra, 47
Marshall, Gen. George, 17, 18, 19, 21–22, 75, 76, 88, 91
Marshall, Brig. Gen. Richard, 18
Martin, Col. Clarence, 165, 166–67, 169, 192, 201, 205, 231
Medendorp, Capt. Alfred, 108
medical problems, 120, 129, 153, 165, 171, 191, 218
Melbourne, 12, 14, 36
Menari, 39, 41, 52, 56, 95
Midway, 4, 32–34, 87
Mikawa, Adm. Gun'ichi, 61–62, 69–70
Miller, Lt. Col. Kelsie, 143, 145, 147
Milne Bay, 26, 28, 50, 59–71, 73, 77, 79, 106, 152, 189, 232
Mindanao, 13
Minnemura, 140
Mission Ridge, 55, 56, 96
Mitchell, Cpl. Harold, 196
MO Plan, 30
Morris, Maj. Gen. Basil, 19, 39, 40, 41, 45, 54
Motieau, 68
Mott, Col. John, 150, 158, 159, 161, 164, 165, 166, 167, 169

Mugoni R., 101
Musa R., 113
Musita Is., 206, 208
Musket (Huggins') Block, 223, 224
Myola, 39, 49, 50, 52, 54, 55, 83, 94, 95, 96, 97, 99, 117

Nagumo, VAdm. Chuichi, 4, 32, 33
Nauro, 39, 41
native carriers, 37, 41, 52–53, 97, 117–19
New Britain, 4, 5, 24, 25, 92
New Caledonia, 3, 4, 28, 43, 87
New Georgia, 87, 112
New Guinea Force, 19, 22, 40, 42, 47, 55, 80, 85, 156
New Ireland, 5
New Zealand, 3
Nimitz, Adm. Chester, 15, 29, 32, 73, 110, 155
Northern Territories Force, 19
Noumea, 3, 91

Oda, Maj. Gen. Kensaku, 190, 226, 230–31
Odell, Lt. Robert, 194–95
Oivi, 117, 118, 119–20, 121, 123
Okada, Seizo, 57, 58, 93, 122, 123
Oro Bay, 140, 213
Owen Stanley Mts., 9, 27, 39, 46, 71, 92, 93, 107, 110, 191
Owen, Lt. Col. William, 46, 47

Paleima, 110
Papua, 4, 6, 9, 26, 36–37, 91, 126, 168
Papuan Infantry Battalion (PIB), 41

Patch, Maj. Gen. Alexander, 90
Pearl Harbor, 1, 2, 3, 6, 10, 20, 30, 232
Philippine Is., 1, 13, 18
Pitt, Lt. Col. William, 42
Porlock Harbor, 113, 152
Pongani, 111, 113, 114, 115, 139, 141, 143
Popondetta, 129, 180, 191, 223, 234
Porter, Brig. Selwyn, 40, 173, 185, 186–87, 221
Port Moresby, 9, 12, 22, 24, 27, 29, 30, 35, 39, 40, 41, 43, 44, 46, 47, 54, 59, 62, 75, 78, 79, 81, 84, 92, 99, 101, 107, 109, 114, 116, 117, 153, 156, 158, 162, 168, 169, 174, 186, 191, 195, 199, 231
Potts, Brig. Arnold, 50, 51, 54, 55, 56, 86, 99
Prince of Wales, 1
Providence Plan, 42–43

Rabaul, 4, 5, 30, 31, 43, 44, 45, 69, 91, 112, 190, 217, 225
Rabi, 60, 65, 68
Rankin block, 224, 226
Renown, 1
Richardson, Maj. Gen. Robert, 36, 76
Rini, Corp. Daniel, 198
Robertson, Col. W.T., 158
Rockkhampton, 36, 101, 102, 156, 161
Rogers, Col. Gordon, 165, 166–67, 194
Roosevelt, Franklin Delano, 13, 18, 20, 74, 76
Rouana Falls, 101
Rowell, Maj. Gen. Sir Sydney, 54,

55, 57, 77, 78, 79–81, 84, 85, 94, 97, 107, 111, 145, 156
Royal Australian Air Force (RAAF), 4–5, 6, 7, 10, 22, 24, 112; Fighter Squadron 75, 60, 66, 67; Fighter Squadron 76, 60, 66, 67
Sakamoto, Lt., 95
Salamaua, 9, 21, 28, 36, 42, 73, 88, 226, 234
Samoa, 3, 43
Sanananda, 36, 37, 94, 115, 116, 124, 125, 126, 127, 131, 133, 136, 141, 159, 171, 176, 177
Sanananda operations, 117–133, 178–87, 220–32
Santa Cruz Is., 36
Sanopa, Lance Corp., 47
Savo Is., 89, 91
Schroeder, Maj. Edmund R., 216, 218
Shirley, Capt. John, 182, 183
Shoho, 30, 31, 32
Shokaku, 30, 31
Simemi Creek, 136, 202, 213
Simpson Harbor, 5
Singapore, 2, 8, 9
Siwori, 150, 206, 219
Small Creek, 172–73
Smith, Lt. Col. Herbert A., 143, 144, 148, 149, 150, 179, 195, 198
Smith, Maj. Herbert, 149, 166
Solomon Is., 4, 26, 36, 87, 91, 92, 126
Sombogo, 228
Soputa, 122, 129, 131, 141, 142, 178, 185, 223
Soputa-Sanananda Trail, 131, 181
Soryu, 32, 33

Southwest Pacific Theater, 13, 15
Spruance, RAdm. Raymond, 33
Strip Point, 202
Sturdee, Gen. Sir Vernon, 19
Sublet, Lt. Col. Frank, 177
Sumatra, 2
supply problems, 51–52, 130, 137, 140, 143, 147–48, 153, 199
Sutherland, Maj. Gen. Richard, 18, 26, 43, 55, 75, 76, 77, 98, 101, 104, 156–57, 161, 162, 164, 167, 198, 215–16, 233
Sverdrup, Col. Lief, 107
Sydney, 8
Symington, Capt. Noel, 48

Tanaka, Lt. Col. Toyanari, 44, 93
tanks, 152, 201–04, 214, 224
Tarakan, 2
Tarakena, 219
Task No. 1, 35, 88
Task No. 2, 36, 88
Tenimber, 44
Templeton, Capt. Samuel, 42, 46
Templeton's Crossing, 39, 95–96, 99
Timor, 6, 11
Timoshenko, 110, 113
Tojo, Hideki, 127
Tomita, Lt. Col. Yoshinobu, 231
Tomlinson, Col. Clarence, 129, 178, 179, 180, 181, 182, 183, 194, 195–96, 207
Torres Straits, 24
Townsville, 3, 62
Triangle, 148, 150, 198, 207, 210
Truk, 5, 35
Tsukamoto, Lt. Col. Hatsuo,

48–49, 126, 131, 178, 180, 181, 224–25
Tulagi, 31, 36, 87, 88, 89
Tupeselei, 107

Uberi, 52
United States Air Corps, 7, 22–23, 24, 25–26; Fifth Air Force, 26, 91, 111, 112, 175, 189, 191–92, 196, 205, 213, 234; 19th Bomb Group, 112; 22d Bomb Group, 24, 25; 38th Bomb Group, 23; 43d Bomb Group, 23; 374th Troop Carrier Group, 191
United States Army units: armies: Alamo Force, 234; 6th Army, 234; corps: I Corps, 36,73, 101, 102, 104; divisions: Americal, 88, 90; 25th, 90; 32d, 35–36, 102–06, 110–11, 127, 133, 157, 158, 163, 169, 171, 192, 198, 219; 37th, 88; 41st, 11, 35,36, 102, 135, 159, 161, 221; 43d, 90; regiments: 126th, 102, 104, 105, 107, 115, 129, 133, 135, 143–44, 148, 151, 157, 178, 179, 185, 197, 206, 221, 223; 127th, 102, 107, 161, 192, 197, 206, 219, 222, 226–27; 128th, 102, 105, 112, 116, 143, 144, 146, 148, 150, 164, 197, 214;132d, 3; 163d, 221, 222, 225, 228, 229, 231; 182d, 3; battalions: 1st/126 Reg., 115, 116, 143, 152, 179, 193, 202–03; 2d/126Reg., 107, 108, 110, 113, 119, 180, 197; 3d/126 Reg., 115, 116, 148–49; 3d/127 Reg., 197,

215–16; 1st/128 Reg., 143, 144, 145, 147, 152, 193, 202, 203; 2d/128 Reg., 143, 144, 148, 197; 3d/128 Reg., 113, 114, 137, 143, 144, 146, 202, 214; 1st/163 Reg., 228; 2d/163 Reg., 228; 43d Engineer, 60; 46th Engineer, 60; 91st Engineer, 105, 107; 114th Engineer, 105, 108; 709th Airborne, 61; companies: B/126 Reg., 126, 224; C/126, 126, 182, 185, 224; D/126, 181; E/126, 104, 105, 107, 164, 207; F/126, 149, 164; G/126, 207, I/126, 182; K/126, 185; L/126, 185; M/126, 182; A/127, 209–10, 219; B/127, 210, 218; E/127, 216, 217; F/127, 209–10, 216, 218; G/127, 208, 210, 219; H/127, 216, 218; I/127, 208, 216; K/127, 208, 209, 216; L/127, 206, 209; A/128, 205; C/128,145, 205, 206; E/128, 149, 194, 198; F/128, 150, 194; G/128, 149, 150, 194; H/128, 195; I/163, 224; L/163, 224
United States-Australian rivalry, 115, 135–36, 155–56, 157, 158, 228–29
United States Marine Corps: 1st Marine Division, 88–90, 155
United States medical problems, 108–09
United States Navy, 1, 3, 7, 28–29, 30–34, 71, 89–90, 201, 213
Urbana Front (Force), 144, 149,

150, 153, 160, 164, 165, 166, 192, 194, 201, 206, 213, 222

Vandegrift, Maj. Gen. Archibald, 89

Van Vollkenburgh, Brig. Gen. Robert, 42, 43

Vasey, Maj. Gen. George, 77, 83, 85, 86, 99, 115, 120, 123, 127, 129, 131, 136, 143, 148, 156, 158, 161, 172, 173, 174, 178, 179, 181, 184, 220, 224, 226, 228–29

Vernon, Capt. Geoffrey, 52

Wadu, Pvt. Kinyoshi, 225

Waga Waga, 60, 70

Wairopi, 37, 45, 92, 106, 108, 122

Wainwright, Maj. Gen. Jonathan, 18

Wake Is., 2

Waldron, Brig. Gen., 139, 140, 147, 160, 168, 169, 195, 199

Wandala, 60

Wanigela, 79, 111, 113

Warisota Plantation, 143

Watson, Maj. W.T., 47

Wavell, Gen. Sir Archibald, 2, 3, 6, 10

weather conditions, 47, 49, 63, 113, 116, 144–45, 153, 173–74, 196, 223

Wedemeyer, Col. Albert, 20

Weeri, 39

Whitehead, Brig. Gen. Ennis, 73, 112–13, 192

Willoughby, Brig. Gen. Charles, 18, 46, 136

Wilmot, Chester, 50, 83–84

Wootten, Brig. George, 61, 201, 202–05, 213, 214, 215, 222

Yamagata, Maj. Gen. Tsuyuo, 127, 175, 190, 230

Yamamoto, Col. Hiroshi, 90, 125, 144, 218

Yamamoto, VAdm. Isoroku, 30, 32, 34

Yamamoto, Maj. Tsume, 125, 129, 130, 131, 171, 176, 217, 226

Yamato, 32

Yano, Cmdr. Minoru, 67, 69–70

Yasuda, Capt. Yoshitatsu, 69, 148, 196, 197, 209, 218

Yazawa, Col. Kiyomi, 94, 100, 119, 121, 127, 175, 217, 219, 231

Yokoyama, Col. Yosuke, 44, 122, 125, 171, 176

Yorktown, 29, 31, 33

Zeef, Maj. Bert, 181, 182

Zinser, Maj. Roy, 197–98

Zuikaku, 30, 31